DANCING WITH DEMONS

The Music's Real Master

by Jeff Godwin

Published by Chick Publications
P.O. Box 662, Chino, CA 91708-0662
Printed in the United States of America

INTERNATIONAL DISTRIBUTORS

Chick-Traktate-Versand
Postfach 3009
5632 Wermelskirchen 3
West Germany

Christ Is The Answer, Inc.
Box 5167, Station A
Toronto, Ont. M5W 1N5, Canada
(416) 699-7800

New Zealand Evangelistic Society
P.O. Box 50096
Porirua, Wellington, New Zealand

Penfold Book & Bible House
P.O. Box 26
Bicester, Oxon, England OX6 8PB
Tel: 0869-249574

Evangelistic Literature Enterprise
P.O. Box 10
Strathpine, Q'ld., Australia 4500
Phone: (07) 205-7100

198/C

Library of Congress Catalog Card No. 88-090860

ISBN 0-937958-28-X

ABOUT THE COVER

Who is that grotesque creature on the cover of this book?

If you are an avid fan of Heavy Metal, "Christian" Rock, rap, or several other forms of today's supposedly "safe" popular music, he is the god YOU worship.

He is the god of Rock & Roll, a Greek deity named Pan. "Pan is represented as more or less bestial in shape, having the horns, legs and ears of a goat . . ."[1] The entire rock world is a massive cult dedicated to him. Multiplied millions of young people are being sacrificed to this master demon as they pass through the fires of rock.

Here are just a few examples of famous rock stars paying tribute to the one they serve, Pan:

Paul McCartney: There is a very interesting picture on his "Pipes of Peace" album. In his left hand, McCartney is holding a musical instrument called a syrinx, or "panpipe." The Encyclopedia Britannica says that an Arcadian deity named Pan was "the lover of a nymph Syrinx (Panpipe)." It goes on to say that Pan can make men "stampede in panic terror . . ."[2] How typical of

Satan's work. McCartney's album is titled "Pipes of Peace," but the demon Paul is paying homage to causes panic terror. The joke's on us.

The Rolling Stones: Their 1981 "Tattoo You" album contained a full inside cover photo of a cloven-hoofed goat's foot. (Pan has the horns, legs and ears of a goat.[3] Former occultist David J. Meyer describes Pan as a principality of Satan who appears at witch coven meetings either in his goat form, or as a violet cloud.)[4]

One of the founding members of the *Rolling Stones* was a wicked man named Brian Jones. In 1969, he journeyed to Morocco, Africa to attend an occult festival dedicated to Pan that was being held by the Joujouka tribe. Drugs and music were a part of the ceremonies to bring up the demons who were being worshiped. Jones later released the "music" in an album titled "Brian Jones Presents The Pipes Of Pan."

Elton John: This bisexual rock star commissioned a special family crest to be made for himself in 1987. Guess who the most prominent figure on that crest is. The Greek god Pan, complete with hoofs, horns and syrinx!

Duran Duran: One of the biggest names in pop/rock during the early eighties. Some members of the group quit to form a new band named ARCADIA, which just happens to be the section of ancient Greece where Pan was worshiped.[5] It was also the seat of Pan's power.

Rush: These Heavy Metal stars put out an album in 1976 titled "2112" with a five pointed star inside a circle on the cover. One song on the record was called, "The Priests Of SYRINX." What a coincidence.

Led Zeppelin: These rock gods wrote the biggest selling single in Rock & Roll history – "Stairway To Heaven." Referring to Pan, The Encyclopedia Britannica says "he is a piper."[6] Keep that in mind as you read these lyrics from "Stairway:"

> "And it's whispered that soon
> If we all call the tune
> Then the piper will lead us to reason . . .
> Your head is humming, And it won't go
> In case you don't know
> The piper's calling you to join him . . ."

How strange that the lyrics from that song and the Encyclopedia Britannica have so much in common.

Many famous rock stars, including *Led Zep* founder Jimmy Page, are followers of the dead satanist Aleister Crowley, who was also a Pan worshiper. At Crowley's funeral in 1947, his disciples were instructed to read aloud a poem he had composed himself called, "Hymn To Pan."

Throughout this book, you will see that the vast majority of today's popular music is pure praise and worship directed towards the Greek god Pan, and his ultimate master – Satan.

Young person, don't you be one of the gullible ones who burn in the flames at the altar of Pan. Please don't dance with the demons.

Table Of Contents

1

BURNING DOWN THE HOUSE

"And they have built the high places of
Tophet, which is in the Valley of the son of
Hinnom, to burn their sons and their
daughters in the fire; which I commanded
them not, neither came it into my heart."

Jeremiah 7:31

"Burn out the day, Burn out the night
I can't see no reason to put up a fight
I'm livin' for givin' the Devil his due
And I'm burnin', I'm burnin', I'm burnin'
For you . . . "   Blue Oyster Cult[1]

If I told you that millions of children have been burned
alive and sacrificed on an altar dedicated to demons,
how would you react? Would disgust and rage fill your

heart? Would you rush out to break up and burn those bloody altars to ashes? Before you say yes, be prepared to hear that the abominations which are destroying your children can be found in your very own home.

The monster I'm referring to is rock music. Three generations have openly worshiped at the high places of Rock & Roll, and a fourth is well on the way. Amid the flames of perversity, blasphemy, obscenity and cruel deception, our children are burning in agony before our very eyes. We allowed those high places to be built. We turned our backs as the high priests of rock reached out for yet another sacrifice – our kids. We've paid the price long enough.

There is one rule we should never forget. Rock is Rock is Rock is Rock. Whether it's called "Soft" Rock, "Acid" Rock, "Punk" Rock or "Christian" Rock, we are still dealing with music more ancient than the classics. Rooted in the Druid demon worship of Celtic England. and baptized in voodoo ceremonies of Africa and the Caribbean, Satan's rock rules the world.

There is a spiritual power to this music, a power that does NOT come from God. Some try to clean it up, tone it down, or even claim it for the Lord, but rock music never changes, no matter how it's perfumed. There are two massive and immovable pillars in rock: REBEL-LION and HUNGER. Rebellion is the coal that feeds that hungry fire. Just like hell, Rock & Roll is never satisfied; it is constantly enlarging itself.

> "Hell and destruction are never full; so the eyes of man are never satisfied."
> Proverbs 27:20

While some debate the pros and cons, stumble through

the moral "gray areas," and preach a compromising tolerance, more young souls plunge headlong into the flames. While we argue, they burn.

This has all happened before. In the Southern Kingdom of ancient Judah during the time of the prophet Jeremiah, God's chosen Jewish race had sunk to the lowest depths of depravity. Thanks to the introduction of pagan Baal worship, Jehovah was left in the dust by His rebellious and hard-hearted children. Hordes of pagan "gods" filled the land, each more brutal than the last – Ashtoreth, Chemosh, Molech. They demanded blood, fire and the tortured death of innocent children. Their worship was celebrated with a mass sexual perversity unknown since Sodom and Gomorrah. Just south of Jerusalem lay the Valley of Hinnom, where the night skies were continually lit by the flames of human sacrifice:

> "Yea, they sacrificed their sons and their daughters unto devils, And shed innocent blood, even the blood of their sons and of their daughters, whom they sacrificed unto the idols of Canaan: and the land was polluted with blood."   Psalm 106:37-38

At the high place of Tophet (the word "Tophet" has to do with the beating of a drum) the pagan priests carefully constructed stairways, altars and fire pits for the frenzied rites of Molech worship. A huge, hulking metal image of this horned demon was the centerpiece of this ghastly place. As the drums pounded like enormous, overworked hearts ready to burst, musical instruments of all kinds were frantically blown and trumpeted to drown out the throat-shredding screams of dying children. Worshipers added their own howls to the chaos as they sang and wailed "hymns" to the

9

demons that were devouring their precious young. It's no wonder that Hinnom eventually became known as "Gehenna" – a term synonymous with Hell.

Today the music still plays while the children go up in smoke. Once perceived to be only a distasteful social phenomenon, Rock & Roll is really one of the most enslaving, destructive and deceptive Devil-tools of all time. It changes colors like a snake shedding its skin. It calls evil good and good evil. It changes titles and terms of description to deceive genuine Christians.

Rock & Roll is the modern equivalent of the Valley of Hinnom. The rock concert stage is today's "High Place" of Tophet. The rock stars are the bug-eyed priests and our young people are the sacrificial babes. By giving up their awesome responsibility to spiritually guard and protect their children, parents are literally throwing their kids into the fire as the music muffles their screams. If God's people ever needed the discernment of the Holy Spirit, mixed with the righteous anger of the Almighty, that time is now.

The following fact needs to be stated clearly and repeated often: Music may be many things but it is NEVER neutral. Rock defenders point to dead objects like an ax or a butcher knife and say, "Those things can be used to chop wood, cut cake or kill your mother-in-law ... it's the intention of a person's heart that makes the difference. The same holds true for music."

No it doesn't!

Music is not a piece of wood or chunk of steel waiting to be used/abused by whoever picks it up. Music has a life of its own. Since music is a spiritual creation, it will always strike a positive or negative chord within our spirits. Enough evidence now exists to clearly show that when rock is played, our bodies, minds and spirits suffer. Proof?

Over a decade ago, a woman named Dorothy Retallack conducted experiments with music, plants and their combined environment. The results are famous. She exposed one set of bean sprouts, Morning Glories and other plants to nonstop rock as they grew. Another set heard placid, devotional "religious" music. Within ten days, the first rock-drenched beans tried to escape from the music by growing away from the source! They became stunted, wilted and eventually died. Group # 2, on the other hand, flourished under their steady diet of godly music, growing TOWARD the source as they thrived and bloomed.[2]

The lesson here is very simple: If rock music attacks, stunts and kills plants, what is it doing to people? The answer is obvious – the same thing! (I don't think the plants really cared about the words, either. It's the music that killed them.)

Rock music has also been found to cause chemical imbalances in the human body. The bass tones and driving drumbeats of modern rock have been proven to demonstrate a reaction with the cerebral-spinal fluid and pituitary gland of the brain. When exposed to rock, the adrenaline and sex glands over-secrete. Their hormonal production is pushed into over-drive. This is why concert-going crowds "bang their heads," raise their fists and destroy the arena. It's also why feelings of lust and sensuality wash over everyone there. Since the body's hormones are imbalanced, it compensates by drawing blood sugar from the brain to bring every-thing back into alignment. Since blood sugar is the primary material used by the brain to feed itself, a lack

11

of decision making ability is the inevitable result.[3]

Rock listeners, take note. You're being hit with a 1, 2, 3 punch! At the same time your heart starts thumping and your sex glands go into warp-drive, you lose your cool, calm, rational ability to think straight. And that's just the physical effects. We haven't yet discussed the spiritual (demonic) attack that follows.

An Australian doctor named John Diamond has conducted physical strength experiments using the "stopped anapestic rhythm" of rock music. Groups that use such beats include the *Rolling Stones*, the *Eagles*, Elton John, the *Doors*, Janis Joplin and Stevie Wonder, plus many others. In hundreds of tests on humans, using rock music and an electronic strain guage, Diamond made three powerful conclusions:

1) More than 90 % registered an INSTANT loss of two thirds of their normal muscle strength while listening to rock.

2) Haitian voodoo drum music has the same rhythms as rock.

3) Above a certain decibel level, the same muscle weakening occurs, regardless of the rhythm.

As if this wasn't enough, Dr. Diamond also concluded that a phenomenon called "switching" occurs in those listening to the stopped anapestic beats of rock music. A mixup in alpha waves between the two hemispheres of the brain results in the same brain wave synchronization found in schizophrenics and babies.[4]

Rock music neutral? Not hardly.

What about the spiritual side of this question? In I Samuel 16:23, we read the famous account of King Saul and the young musician David. Saul was changed when David played. This was GODLY music. Why? First, Saul was "refreshed," the Hebrew word being "RAVACH" meaning "to breathe freely." This shows that the music refreshed the king's PHYSICAL BODY.

We also see that Saul was "well" (Hebrew "TOWB") which means "to be (make) well, good, or better."[5] Thus, Saul's MIND was made well by David's music.

Thirdly, the "evil spirit departed" as a result of David's harpistry. The meaning here is literal and self-evident. Conclusion?

Godly music refreshes the body, makes the mind well and drives away evil spirits. (See I Thessalonians 5:23.) What about UNgodly music then?

> 1.) Rock has been proven to harm and
>   destroy the body.
> 2.) Rock hypnotizes the mind.
> 3.) Rock attracts evil spirits, as anyone
>   who has ever repented of it knows only
>   too well.

How then can something as ungodly as rock music be made holy and good with a change of lyrics, as defenders of "Christian" rock claim? It can't.

THE BIG THREE

Satan has a three-pronged process he uses through all of rock music to destroy young people and their families: Sex, Drugs and Rock & Roll – the battle cry of an entire generation. While youngsters fight for their right to have all three, Satan is using these weapons to wipe out millions of unsuspecting souls. Here's how:

SEX

All the smutty and degenerate emphasis on sexual lust in rock music is designed to fire up teenage imaginations and hormones, leading to active fornication. Why is Satan so interested in getting kids sexually active? Because immoral sex serves a specific purpose – to spread demons. Demons are a venereal disease in the truest sense. Since those engaged in sexual union are "one flesh" physically, whatever demons are lodging in either body are free to pass back and forth, attracting others at the same time. That's why we have such dire warnings against consorting with adulteresses and prostitutes in Proverbs 6:20-32 and 7:1-27:

> "But whoso committeth adultery with a woman lacketh understanding: he that doeth it destroyeth his own soul."
>
> Proverbs 6:32

The Apostle Paul further explains this thought of bodily and spiritual pollution through fornication in I Corinthians 6:15-20:

> "Know ye not that your bodies are the members of Christ? shall I then take the members of Christ, and make them the members of an harlot? God forbid. What? know ye not that he which is joined to an harlot is one body? for two, saith he, shall be one flesh. But he that is joined unto the Lord is one spirit. Flee fornication. Every sin that a man doeth is without the body; but he that committeth fornication sin-

14

neth against his own body . . . For ye are bought with a price: therefore glorify God in your body, and in your spirit, which are God's."

Wild and unchained sex is a hallmark of both the rock lifestyle and true satanism. Witches call it "allowing the astral forces to move more freely among us," but demonic infestation is the real objective. Keeping sons and daughters sexually pure until marriage is one of the greatest challenges facing parents today. One good way is to pull the plug on rock music.

DRUGS

There is a perfect parallel between drugs, rock music and bona-fide satanism. Hallucinogenic drugs are a basic part of satanic rituals and devil-orgies. Rock music has openly promoted mind expanding drugs for over twenty years, but not because they're a good way to expand your own consciousness. A person's "altered state of consciousness" when they are high on drugs is just a fancy way of describing a rocket ride straight into the spiritual world, where demons exist and travel. The more often you vacation in this deadly fairyland, the closer you get to Hell.

Some of the biggest names in rock have died of drug overdoses during such hallucinogenic dreams. Now they'll burn in eternal flames with Satan forever. Every parent's greatest fear is to learn that their child is on dope. Take action today by banning rock music from your home, school and church.

ROCK & ROLL

Rock music is the first and last step in Satan's destruction of youth. Piped in from Hell, rock's pounding rhythms are the same as those used in voodoo rituals:

> " . . . The follower of Voodoo seeks to incor-
> porate a LOA (lesser god) into himself by
> writhing and leaping through a dance,
> while drums bang out complex rhythms.
> When just the right rhythm is found for an
> individual LOA, the dancer takes it up,
> and the LOA enters his soul. His physical
> and mental powers are immediately height-
> ened; he becomes god – like himself. Ani-
> mals will often be sacrificed to appease the
> spirits. . . The religion is strictly Dionysian,
> and dances often end in wholesale copula-
> tion . . . "[6]

The bridge between actual voodoo and modern rock came through a style of music known as "the blues." Filled with themes of fornication, murder, adultery and hopeless despair, the blues was made popular in the 1930's, 40's and 50's by dozens of black performers. Many of these men met the same violent deaths they so frequently sang about. These blues pioneers took the ancient tribal sounds of their African ancestors and turned them into a new and widespread form of musi-cal voodoo. The message was utterly negative and the music was rooted in witchcraft. When white rock superstars like *Led Zeppelin*, the *Who* and the *Rolling Stones* recycled the blues into their own electrified blast, a whole generation of young people fell under the spell of Satan's special beat. As blues trailblazer Muddy Waters tells it:

> "The big drop after the beat on the drum
> formed the foundation of my blues. Noth-
> ing fancy – just a straight heavy beat with

it... But you see blues, it's tone – deep tone with a heavy beat. I kept that backbeat on the drums plus full action on the guitar and harmonica and the piano in the back, then you've got a big sound . . . "[7]

Here's how rock guitar god Jimi Hendrix described his own brand of electric blues:

"The blues are easy to play but not to feel. The background of our music is a spiritual – blues thing. Blues is a part of America. We're making our music into electric church music – a new kind of Bible, not like in a hotel, but a Bible you carry in your hearts, one that will give you a physical feeling. We try to make our music so loose and hard-hitting so that it hits your soul hard enough to make it open. It's like shock therapy or a can opener. Rock is technically blues-based . . . We want them to realize that our music is just as spiritual as going to church."[8]

A beat hard enough to crack open your soul – what more needs to be said?

Many Christians know the story about an American missionary who took his family to Africa. One day, as the man's children blasted their rock records they had brought with them, terrified native tribesmen rushed up to the preacher, their faces full of fear. They asked him why he allowed his children to play music that was used to call up demons during voodoo rituals. This account has long been given the horse laugh by rock addicts, especially by "Christian" rock defenders.

An event in the wasted life of guitar god Jimi Hendrix, (who suffocated to death on his own vomit in 1970) strikes at the heart of this "beat can't be evil" controversy. In David Henderson's book, "Scuse Me While I Kiss The Sky," we read about a young African musician who was much in demand on rock recording sessions. Kwasi Dzidzornu, whom Hendrix called "Rocki," was a gifted conga drum player that Jimi met in London. Rocki was from the African country of Ghana. His father was the chief drummer and a voodoo high priest in a small village there. Rocki jammed often with some of the biggest names in popular music – stars like the *Rolling Stones*, Jimmy Page of *Led Zeppelin*, and of course, Hendrix himself.

Early in their relationship, Rocki asked Jimi where he learned the voodoo rhythms and dances that he used on stage and in the studio. Hendrix wouldn't say. According to Rocki, the rhythms of Hendrix's "music" were IDENTICAL to those used by his father during demon raising voodoo ceremonies. Rocki said that Jimi's wild, in-concert leaps and primitive rhythmic movements were the same as those used to worship Oxun, the pagan god of thunder and lightning (a demon).[9] Skeptics want proof? Here it is: The son of a voodoo high priest saying Rock & Roll and a satanic song service to call up demons are the same thing.

Rock's incredible volume, coupled with screeching dissonance and the rhythmic beat of voodoo, form a battering ram that smashes into the listener's mind and spirit. Subliminals and backmasks pump Satan's messages into the brain, and are combined with a fairly new development called ELF (Extremely Low Frequency). These are subsonic tones that cannot be heard, but are felt in the physical body. Go to a rock concert and you'll feel the ELF literally move your internal organs around. Depending on the number of cycles per second, ELF can produce euphoria or violent, murderous reactions in those listening.[10]

Physically and mentally beaten to a pulp by all this, the rock listener is left wide open for spiritual attack by demonic forces. That's been the purpose of Rock & Roll all along – to reprogram young minds along satanic lines through the spiritual assault of demons. Satan's plan is to wipe out entire generations of youth, turning them against their parents and more importantly, against God.

The devil is also using the same tactics to destroy Christian youth through so-called "Christian" rock. Young believers now bow before the altar of C-Rock just as their unsaved counterparts worship the *Motley Crues* and Ozzy Osbournes. A clean-cut image and some religious words sweeten the deception. Satan doesn't mind one bit – since he's still the one in charge.

FIRE

Rock music today is the modern version of Tophet's ancient cremations. Rock & Roll relies heavily on scenes of fierce, flaming, fiery destruction in all three phases of its production – live concerts, song lyrics and album packaging. Here are some examples: In 1968, an obscure English weirdo named Arthur Brown was one of the first Devil-Rockers to integrate pyrotechnics into his stage show. As part of his hit single, "Fire," he proudly paraded onto the stage, having just set his head on fire!

A dozen years ago, Heavy Metal hate mongers like *KISS* began the trend of blowing great billowing bursts of flames during their concerts. Today none of the big names in rock would dare hit the road without their flamepots. They have been well trained to vividly recreate Hell in those concert halls.

Motley Crue's 1983 "Shout At The Devil" album centerfold features the group posed before burning brimstone amid the caverns of Hades. The promotional package for the 1986 *Judas Priest* "Fuel For Life" tour showed the boys in front of walls of licking flames as a monstrous hand prepares to pour gas on the fire.

The Molech mentality of rock song lyrics both new and old could fill pages. Here are just a few examples:

"Gimme Shelter" by the *Rolling Stones*: (1969)

> "Oooh, see the fire is sweepin'
> Our very streets today
> Burns like a red coal carpet
> Mad bull lost its way . . . "

"War Pigs" by *Black Sabbath*: (1970)

> "Generals gathered in their masses
> Just like witches at Black Masses
> Evil minds that plot destruction
> Sorcerer of death's construction
> In the fields the bodies burning
> As the war machine keeps turning . . ."

"Cities On Flame" by *Blue Oyster Cult*: (1975)

> "My heart is black, and my lips are cold
> Cities on flame with Rock & Roll
> 3,000 guitars they seem to crush
> My ears will melt
> And then my eyes . . . "

"Flaming Youth" by *KISS*: (1976)

> "My parents think I'm crazy
> And they hate the things I do
> I'm stupid and I'm lazy
> Man, if they only knew
> How flaming youth will set the world on
>   fire
> Flaming youth, our flag is flying higher"

"Cook With Fire" by *Heart*: (1978)

> "I got the soul that's got the spark for you
> Holding a real hot wire
> We've got a hungry flame in the dark and
> Lord, we're gonna cook with fire
> Oh, listen to me . . . "

"Light Up The Sky" by *Van Halen* (1983)

> "I heard the wind a whisperin'
> Saw magic comin' out, Comin' out for sure
> Come see your children, They're lighting
>   up the skies
> You won't recognize them anymore . . ."

"Fight Fire With Fire" by *Metallica*: (1984)

> " . . . We all shall die
> Time is like a fuse, short and burning fast
> Armageddon is here, like said in the past
> Fight fire with fire, ending is near
> Fight fire with fire, bursting with fear. . . "

"Sleeping In The Fire" by *W.A.S.P.*: (1984)

> "Taste the love, the Lucifer's magic

21

That makes you numb, you feel what it
    does
And you're drunk on love
You're sleeping in the fire . . . "

"Light The Flame" by *Barren Cross* ("Christian"
    Rock group): (1986)

"Light the flame
Take hold and know my name
I long to give you the love that's in my hand
Light the flame
My gift to you's been paid
Receive the King
His crowns await your stand . . ."

"Venus" by *Bananarama*: (1986)

"I'm your Venus
I'm your fire
Your desire . . . "

In the occult, Venus, the "bright morning star," is
another name for Lucifer.

This nightmarish picture of burning souls trapped in a
world aflame is blaring from millions of stereos in
teenage bedrooms all across America. Each one is an
altar to Satan, dripping with the doctrines of devils. Is
one of these blackened altars set up in YOUR home?

Even Christians are being sucked into this trap by mop
headed, spandexed "Christian" rockers who sell Jesus
like a new and improved brand of soap. This idol
worship will continue to flourish until Christian parents (especially fathers) rise up in righteous anger and
say, "Enough!" The words of the prophet Jeremiah are

just as true today as when they first came from his lips:

> "Thus saith the Lord, Stand ye in the ways, and see, and ask for the old paths, where is the good way, and walk therein, and ye shall find rest for your souls. But they said, We will not walk therein. Also I set watchmen over you saying, Hearken to the sound of the trumpet. But they said, We will not hearken."   Jeremiah 6:16-17

To confront evil is to fight it. To ignore it is sin. (See James 4:17.) Every parent, pastor and youth leader reading these words should immediately seek the Lord's guidance, strap on the whole armour of God, (Ephesians 6:12-18), hold tight the sharp Sword of the Spirit and go forth to cleanse our land of the suicidal plague of Rock & Roll. The battle is spiritual (II Corinthians 10:3-5) and it begins at home (Matthew 10:36). The alternative is the music, the flames, and dead children.

The outcome is up to you.

2

AND THE CRADLE WILL ROCK

"Train up a child in the way he should go:
and when he is old, he will not depart from
it."   Proverbs 22:6

"Listenin' to the teacher
Bosses and the preacher
Ain't never done nobody good . . . "
                                    KISS[1]

At the very core of Rock & Roll music is the steely rule
of rebellion. It has always been so, and will never
change as long as rock exists. When hip-wiggling Elvis
Presley flaunted his pink and green coats, blue suede
shoes and grease-dripping mop of Brylcreemed hair,
he lit the fuse of rebellion against everything the
1950's generation held decent.

When the *Beatles* publicly acknowledged smoking pot and tripping on LSD, an open revolt against the laws that made those drugs illegal was thrown into motion. Many millions of young lives world-wide have been utterly ruined as a result.

When bisexual David Bowie went public with his perversion in the early 1970's, he okayed the rebellion against God's law for the natural use of the man and woman. The rotten fruit of his influence is found today in men who think God gave them the wrong hormones at birth, and lesbian groups who publicly praise their degraded lifestyles.

As the decade of 1980 dawned, outright satanism, coupled with the intense glorification of wickedness, boldly lashed out through rock music. Spearheaded by groups like *Venom, Slayer, Impaler, Motley Crue, Twisted Sister, KISS* and dozens of others, the rebellion of our dying world has been clearly reflected in the mirror of modern rock – open warfare against God. The Bible says:

> "For rebellion is as the sin of witchcraft, and stubbornness is as iniquity and idolatry . . ." I Samuel 15:23

Rebellion was the crime for which Satan was cast out of Heaven as he exalted his own prideful will above the will of God (Isaiah 14:12-20). Rebellion is the foundation on which rock music is built, and a satanic Tower of Babel has been erected on rock's rebellious foundation with only one purpose . . . to spit in God's eye.

As long as the Lord tarries, we still have time to expose this perverse music to the penetrating light of open examination, guided by the Word of God. Though rock music is inspired by Satan and his demons, it is still produced by people – men and women with hearts, minds, spirits and souls. The bitter root of rebellion that led them into the slavery of the rock scene often began in their childhood homes.

If we can trace the rebellion in those early lives, it will be a lesson for every mom and dad. The kings of Rock & Roll didn't just appear out of nowhere. Everything they say and do is tied in part to the way their parents raised them. Let us closely examine their mistakes so that our own children won't follow in their footsteps.

In researching their families, I found that all rock idols, past and present, share one common thread. Though separated by time, wealth, distance, intelligence and opportunity, the seed of REBELLION was firmly planted in them years before fame and fortune overtook them. It often came through famous rockers, who infected those kids with a desire to create Rock & Roll music on their own.

Some parents tried to beat these obsessions out of their children. Others simply looked the other way, hoping the "phase" would pass. Some actually encouraged their kids' musical careers, though they must now tremble at what they helped create. Let's take a look at some of these children rocked in the cradle of hell.

DEE SNIDER OF TWISTED SISTER

Danny "Dee" Snider is the oldest of six children, the son of a New York police officer who refuses to keep any pictures of his son past the age of 12. Dee says often in various Heavy Metal books and magazines that his father was a mean-spirited and uncaring drill sergeant of a dad, quick to dispense brutal punishment for the slightest infraction of household rules. Dee comments:

> "He once beat me with a wiffleball bat. . . I am a total paranoid because of my father."[2]

> ". . . When they said they were sorry, I said, 'It's ok, Dad, I'm making a living out of being so messed up.' "[3]

At 15, Dee's dad forced him to have his long hair buzzed to the scalp. The boy never forgave him, quietly sulking as he fed the murderous hatred which would erupt years later in the lyrics of *Twisted Sister's* most famous song, "We're Not Gonna Take It:"

> "Oh you're so condescending
> Your gall is never ending
> We don't want nothin', not a thing from
>   you
> Your life is trite and jaded
> Boring and confiscated
> If that's your best, your best won't do . . . "

As the gap between them widened, rebellious Dee sought refuge through Rock & Roll. Any time a void exists within a family, Satan and his rock pawns rush to fill the gap. Snider's first taste of rock worship came with the *Beatles*:

> "I remember I made a conscious decision to be a rock'n'roll star the day after the *Beatles* appeared on the Ed Sullivan Show (February 9, 1964). I didn't even see them. I was at the bus stop, I was in the third grade, and a kid told me about it, and I just said, that's what I want to be . . . "[4]

After Satan's doorway opened through the Fab Four foothold, Dee quickly graduated into an all-out worship of his newest "god" – rock star Alice Cooper:

> "Alice Cooper is my hero. I used to have this picture of Alice over my sink, and every morning I would bow down to it."[5]

> "Cooper went straight to the #@%! point . . . I realized that this was what I needed – plain talk, words I understood . . . Speak to me, Alice. Let me watch you and forget about my problems, Alice. Let me get out my frustrations, Alice. I couldn't put it into words myself."[6]

> " . . . I used to come home from school and put on Alice Cooper. Because I was a very unpopular person, and I'd go home every day and put on Alice. I'd stand in front of that mirror and I'd mouth, wiggle around, and be a rock & roll star. And I'd GO someplace. In that place, the party was going, Alice was there, the band was there, and everybody was having a great time."[7]

With Alice Cooper's music fueling his hatred, this young alienated misfit became a rock-obsessed monster. Fights in school and raging arguments at home led Snider to strike out on his own at age 19. Dee's antisocial viciousness and one-track obsession drove him to join a series of Heavy Metal glitter groups. Done up in women's clothing, their beard-stubbled faces caked with mascara and makeup, the last of these abominations was called *Twisted Sister*.

A ragged remnant of ex-street gang thugs and juvenile

delinquents, (one is nicknamed "The Animal") *Twisted Sister* soon became known in every beer joint and dive on Long Island. Spewing out a foul-mouthed tirade of gutter oaths backed by thundering Heavy Metal, Dee and his band had even hard core bikers blanching at their on-stage antics. Year after year they slugged their way through New York's seedy club circuit, growing rich in the process.

Dee descended further and further into the violent and perverse personality he had built for himself until finally, like Alice Cooper before him, Danny Snider disappeared entirely, swallowed up by the monster he had created. Here is a description of what ultimately happens, as described by his idol, Alice:

> " . . . I get all my Alice drag [female clothing] on, and then nobody's allowed in for an hour before I go on stage. That's when I do my transformation into Alice. Nobody knows where he comes from, but he shows up every night in my dressing room."   Alice Cooper[8]

The song "Gail" from his 1987 album "Raise Your Fist And Yell" is an example of the demented ideas bubbling up into Cooper's mind after "Alice" takes over:

> "A tree has grown on the spot
> Where her body did rest
> Blood seeped in the soil
> From the knife in her chest
> The bugs serve time in her skeletal jail
> I wonder how the bugs remember Gail. . ."

Where Alice's insanity led, Dee quickly followed:

"I was the most obnoxious, egocentric, irritating son-of-a-bitch you ever saw. I walked into the Palladium and it was, 'Get out of my way! You are near the next superstar of this planet.' Evil is not the word for what I became, but just ... dark. My whole mind was dark. Night after night I was a real horror show. I had a bodyguard, and he was dark, and I was dark, and we just walked around being dark." Dee Snider[9]

"Four years ago, I went through a very dark period of my life when I was very . . . bad. That was during the ego trip. I was into being omnipotent. I had this whole concept that I was a superbeing. I had this friend I hung around with. He was very physically powerful, legally insane, and a genius. We kept patting each other on the back and telling each other how brilliant and powerful we were. We abused people, played head games. We referred to everybody as 'our humans.' "[10]

What Dee is describing here is the possession of his mind and body by demonic spirits. Trained deliverance ministers know that children are often indwelt with demons because of parental rejection. Hatred and an unforgiving spirit are also powerful tools Satan and his demons use to take over a person.

As a teenager, Snider opened wide the doors to such possession. Because of his undying hatred and stubborn refusal to forgive his father, Dee's soul became dead meat for Satan. Snider was flung headlong into the darkness by bowing down to Alice Cooper as god. The results are obvious:

"I tap into everything negative in my personality. I think about the things I hate, the things I'm angry about. I let it all out – I curse, scream, roll around – and afterwards, I feel good."[11]

In 1984, *Twisted Sister* released "Stay Hungry," a bone-chilling fright-fest of a record, dripping with evil chaotic revolt against all authority. Here are some lyrics to one of the songs on that album:

"Burn In Hell"

"Welcome to the abandoned land
Come on in child, take my hand
Here there's no work or play
Only one bill to pay
There's just five words to say
As you go down, down, down
You're gonna burn in Hell . . . "

The twisted visions being demonically pumped into Snider's head were showcased in another "Stay Hungry" song – "Captain Howdy:" (Captain Howdy was the name of the demon who possessed Regan MacNeil in the movie, "The Exorcist.")

After the runaway success of the "Stay Hungry" album, (over 4 million copies sold) *Twisted Sister* began their video follow-ups to the record. The minifilm that put them on the MTV map was "We're Not Gonna Take It." Still seething with hate fifteen years after the fact, Snider's video shows an overbearing, loud-mouthed father being bashed in the face and dragged down a flight of steps by the *Twisted Sisters*. This parental punishment was given because dad had chewed out his rock-loving teenage son. Dee Snider's long range

31

revenge on his father was finally complete. Dee explains his battle plans this way:

> " . . . The type of music we play and the way we look is every parent's nightmare, so I guess in some ways we are standing up for the kids against their parents. That comes across in the video, and it's in the songs as well. But that's the basic attitude of rock and roll; you like it because your parents hate it . . . "[12]

> "The third year of *Twisted Sister* (1978-79), we developed our audience to a huge number of people. We'd get up to 3,000 people a night. That's when my parents stopped hassling me, 'cause I started making more than my father."[13]

> "That's why Heavy Metal exists. It is the only form of rock'n'roll besides punk where that essential element of rebellion still exists. My parents did to me what happens to that kid in the video. Maybe some kid somewhere who's getting beat up on can feel better thinking about me dragging that father downstairs by his hair. The message of *Twisted Sister* is personal freedom. If you like what you are, #@%! what everybody else thinks . . . "[14]

In October, 1984 at a *Twisted Sis* concert in Amarillo, Texas, foul-mouthed Dee was arrested for public profanity, due to parental complaints. Though he tried to laugh it off, not even a "dirtbag" (Snider's favorite name for himself) enjoys having a police record.

The question of verbal vulgarity came up again in September of 1985 as Snider addressed the Senate Committee on Commerce, Science and Transportation in Washington, D.C. Influenced by the Parents' Music Resource Center (PMRC), key senators were contemplating the possibility of rating rock records. Senator Albert Gore questioned Snider about *Twisted Sister's* SMF (Sick Mother #@%! Friends) fan club. Dee made no apologies for the obscenity; instead he declared he was a CHRISTIAN, as if that settled the matter!

> "Who is he trying to tell me I'm not a Christian because I curse." Dee Snider[15]

If Dee Snider was truly a Christian, he'd do himself a favor and read and obey Ephesians 5:3-6! Does Dee really want to serve God? Not hardly. In the following quote, he smugly declares what he's really after:

> "This is my only shot to be rich and famous. And I WANT to be a rich and famous rock star . . . I'm obsessed with proving to the world I'm cool on my terms. I want to walk into fancy restaurants and look like a dirtbag and have them serve me caviar . . . "[16]

As 1985 drew to a close, *Twisted Sister* released a new album called, "Come Out And Play." The cover perfectly revealed the bent ideas bubbling through the band's brains. It featured a half-naked Dee Snider crawling up out of a sewer hole. For the picture, he shaved his chest and had his two front teeth filed to sharp points, like some kind of mindless cannibal.

With wealth and fame came new boldness for the demonic spirits controlling Snider's song writing. The tune "Come Out And Play" is a prime example:

"Join our cavalcade
Enter the world you made
We're only here for you
To do what you won't do . . .
A place where fallacy
Becomes reality
We'll spin your head around
We're programmed to astound . . .
Welcome to our life
Just follow me and you'll think that
You're free . . . "

Rock has always promised total freedom, but all it ever
delivers is bitter bondage. Like hound dogs on a trail
of blood, misery and slavery follow the rock stars and
their spellbound fans. The words of II Peter 2:19 ring
solidly true, exposing rock's lies. Hear them!

"While they promise them liberty, they
themselves are the servants of corruption:
for of whom a man is overcome, of the same
is he brought in bondage."

"I Believe In Rock'N'Roll" is another song from the
album – a chilling slice of Satan's lies trumpeted forth
from Dee Snider's mouth:

"I pledge allegiance to the flag
Of the United States of Rock
And to the point of view for which it
    stands
One music under God
Yes, even God loves Rock'N'Roll . . .
But as for me, I know that Heavy Metal
    lives
And that it will at last stand forth upon the
    dust . . .

And from my flesh I shall see it Rock
My inmost being is consumed with longing
This is the Word of the Rocker."

Those words are pure blasphemy. The "god" who loves
Rock & Roll is NOT the great I AM, the Lord of Hosts
and Father of all Creation! Rather he is a thief,
murderer, destroyer and the father of lies – Satan. A
decade earlier, Alice Cooper spewed out the same
sneering hatred in his song "Hallowed Be My Name."
Recycled and covered with a fresh coat of paint, the
identical mockery of God's power once again drips from
Twisted Dee and his Sisters. In the end, both Snider
and Cooper will share a double date in Hell, unless
they repent. (See Matthew 25:41.)

After years of awestruck idol worship, Dee finally met
his "god" face to face. Alice Cooper guested on two
songs from the "Come Out And Play" album, as well as
appearing in the video "Be Chrool To Your Scuel,"
(banned by MTV). A year later, this powerful exposure
allowed Alice to mount his own blood-soaked comeback
into rock arenas around the world. Both Cooper and
Snider have scratched each other's backs, and why
not? They both serve the same master.

Because of the publicity generated by the police and
PMRC, *Twisted Sister's* career quickly took a screaming nosedive. "Come Out And Play" sold millions less
copies than "Stay Hungry." Parents and vice squad
officers across America were ready for Dee and his boys
when their concert rolled into town. As they continually stared out at half-empty halls, *Twisted Sister* was
forced to cancel their tour midway through rather than
go bankrupt. Suddenly Dee Snider had to face the fact
that even a rock god can be brought low by the united
efforts of Christians and parents.

In a mad scramble to retain some credibility in the Rock & Roll jungle, Snider and his Twisted boys released a 1987 album, "Love Is For Suckers." He also co-authored a book, "Dee Snider's Teenage Survival Guide." Besides detailing his own personal masturbation, sexual and abortion experiences, Snider's book gave this advice to his army of adolescent followers:

> "Masturbation is a healthy, normal sexual release practiced by more than nine of ten teenagers – boys and girls alike – and during your teen years it may be your only sexual release . . . It is normal to fantasize, or to think sexual thoughts, while masturbating: about your girlfriend or boyfriend, an acquaintance at school, celebrities, Dee Snider (for you girls), strangers . . . "[17]

Here are his thoughts on homosexuality:

> "Just as inevitable is sexual experimentation with members of your own sex . . . According to Dr. John Money, no human being can be labeled exclusively male or female. We all have traits – and hormones – of both sexes and are all capable of bi-sexuality . . . "[18]

When asked why *Twisted Sister's* albums were no longer selling well, a haughty Dee snidely huffed:

> "Hey, you can't hurt my feelings. I'm rich, I've got a nice big house, seven cars, two boats . . . I live on the water. I'm set for life. And if this thing all falls apart, I'll still be set for life, while writers, photographers, etc., are still making peanuts. So really, I

care about it, but thank God that now I'm in a position not to operate out of desperation, but out of love."[19]

Snider ought to heed this warning from God's Word:

"Whereas ye know not what shall be on the morrow. For what is your life? It is even a vapor, that appeareth for a little time, and then vanisheth away."   James 4:14

Raised in rebellion and molded by the worst Heavy Metal has to offer, *Twisted Sister's* head honcho is indeed "every parent's nightmare." But here's something guaranteed to give Dee some sleepless nights as well – 100,000 *Twisted Sister* albums thrown into the trash by parents who are fed up with his rot-rock. In fact, as long as Christians continue putting on the pressure, Snider and his metal monsters might just fade out of the picture entirely. Like a vanishing vapor, Dee Snider could be gone before you know it. (*Twisted Sister* broke up and disbanded in April, 1988.)

LITTLE RICHARD

Mick Jagger called him King. To John Lennon, Elvis Presley was bigger than Christ, and Little Richard was bigger than Elvis. Paul McCartney was so star-struck when they met, he wouldn't touch this black rock god. Almost every rock star of the past 30 years has paid tribute to Richard W. Penniman, a man who was making hit records when Elvis was still a truck driver. Homosexual, peeping Tom, drug addict, jailbird and would-be pimp, Little Richard is the musical role model for two generations of powerhouse rock stars and their fans. He too, started down the ugly path to perversion while still a child.

37

With eleven brothers and sisters, Richard's mother, Leva Mae, was often too preoccupied to ride shotgun on her delinquent son as he terrorized the neighborhood with his perverse and dangerous practical jokes.

> "I don't know why he does such evil dirty things like that. It must be the Devil."
> Leva Mae Penniman[20]

By day, Richard's father was a construction laborer. At night, he ran bootleg whiskey. Free with the belt and disgusted by his son's feminine attitudes, Bud Penniman whaled the tar out of his boy often.

Wickedly rebellious, Richard soon crossed the line into true homo and bi-sexuality. His perversion began with sneaking into his mother's bedroom to secretly apply makeup and perfume. This quickly led to sexual contacts with loose women in the neighborhood. Soon, while barely into his teens, he had his first homosexual encounter. (The first of hundreds.)

Leading a bizarre, schizophrenic lifestyle, Little Richard divided his time between sexual deviance and old-time religion. He haunted the local Baptist churches of Macon, Georgia where he bellowed and screamed the hymns like a maniac until the congregation booted him out the door. Religion to Richard was a stage, an audience and a chance to perform.

Accepted by a traveling band that was passing through the area, he quit school and left home to hit the road at age 14. Leva Mae's heart ached that her son was throwing his future to the wind, but Richard's dad wasn't sorry to see him go. Deep inside, no dad wants a homosexual son. Bud Penniman was no exception.

In 1950, Richard became a full-fledged drag queen, performing in dresses and make-up. Since Rock & Roll didn't exist yet, he drew on the styles and influences of the blues and R&B artists of the day. The blues, along with his ear piercing caveman yells and female attire, made a Little Richard performance one very strange event indeed. Talent scouts began approaching the budding rock star with recording contracts and soon Little Richard started making records.

Driven by the wicked spirits of fantasy lust within him, Richard was jailed, then run out of Macon, Georgia for a sexual crime (lewd conduct). Later he was arrested in California for hanging out in a public men's restroom, looking for "action."[21]

In 1955 his first big hit ("Tutti Frutti") smashed into both the white and segregated black radio stations, something unheard of at the time. The words to the song were so filthy they had to be rewritten. In concert, Little Richard half howled, while pounding the piano with his feet. Fans, both black and white, flocked to his musical altar as their parents looked on in shock. Preachers denounced him from their pulpits and were promptly labeled as racists. Rock & Roll was born.

As the money rolled in, Little Richard went nuts. Hollywood mansions, mountains of cash and big-finned Cadillacs merged with a brutal whirlwind of hotel room orgies and bisexual depravity as he blazed a trail of sin from coast to coast:

> "I used to like to watch these people having sex with my band men. I would pay a guy . . . . and have sex with these ladies so I could watch them. It was a big thrill to me . . . ."
> Little Richard[22]

The nonstop Rock & Roll decadence finally became more than Penniman could take. He reached rock bottom in 1957 while his singles were still racing up the charts. Turning his back on it all, he made a highly publicized religious conversion and joined the Church of God of the Ten Commandments as a traveling evangelist.

Lee Angel was a professional stripper as well as a sexual companion on Little Richard's rollicking Rock & Roll tours. He continued to see her even after joining the Church. What did she think of his "conversion?"

> "I keep hoping I can trust him, but I know better, so I'm not going to waste my time . .. He's saying one thing in public and doing another thing in private."[23]

Though changed outwardly, demons of homosexuality still ruled Richard Penniman with a grip of steel. He resigned from Bible College after being accused of taking evil liberties with a deacon's son on the campus. Unwilling to give up singing, Little Richard began recording gospel songs. But millions of rock fans demanded that he revive the Hell-raising, loud-mouthed Little Richard they remembered and worshiped. He gave in to the pressure, resurrected his rock career, and by 1965 the Lord was forgotten.

Years of sickening debauchery came and went. Penniman added drugs like cocaine, PCP, marijuana and heroin to his suitcase stuffed full of sins. A roller coaster ride of albums, orgies, tours and dope lit Little Richard up like a Christmas tree:

> "I became very nasty, which I never used to be. Cocaine made me paranoid. It made

me think evil . . . . When I got real high I couldn't sleep . . . I spent my time locked up in a hotel room . . . The drugs brought me to realize what homosexuality had made me. When I felt that, I wanted to hurt. I wanted to kill . . . They were SCARED of me cos my homosexuality was so heavy they could see it in my eyes . . . "[24]

In the late 1970's Richard again "retired" from rock to seek the Lord. Feeling near death, he dumped drugs cold turkey and threw himself into personal evangelism for Jesus Christ. It was during this period that he gave this solemn warning about rock:

"My true belief about Rock'N'Roll – and there have been a lot of phrases attributed to me over the years – is this: I believe this kind of music is demonic . . . A lot of the beats in music today are taken from voodoo, from the voodoo drums. If you study music in rhythms, like I have, you'll see that is true. I believe that kind of music is driving people from Christ. It is contagious . . . "[25]

But Little Richard ignored his own advice and appeared in the 1986 movie, "Down And Out In Beverly Hills." The accompanying MTV video showed him seated at the piano with a big grin on his face as his hands pounded out the piston-pumping rhythm. With a new album in the stores, Little Richard was once again in his well-worn driver's seat, stoking the fires of Satan's Rock & Roll . Some people never learn.

DAVID LEE ROTH

"Women are my hobby. Every man needs
something to keep his hands busy."[26]

David Lee Roth has the dirtiest mouth in rock. His
lewd and disgusting conversations have been end-
lessly reprinted in every music magazine in the world
for almost a decade. He spent over eight years as front
man for Heavy Metal mega-stars *Van Halen* before
jumping ship in 1985 to begin a solo career. The fans
cheer, holler and howl at his dirt-caked dialogue:

> "I am one of the recreational directors for
> the immoral majority."[27]

> "I'm a very family-oriented guy. I've per-
> sonally started three or four in 1983
> alone."[28]

> "I am primarily motivated by fear and
> revenge . . . you'll find it in all my presen-
> tations: my songs, my interviews, the way
> I dress, the way I walk down the street
> . . . There are some things I wish I'd done
> differently, but as far as guilt and shame
> go, no. . . you burn a trail around the world,
> leaving a permanent shadow of groupies
> and rubble as never before in the history of
> rock'n'roll, and one day, it's Miller Time."[29]

Roth's mindless pursuit of pleasure at any price can be
traced all the way back to his childhood. He was born
in Bloomington, Indiana on October 10, 1955. The son
of a Jewish eye doctor and school teaching mother,
Dave's emotional problems and complete lack of conscience began surfacing at an early age:

"When I was a little kid my parents were really worried about me. I used to run around the house climbing on the furniture and singing along with all the TV commercials. I guess it was getting my folks a little crazy because they took me to a doctor who told them I was hyperactive . . . "[30]

"I threw off my parents super early. They sent me to a child guidance clinic when I was seven. So I disposed of all those vestiges of society way back . . . No guilt . . . Whatever it was, I just wasn't ashamed of it. That's what really threw them."[31]

By 1962 the Roth family had moved to New England and young Dave was spending summers with his Uncle Manny, owner of the famous New York folk-rock club, the "Cafe Wha?" For almost three years, David Lee Roth saw some of the biggest names in popular music perform at his uncle's place. Like thousands of infatuated rock bums before him, Dave instantly knew what he wanted to do with his life:

"That's when I decided I wanted to be a singer. I saw the excitement that the performers were generating, and I knew that was for me . . . "[32]

"I used to watch people like Hendrix or a soul band and then I'd practice in the mirror what I'd seen them do . . . I was exposed to lots of good music when I was young, and that influence has stayed with me all my life."[33]

The restless Roth family relocated once again, this time to Pasadena, California. Fueled by the music of the 60's British Invasion, Dave's high school years were spent in a rebellious fog:

> "I never was much of a conformist. I used to love to take my guitar to school and just sit under a tree and play. I'd always forget what time it was, and I'd always miss class, but I found out very quickly that you could meet a lot more girls sitting under a tree with a guitar than you could in chemistry class."[34]

> "[I was] just one of the #@%!-ups, cutting class and lying out in the sun."[35]

> "Around the end of my junior year in high school, I was sent to a work ranch for bad boys . . . That's when I started wearing denim jackets and #@%! . . . "[36]

Having spent almost six months paying for his juvenile delinquency, Roth somehow made it out of high school and into Pasadena City College. Higher education was the furthest thing from his mind:

> "[College] was treading water until a band got launched."[37]

It was in those hallowed halls of academia that Roth met Eddie and Alex Van Halen, two Dutch boys who had immigrated to the U.S. years earlier with their musician father. A guitar marvel even in his teens, Eddie blasted out electrified shock-rock while Alex bashed his drums into quivering piles of jello. Dave was impressed. The trio formed a band, added bass player Michael Anthony and hit the California bar and booze circuit. *Van Halen* was on its way.

The group escaped years of musical bar-busting on the stages of dirty liquor dives by the appearance of the fire breathing bassist from *KISS* – Gene Simmons. Early on, this blood-spitting bozo with the seven inch tongue offered to produce demo tapes for *Van Halen*. Simmons had seen them perform and wanted to give them their first big break. Thanks a lot, Gene.

Eddie's red hot guitar, combined with Roth's notorious motor mouth, helped land them a Warner Brothers recording contract in 1977. The song, "Runnin' With The Devil," became one of the biggest hits from their smash debut album. (Every Van Halen album with Roth as singer has sold well over a million copies.)

"Runnin' With The Devil"

"I live my life like there's no tomorrow
All I've got I had to steal
Least I don't need to beg or borrow
Yes, I'm living at a pace that kills
Oh yeah, we're runnin' with the Devil. . . "

As their first taste of fame and fortune set in, David Lee Roth cranked his foul mouth into high gear. Smut quickly became his favorite topic:

"A lot of people think that a Van Halen tour is just one long orgy with a few stops on stage in between. Well, let me tell you . . . they're right."[38]

"I like women to be my friends after sex . . . I'm just acting out the old male dream.

45

Nothing lasts forever, but I'm good for the entire night."[39]

"[Van Halen] is a group of barbarians who are sweeping around the world non-stop and have a few basic goals in mind and when it's done have a good old barbarian party – after each city is conquered . . . And after it's over, we sack the village. We go looking for women and the children."[40]

"We want to go to every town and leave a bit of Van Halen there – as long as I don't have to pay the paternity bills."[41]

(Roth was the first rock star to take out a multi-million dollar insurance policy against paternity suits.)

In a 1984 interview, "Dirt Mouth Dave" revealed how he procured young girls from the concert crowd to take part in his back stage activities:

"We have our own custom barricade that we bring from city to city, and fellows behind it with walkie-talkie headsets connected to fellows in the pit . . . I'll dance over to one of the guys and say, 'Red right, red T-shirt, out of sight, six feet back!' I'll dance back on stage, and he'll radio, and a big gorilla will crawl over the barricade and slap a pass on her. You do that 15, 25 times a night, and you'll have some new friends, too."[42]

Like goods on display in a perverse meat market, any pretty young girl attending one of Roth's concerts is fair game for his lust. Star-struck by their idol worship, many girls end up in situations they hadn't bargained for. When pregnancy occurs, they needn't bother looking for help from Dave; he'll be on to another town and other "conquests."

Drugs naturally followed Roth's other debaucheries as the *Van Halen* war machine continued to soar to even greater heights of wealth and popularity:

> "The National Enquirer is the only paper I use for more than rolling joints."[43]

> "I promised everyone if we'd make it, we'd all do Blow together."[44] ("Blow" is druggie code for cocaine.)

> "You have to decide, am I going to get high tonight and miss tomorrow? Sometimes, yeah. But not as much as people think. There's definitely a place for it . . . "[45]

> "I used to have fantasies, but they all came true, so now they're vices. I have six or eight vices now, distilled from the 20 or 30 I originally involved myself with on the road. Now I just do those six or eight all the time."[46]

Following in the mucky footsteps of scores of degraded rock scum before him, the wickedness of Roth's life-style eventually led to outright blasphemy of the Lord:

> "The night life balances my scheme of things. I love watching the sun come up while you're coming in. It's like God saluting me for having an evening that would do him proud."[47]

47

Sexual perversity, the next stop on *Van Halen's* sicko express, came in the form of a poster tucked inside their "Women And Children First" album. David was suspended in chains, bondage style, his hairy chest draped in black leather like a sado-masochist sacrifice:

> "We put the poster in because it UPSETS people. It's disturbing. It's one of those beautiful things where there's actually nothing going on in the picture and you're forced to use your FILTHY LITTLE IMAGINATION . . . "[48]

Under Roth's guidance, *Van Halen* received the largest single payoff in the history of rock. The Guinness Book of World Records named them the highest paid group for a single performance after their 1982 show at California's US Festival. Their fee? $1.5 MILLION! (That's $375,000 each; or almost $188,000 an hour!)

By this stage of their career, the *Van Halen* road show included a 60,000 watt sound system with 600 speakers putting out a mind-mashing 134 decibels (dbs). (The human pain threshold is somewhere around 90 dbs.) The 16,000 watt monitor speaker set-up they used just to hear themselves was louder than the entire system of most groups!

Noises of this intensity can quickly bloody the ears. Who knows what effect it has on the body and the brain? Drummer Alex Van Halen has lost over 30% of his hearing, but still continues destroying himself, hoping that a solution will be found some day. Too bad he won't be able to hear about it by then. This is the same man who bet $50,000 dollars that he wouldn't allow two packs of burning cigarettes to drop from his bare forearms until they went out . . . and won![49]

By 1984 Roth and his *Van Halen* lunkheads were making MTV videos. One of their most disgusting was "Hot For Teacher." The "plot" consisted of Dave and his partners-in-smut invading a high school classroom. The music roars as they watch the teacher strip and parade lewdly in front of dozens of cheering, drooling boys. Lyrics to the song go like this:

"Hot For Teacher"

"Maybe I should go to Hell
But I am doin' well
Teacher needs to see me after school
I think of all the education that I've missed
But then my homework was never quite
   like this
Got it bad, Got it bad, Got it bad,
I'm hot for teacher . . . "

In 1985, Roth went solo, claiming the other *Van Halens* were too lazy to get out of bed long enough to collect their million dollar fees. In return, they called Dave a jerk (or words to that effect).

Freed from all restraint, and with plenty to prove musically, Roth threw himself into making videos, hoping that a nonstop barrage of bare female flesh on film would hide his horrendous singing. "California Girls" was chock full of half-naked bathing beauties for Dave to ogle and fondle while the cameras rolled. It became one of the most requested videos on MTV.

In his next minifilm, "Just A Gigolo," Roth danced an obscene bump and grind before a shocked panel of TV censors, one of whom had a heart attack on the spot. These videos propelled Roth into the solo superstar stratosphere. He became the darling of prime time entertainment shows and musical awards banquets from coast to coast.

In 1986 David Lee hired three new flunkies to replace his ex - Van Halen buddies and cleverly named his new group "The David Lee Roth Band." Their chart busting debut record, "Eat 'Em And Smile," sold over 2.5 million copies. A new video, "Yankee Rose," followed. It quickly penetrated MTV's 24-hour rotation slot. In concert, Roth held a six foot long inflatable microphone between his legs. He sticks his wiggling backside straight into the camera lens and keeps it there. The theme of the tune? Dave's favorite prostitute:

"Yankee Rose"

"Are you ready for the new sensation
Well here's the shot heard round the world
All you back-room boys salute
When her flag unfurls
Well, guess who's back in circulation
Now I don't know, but you may have heard
But what I need right now
Is the original good time girl . . . "

Dirty Dave and his buddies produced a follow-up record in 1988 called "Sky-scraper," and the usual cycle of hit singles and Top 10 videos repeated itself. The lyrics are so filthy, they cannot be printed. According to Eddie Anderson, Roth's personal bodyguard, here is what David Lee likes to do on vacation:

"Actually we went to the Birthday of the Devil in Haiti, and that scared the #@%! out of me. Every year, they celebrate the Birthday of the Devil there. They sacrificed a chicken. One high priest puts the

50

body of the chicken in his mouth, the second high priest puts the head in his mouth, and they rip it apart . . . [Dave] just watched. It was very scary. But it was fun."[50]

A hot-headed rebel from his earliest youth, today David Lee Roth has gone to the ultimate limit. The rebellion that was planted in him in his youngest days was a gift from Satan himself. Throughout his life, the devil has used that rebellious spirit to drag David further and further into his blood-soaked clutches. Now David is openly celebrating the devil's birthday. His awestruck reverence for his real master has finally been laid bare. While still a young child, I bet he never dreamed he'd one day spend his vacations watching satanic high priests stuffing live chickens into their mouths and tearing them to pieces. But when Satan is your master, it never ends up like you thought it would. By this point in his "career," I'm sure David Lee Roth knows that only too well.

JOHN PHILLIPS

As the head honcho of the 60's recording group, *The Mamas And Papas*, John Phillips re-defined a musical era by mixing folk with rock to produce what became the "California Sound." Superstar bands like *Fleetwood Mac* and *ABBA* would later follow the Mom & Pop's example of soap opera song writing, mixed with double boy/girl harmonies.

Phillips was personally responsible for organizing and staging the first major rock festival ever held in the United States, 1967's Monterey Pop extravaganza. Without Monterey's exposure, Jimi Hendrix, Janis Joplin and British mega-stars, *The Who*, might never have become the monstrous legends they did.

The head Papa also wrote one of the biggest songs of the sixties, the huge international hit, "San Francisco (Be Sure To Wear Flowers In Your Hair)." Rock's royalty were some of his closest friends. He spent many a drugged and drunken night making music with the likes of *Rolling Stones* Keith Richards, Ron Wood and Mick Taylor.

Phillips' 1986 autobiography, "Papa John," is not for the squeamish. I thought I had a cast-iron stomach after spending months researching the filthy lives of Heavy Metal monsters like *KISS* and *Motley Crue*, but "Papa John" takes the nausea cake. Phillips coldly describes in vivid detail his decades of sexual depravity and wild drug abuse. He reminisces about such memories as broken, bloody syringes, group sex orgies and injecting his own daughter with cocaine. This is the same man who produced such mellow mid-sixties "safe" songs as "California Dreamin" and "Monday, Monday."

For over forty years, John Phillips' wasted and degraded existence has been spent in a frenzied rebellion. Conventional morality is a joke to him. His cold-blooded philosophy is that ALL laws were made to be broken. As usual, the seeds of such self-destructive bitterness were sown at home.

John's father was a hard-drinking career officer in the Marines. A series of heart attacks forced him out of the service and into the slow, agonizing decay of alcoholism. He spent the rest of his life dying in the cellar of their Virginia home, a terminal drunk. The Phillips family fell apart and six-year-old John's upbringing was left to the wind.

During his teens, the boy learned life's lessons on the

streets, though he was forced to attend strict military schools part of the year. Early on he developed an icy hatred of authority that was to guide him through the next two decades. Blessed with a brilliant IQ, Phillips intentionally flunked every class he could, preferring the company of a gang of juvenile delinquents. He became a petty thief, boldly shoplifting from neighborhood stores. By the time he was kicked out of high school, he had moved up to muggings, robberies and stealing cars.

When he received his first guitar, the spell of making music totally engulfed John's mind, body and spirit. John describes the spell:

> "I emerged from the room as if I had come out of a trance. My head and body felt weightless. Only then did I notice it was dark outside and the house was empty. I was hooked. I was spending more and more time down there with the guitar . . . Music became a refuge, an outlet of self-expression. With the guitar I could create and explore my own world of images and sounds without any hassles from the outside. No one could touch me; I felt safety, privacy, strength, and beauty through music . . ."[51]

Strumming a guitar didn't pay the bills, however, so he sold graveyard plots until he was fired for stealing the down payments. He then became a postman but was nearly jailed for throwing away a sack of mail. (He didn't like carrying heavy bags in the summertime.)

Phillips married after getting one of his girlfriends pregnant. After the baby was born, he celebrated by deserting his newlywed wife. Papa John just couldn't handle the responsibility. Weeks later, he came back like a whipped pup, begging to be forgiven. She agreed and they produced another child, a daughter named Mackenzie. (Mackenzie Phillips starred in the hit TV sitcom "One Day At A Time." She was fired because her raging cocaine addiction made her an embarrassing liability to the show.)

With two children and a wife to support, Phillips did what any caring husband and father of two would do. He ran away to Los Angeles! Establishing a pathetic pattern he would use again and again, he came crawling back to his family whenever the money ran out. Drugs, prostitutes and countless illicit affairs were the core of his sick lifestyle.

John later formed a pop quartet good enough to land on Dick Clark's American Bandstand. The ceaseless grind of traveling to every two-bit backwoods club in the country soon killed that band, but lean, lanky, street-wise John Phillips had gained a wealth of knowledge along the way. Thanks to his freshly made connections, a new group quickly formed and hit the road. Their first stop – California.

Having dragged his longsuffering wife and children clear across the country, proud Papa J. promptly dumped them all to set up house with a 17-year-old high school student named Michelle Gilliam. (He was almost 30 at the time.) Before his divorce was final, he gave his wife one last thing to remember him by – yet another pregnancy. The baby was aborted.

In 1962, folk was still a driving musical force and Phillips' band took full advantage of it. But when the *Beatles* hit American radio in 1964, the traditional folk music Phillips had based his career on died with a mighty thud. Electrified Rock & Roll was now the rage. He suddenly found himself without a band or a job, so he groomed his new bride to take their place. They spent weeks writing songs and perfecting vocal harmonies together.

One night in the winter of 1965, John and Michelle took LSD for the first time with two of their oddball musician friends. Dennis Doherty was a hard drinking Canadian misfit with a voice like a choir boy. Cass Elliott (real name Ellen Naomi Cohen) definitely stood out in a crowd, weighing 300 pounds and wearing tent-like purple muu muu dresses. Together, this whacked-out group of weirdos ingested enough "acid" to make an elephant turn somersaults.

During one of many technicolor hallucinations that followed, Phillips became too stoned to walk. Doherty led him to the stereo where "Meet The Beatles" was resting on the turntable. As his senses shimmered somewhere between reality and the planet Pluto, Phillips fixed his wildly tripping brain cells on the sounds that were blasting from the speakers. His soul merged with the music until the two became one.

Thus *The Mamas and Papas* were formed. After that Fab Four LSD trip, their lives were changed forever:

> "It had been an extraordinary mind-blowing trip. When the four of us tried to start the day, we all knew two things were clear: one, that our lives would never be the same; and two, that we immediately wanted to score more acid. There was no going back now. Within a month, I had written about thirty new songs. Acid,

Denny's hypnotic spell, ambition, Lennon
and McCartney – SOMETHING had unleashed my creative energy . . . "
John Phillips[52]

I have news for John. That "something" was Satan.

The Mamas and Papas became one of the most mind-
boggling supergroups of all time. Though they were
only together a little over three years, their records
sold so many millions so quickly, no one could count the
incoming dollars fast enough to keep up. In two short
years the group won a Grammy and produced six Top
5 singles and four Top 5 albums. They also appeared
at the Hollywood Bowl, something only rock gods like
the *Beatles* had previously done.

In concert, no one could quite believe what they were
seeing. Sherman tank Mama Cass bellowed tunes like
an opera singer, while sweet little blonde sex pot
Michelle cooed delicious, honey-dripping harmonies
into the microphone. John Phillips looked nine feet tall
standing next to the others, his puckered, perpetually
frowning face hidden under a furry pillbox hat. Denny
Doherty rounded out this musical freak show. They all
were usually tripping their brains out when they
performed. Together they resembled an MGM casting
call for "The Three Stooges Meet Frankenstein."

But still the multi-millions poured in. As it did, Phillips cultivated a lifestyle of wasted decadence and
utter hedonism that would have made Roman emper-
ors blush. Huge mansions stuffed with priceless art
and antiques, a driveway full of expensive limousines,
drugs so pure that the brain reeled. Depraved sex
every wicked way possible filled his endless days and
shameful nights.

Like so many other rock stars, the abundance of his sins only created an overwhelming desire for more. He hobnobbed with Hollywood movie stars and rock royalty alike. *Beatle* Paul McCartney was a guest at Phillips' Bel Air estate. John Lennon procured dope for the head Papa while in London. McCartney actually delivered the drugs. Even Elvis became a good friend.

Having climbed every peak the world had to offer, the only way Phillips could go was down. Way down. In 1969 *The Mamas and Papas* broke up. After a series of multiple affairs and brutal fist fights, Michelle divorced him. His money could have kept John in clover for the rest of his life, but an unquenchable thirst for bigger and better highs soon led him to the drug that destroys most all rock stars eventually – heroin.

High grade marijuana, mescaline, speed and LSD were enough for quite awhile, but like all junkies, Phillips needed something more. Snorting pharmaceutical cocaine by the bag while smoking cigar-like sticks of sensemilla pot gave a slight thrill, yet the ultimate high still eluded him.

It was during this dope-drenched period that his teenage children from his first marriage came to live with dear old dad. Jeff and Mackenzie had easy access to the piles of narcotics that were lying around the house. Papa John watched lovingly from a drug-dimmed daze as his kids built sizeable addictions of their own. Both eventually became needle junkies.

In the classic pattern of slow building heroin addiction, Phillips would "skin pop" cocaine, barely sliding a syringe into a thick muscle. But this was not as much fun as sticking the needle straight into a vein (mainlining). Since injections of liquid cocaine turn the user into a glassy-eyed, teeth-chattering, nerve-snapping bundle of hyperactivity, a few snorts of heroin are usually necessary to calm things down. Phillips was soon telling himself that the shakes, sweats and nausea he felt in the mornings wasn't really addiction.

Since inhaling "smack" through the nostrils was so slow and such an expensive waste of material, heroin replaced the cocaine in Papa John's needle. Every minute of every day now revolved around the "rush" – how to obtain it, how to maintain it. Mainlining "smack" became a way of life.

Attracted by the lure of good dope, *Rolling Stone* Keith Richards became Phillips' inseparable drug buddy. Keith's palatial home was quite cozy; he even kept fresh syringes on his bathroom sink, ready for use.

Within a matter of months, Phillips was so strung out on heroin and cocaine that veins had collapsed in his arms and legs. Needle related infections threatened gangrene and amputation of his foot. His drug hunger now completely ruled what was left of his wretched life. This composer of some of the biggest hits of the 1960's was reduced to a common junkie. The millions of dollars made with *The Mamas and Papas* evaporated like cold fog in the hot morning sunlight. Phillips sold anything that wasn't nailed down for cash to buy dope. His bathroom walls were covered with blood from testing his needles. Every 15 minutes of every day of every week of every month for a very long time, John injected himself with narcotics.

Cocaine psychosis finally took over. As he hallucinated, he thought he saw bugs crawling under his skin. He dug at himself with a scalpel and tweezers, trying to kill the parasites which existed only in his mind:

> "The more I shot coke, the more often I saw them: horrible white bugs, like maggots, that wiggled and crawled just below the surface of my skin . . ."   John Phillips[53]

In July of 1980, Phillips was arrested by Drug Enforcement Administration agents. Much of New York state was being flooded with drugs moved by the mob with Phillips as a go-between. He faced a possible 45 year prison sentence, but received a month in prison and a $15,000 fine, plus probation. He eventually beat his drug addiction, only to become a full-fledged alcoholic. The battle against the bottle was also broken, but not before he doled out more than $150,000 in fees and fines and spent five years on probation.

Because of his deep-seated rebellion, this pawn of the devil endured almost forty years of misery. His fights, lusts, drugs, women, alcohol and self-destruction can all be traced back to the rebellion Satan bred into him as a child. Phillips sums up his philosophy this way:

> " . . . I guess if I liked goin' by the rules I wouldn't have this problem to begin with, would I?"[54]

> "Be not deceived; God is not mocked: for whatsoever a man soweth, that shall he also reap."   Galatians 6:7

Here's how a few other rock rebels look at life:

> "I got sent to a private school when I was thirteen. I enjoyed it but didn't like most of the people there. It was a great chance to be away from your parents for four years. It was a brilliant way to #@%! about

and get in trouble a lot. And, I was a very irritating pupil, I was a poorling, I got thrown out! I was a terrible student! I applied myself to everything except the things I was SUPPOSED to apply myself to. To say I was rebellious would be an understatement."

Bruce Dickinson of *Iron Maiden*.[55]

"When I rebel, I don't really take it out on anybody. I just rebel. And I'm the only one who gets miserable . . ." Joan Jett[56]

"I realized at that point that my destiny was to be a #@%! - up . . . We used to go out absolutely defiant. All of us seemed to have one thing in common, some sort of crazy drive. Everything was always in excess. You can't just drink five beers, you've got to drink fifteen. Can't just smoke a little pot, got to smoke a whole bunch. Can't do LSD once . . . got to take it twenty times. Can't have one girl, have to have one a week. To someone who considers himself an intellectual, all this would seem stupid. They'd think the mentality was real low, but it's a real mentality, the real world . . ."

John Cougar Mellencamp[57]

"We love the kind of lives we lead. There's always something exciting going on. Either we're getting into fights with gangs outside of our hotel, or we're wrecking a bar, or we're driving our cars at 100 miles an hour with a trooper on our #@%! That's all part of rock and roll to us . . . We're the same all the time. We truly are a motley crew, and we're proud of it."

Nikki Sixx of *Motley Crue*[58]

"If a guy turned right in front of us we'd smash his car up, block their way. We'd get out and smash the headlights. It would be a family going to the movies, and the kids would be screaming in the back of the car. That's what we did for fun."

Mick Jagger[59]

"Survival's gotta do with believing in yourself, period. People are going to tell you, 'You can't do this. You can't do that.' They can all go #@%! themselves collectively. You don't need those people around, and that includes your parents. If people aren't supporting you, they are your enemies . . ."

Gene Simmons of *KISS*[60]

Rock music in the 1980's is stuffed to the bursting point with rebellious revolt and a scornful mockery of God. Today's stars have learned their lessons well from the Little Richards and John Phillips of the past. Anything goes. The sicker the better. But there will be a day of reckoning, perhaps sooner than they think. God does not leave sins like these unpunished:

"Therefore thus saith the Lord; Behold, I will cast thee from off the face of the earth: this year thou shalt die, because thou hast taught rebellion against the Lord."

Jeremiah 28:16

ALL rock music is rooted in rebellion. To follow rock and the monsters who create it is to turn your back on the Lord and bring judgment upon yourself. No child of God should have anything to do with the spirit of rebellion. It is the spirit of antichrist and glorifies only Satan. I wouldn't want to be standing in these rock stars' shoes when God pronounces judgment on them.

I urge you to repent from Rock & Roll worship, no matter what your age. Please don't persist in breeding rebellion by involvement in rock music. If you do, the promises of scripture will surely become your curse:

> "An evil man seeketh only rebellion: therefore a cruel messenger shall be sent against him." Proverbs 17:11

> "Woe to the rebellious children, saith the Lord, that take counsel, but not of me; and that cover with a covering, but not of my spirit, that they may add sin to sin." Isaiah 30:1

> "It is a fearful thing to fall into the hands of the living God." Hebrews 10:31

PLAYING IT SAFE

"I know thy works, that thou art neither cold nor hot: I would thou wert cold or hot. So then because thou art lukewarm, and neither cold nor hot, I will spue thee out of my mouth."   Revelation 3:15,16

"Well, it may be the Devil
Or it may be the Lord
But you're gonna have to
Serve somebody . . . ." Bob Dylan[1]

Though no one enjoys having their toes stepped on, the Lord allows our tootsies to be trampled once in a while to drive the complacency and self-satisfaction out of our lives. Otherwise too many of us would continue blindly going our merry way until overtaken and bushwacked by a cunning and ruthless enemy – Satan.

Two questions have been asked over and over in the many letters I've received since writing **"The Devil's Disciples."** So many write and ask, "Not all rock is bad, is it?" Others wonder, "Is my favorite group O.K.? They're not as bad as the rest, are they?" These fans just don't understand that the Top 40 radio dial is not the dividing line between good and evil. For example, is *ZZ Top* as "bad" as Ozzy Osbourne? At last report, no one in *ZZ Top* had chewed the head off a bat or urinated on the Alamo. (Ozzy has done both.) But that still doesn't excuse *ZZ Top's* songs about drunkenness, prostitution and fornication.

The same holds true for the seminars on rock music I've presented at church meetings. Young people of all ages desperately want the reassurance that their favorite band or singer is "O.K." But the excuse that "my favorite isn't as bad as some others" is just a cop-out. Finding someone unfavorable to compare ourselves with really doesn't prove anything. The bottom line is this: everyone is willing to point fingers, but to give up the groups we really love is another story entirely.

When the fans stop trying to defend the groups or singers they happen to like, and look at rock music as a whole, they quickly realize that ALL of rock is rotten from top to bottom and beginning to end. To admit that means we have to do something about it, and very few are willing to go for that.

To make matters worse, Satan has now penetrated the church and deceived many thousands of young people through "Christian" rock. Young believers fresh in the faith and lacking in spiritual discernment are some of the most rabid defenders of rock music, when the exact opposite should be the case. Of course, they insist they're not into the "bad stuff," just their own pet groups, idols and stars. Again, the hard reality is . . . they like it.

But what does the Bible say? All our opinions are equally valid or worthless until matched against the Word of God. The Bible alone should determine our likes and dislikes, not society's current trends. The following scriptures couldn't be plainer:

> "And be not conformed to this world: but be ye transformed by the renewing of your mind, that ye may prove what is that good, and acceptable, and perfect, will of God."
> Romans 12:2

> "Love not the world, neither the things that are in the world. If any man love the world, the love of the Father is not in him. For all that is in the world, the lust of the flesh, and the lust of the eyes, and the pride of life, is not of the Father, but is of the world." I John 2:15,16

> "Ye adulterers and adulteresses, know ye not that the friendship of the world is enmity with God? whosoever therefore will be a friend of the world is the enemy of God." James 4:4

> "God forbid: yea, Let God be true, but every man a liar; as it is written, That thou mightest be justified in thy sayings, and mightest overcome when thou art judged."
> Romans 3:4

You may hate Heavy Metal with a passion and listen only to the "safe" stuff on Top 40 radio. Or maybe you despise "Wimp Rock" and consider yourself to be the last real headbanger alive. Perhaps "Christian" Rock is your thing and that's where your true devotion lies. It all adds up to the same stinking pile of worldly garbage – rock music. Quit trying to play it safe. Take out the trash and clean up your spiritual rooms. You'll be amazed at how sweet the air can smell when rock is thrown out of the picture.

Let's zoom in on some of the most popular rock music stars from the past and present. Let's take a look at just how "safe" they really are. As in all deep things of Satan, looks can be deceiving.

PAUL McCARTNEY

Few people in the music business today are more revered than James Paul McCartney. The 1987 Guinness Book Of World Records lists him as the most successful musical composer in history. Since 1962, he has written and co-authored over 40 songs that sold over one million copies each. His personal fortune is estimated at well over $500 million and growing by the year. With his boyish good looks and ever chuckling, thumbs-up goofiness, "Paulie" broke hearts from coast to coast and helped sell *Beatles* records by the truck load when the Fab Four first invaded the U.S. in 1964.

His father became a widower when wife Mary McCartney died in 1955; Paul was only 13 years old. Almost two decades later, one of his most famous tunes contained these lines:

> "When I find myself in times of trouble
> Mother Mary comes to me

66

Speaking words of wisdom
Let it be . . . "

At the time, these words were widely thought to be
evidence of some kind of religious awakening in Paul,
but in reality, McCartney has always been an outspoken agnostic:

> "I don't know what I was before I was born.
> I was the sperm that won out of those three
> hundred million. I can't remember that
> far back but there was something working
> for me, some incredible thing that did it.
> So for me the wonder of that, of knowing
> that something got on with it before my
> conscious memory existed, leads me to
> believe that when you die maybe some-
> thing gets on with it, too. Which gives me
> this vague faith that I can't pinpoint. I
> don't say it's so-and-so doing it. But it's
> just IT, and whatever IT is I have an
> optimistic view about it . . ."[2]

I've got news for Paul McCartney – optimism won't get
him to heaven. What he so stubbornly refuses to admit
is that God knew his personality and formed his body
before he was even born! (Psalm 22:9,10)

An honor student all through his elementary and
junior high school years, by his mid-teens, McCartney's
firm grip on his studies started to slip noticeably.
Why? He had discovered Rock & Roll. To his father's
shock, he gave up his promising academic career geared
towards becoming a teacher while taking his A levels
(the British equivalent of America's high school).

On July 6, 1957, McCartney was introduced to a foul-mouthed, drunken delinquent named John Lennon, and Rock & Roll history was made. The introduction came while Lennon's group played at a CHURCH dance! (St. Peter's Parish Church in Woolton, England.) The two boys became inseparable as they honed their budding musical skills together day and night. George Harrison, a star-struck kid three years younger than Lennon, quickly came into the fold and the nucleus of the *Beatles* was formed.

Together, they avidly worshiped at the shrine of rock, adoring Elvis, Little Richard and Buddy Holly. The group's first big musical break came when they were offered a six week booking in Hamburg, Germany. They stayed there five months, sleeping in the back of a porno theater and washing up in the cinema's public rest room. At night they played Rock & Roll at a filthy strip joint called the Indra Club, famous for its live sex shows. Their "fans" consisted of prostitutes, drunks, transvestites and other assorted German criminals.

The boys lived in an area of Hamburg called the "Reeperbahn," a decaying ghetto full of brothels and drug houses. The young *Beatles*, including "sweet" little Paul, explored these dens of iniquity to the fullest. Like kids let loose in a candy store, they filled up on booze, pep pills (speed) and illicit sex.

Paul, John and George were crawling with venereal diseases when they finally returned to England. Harrison had been deported for being in Germany illegally without a work permit. Paul was kicked out under suspicion of committing arson. He started a fire in the porno palace the *Beatles* called home. After the police arrested and released him, poor Paul wasted no time in hopping a plane back to Britain.

Back home, the *Beatles* found that their musical reputation had preceded them. They were given a steady gig in a dank and dripping Liverpool basement club, (The Cavern). It was here that a rich young homosexual dandy named Brian Epstein fastened his lecherous eyes on John Lennon. Excited by what he saw and heard, Epstein offered to manage the group. Under his Svengali-like leadership, the *Beatles* cleaned up their act, put on suits and proceeded to penetrate the record charts. Though Epstein died of a drug overdose in 1967, his work with the *Beatles* helped their power, popularity and influence over teenagers to first snowball, then avalanche. *Beatle*-mania had arrived.

Tremendous amounts of cash rolled in. Their bank accounts doubled, tripled and quadrupled. It just kept coming. They embarked on massive, mind boggling world tours filled with every sinful vice known to man. Satan had given them everything they had ever wanted. They had it all. But oh, was there an awful price to pay:

> "I've sold my soul to the Devil."
> John Lennon[3]

It was during their initial American conquest in August of 1964 that Paul McCartney and the other *Beatles* smoked marijuana for the first time. They were "turned on" by popular folk music protester Bob Dylan. Flying high through a dizzy cloud of pot smoke, Paul flipped his gourd. He was so heavily stoned, he demanded that a *Beatle* flunky immediately write down every word he spoke, to preserve his genius for future generations! (The flunky did as he was told.)

Marijuana was the key that opened the door to a whole Pandora's box of hallucinogenic brain-busting by the *Beatles*. Their albums were suddenly full of dope

69

imagery and counter-cultural catch phrases. Their every waking moment was spent in a haze of joint-smoking, pill-popping, and eventually, LSD use. They were so addicted to marijuana, they even got stoned in a Buckingham Palace bathroom as they waited to meet the Queen of England on October 26, 1965.

Cute and cuddly Paul shocked the world when he admitted using LSD in Life magazine two years later:

> "It opened my eyes. It made me a better, more honest, more tolerant member of society."[4]

A hailstorm of critical outrage almost immediately burst over McCartney's befuddled head. His response?:

> "If you'd only shut up about it, so will I. It's your fault for putting it in the papers. You've got the responsibility not to spread it."[5]

Beatle Paul also snorted cocaine years before "crack" hit the streets:

> "Again, I was lucky, because I was into that just before the entire record industry got into it. I was into it at the time of Sgt. Pepper, actually. And the guys in the group were a bit, kind of, 'Hey, wait a minute, that's a little heavier than we've been getting into.' And I was doing the traditional coke thing – 'No problem, man, it's just a little toot, no problem . . . ' "[6]

Although he claims to be drug-free today, McCartney still sympathizes with dopeheads everywhere. Witness these comments from a 1986 interview in Rolling Stone Magazine:

> "I think a lot of it's (today's drug problem) been caused by people's ignorance of the drug scene – like lumping marijuana with heroin, saying, 'Well, one leads to the other.' I always say to them, 'Well, booze leads to it just as easily, and cigarettes lead to booze, and so on. It all leads to each other.' "[7]

A very interesting tidbit from McCartney's misguided morality! In one brief quote, he both denies drug use and admits it at the same time. Maybe his mind is too frazzled to figure out what he really believes. Has pot been "harmless" for Paul? Let's check the record:

In August of 1972, almost two full years after the *Beatle* break-up, Paul, his wife Linda and their new group *Wings* were touring Europe and toting pounds of pot with them from country to country. When the dope ran out, they ordered more to be sent to them through the mail. In Gothenburg, Sweden, customs officials nabbed one of the parcels meant for them. The contents? Half a pound of lush, fat-budded marijuana. The McCartneys were arrested and fined.

In 1973, Paul was busted again – this time for GROWING dope at his farm in Campbelltown, Scotland. He claimed he didn't know what the seeds were when he planted them. How about when they started to grow, Paul?

Two years later, Paul and Linda were detained by police in Los Angeles, California. Their erratic driving alerted an L.A.P.D. prowl car, which quickly pulled them over. The McCartney vehicle reeked of dope and a stash of marijuana was found in the glove box. Linda took the rap, since Paul could have been immediately deported due to his previous drug convictions.

The best evidence of marijuana's dulling effects on the brain came in January, 1980. In a move of stunning stupidity, the McCartneys tried to smuggle a half pound of pot placed in a common suitcase through Japanese customs. A *Wings* tour was to begin, but the concerts were cancelled when Paul was arrested and sent immediately to jail. He spent a total of nine days behind bars, then was booted out of the country:

> "We were just taking the flight and without thinking bunged some in. The minute it was discovered at the airport I thought, 'Oh no, goof, goof.' It just banged in my brain the first few days: 'Goof, goof, error.' We didn't really need to take it in. For most people who smoke pot, it's not that big a deal if they haven't got it for a few days. I think of my kind of drug involvement as harmless, so I walked straight into Japan after a fourteen-hour flight thinking, 'It's not that bad . . .' "[8]

Harmless when you can't go for more than a few days without your dope, Paul? Harmless when your brain is so muddled from pot that you stuff a half a POUND of marijuana in your baggage?!

In January of 1984, Linda McCartney was busted for pot possession twice in three days, once in Barbados, and again in London, as she tried to smuggle more marijuana through English customs. This kind of drug-induced desperation should offer ample proof that "grass" is indeed an addictive narcotic.

The McCartneys claim their drug use is under control, merely a harmless giggle. But their bone-headed, dope-fogged actions reveal the true depth of their destructive enslavement to marijuana. How sad that millions of young people cheer them on as they eat up more and more of their minds with every blackened joint consumed.

McCartney's 1983 album, "Pipes Of Peace," featured all kinds of pot pipes pictured on its cover. (See Figure 1.) Paul is also holding the "Pipes of Pan" (Syrinx) in his left hand. (See "About The Cover.") If there was ever a slave to pot, (and Pan) it's Paul McCartney.

PIPES OF PEACE

Figure 1
What have you been smoking in those Peace Pipes, Paul?

73

Paul McCartney's fans will say, "It's his life to live . . . it has nothing to do with his music!" I disagree. The lifestyles of popular rock performers cannot be separated from the music they make. Their private lives are not only a reflection of their output, but are the very SOURCE of their inspiration!

We must understand that all the mystique about "getting high" is Satan's smokescreen hiding a very gritty reality. One toke of a marijuana joint is enough to break down the protective hedge the Lord has placed around us, spiritually speaking. The euphoria, weirdness and lightning quick flashes of inspiration that hit all dopers (including Paul McCartney) are the work of demons. As kids seek a thrill through drug use, these evil spirits come clinging and singing into the mind of the dope smoker. This is why drugs play such an important part in Rock & Roll – they are the main source of inspiration in the music making process.

Think about it, young person – one joint is all it takes to send you straight into the spiritual world that surrounds us. Satan doesn't care what your reasons are; you're in HIS territory now, and he is a cruel and ruthless assassin of trespassers. In McCartney's case, his dope dreams put to music are often covered with a sickly sweet, candy-coated syrup made with synthesizers and lush string arrangements. But there is more than meets the ear in such musical mushiness.

In his book, "Media Sexploitation," Wilson Bryan Key says this about the *Beatles*' music:

> "The *Beatles* popularized and culturally legitimized hallucinatory drug usage among teenagers throughout the world. The *Beatles* became the super drug culture

prophets and pushers of all time . . . "⁹

Key is a pioneer in exposing subliminal seduction and manipulation through film, television, advertising and popular music. In "Media Sexploitation," he specifically dissects the song, "Hey Jude," which was penned by Paul McCartney and performed by the *Beatles*. Here are his findings:

> " . . . 'Jude' could have referred to Judas who betrayed Christ under the guise of friendship. Heroin, of course, at first seems to be a friend before it betrays the user into addiction . . . McCartney sang, 'Let her into your heart,' 'Her' meaning the drug and 'Heart' the pump that circulates drug-laden blood through the body . . . During the lonely opening verse, the drug injection occurred . . . The lyrics tell us, 'Don't be afraid.' 'The moment you let her under your skin, you begin to make it better. . .' 'The movement you need is on your shoulder,' suggesting either the arm for the injection or the monkey (heroin addiction) on your back or shoulder."¹⁰

McCartney swears that "Hey Jude" was inspired by John Lennon's son, Julian. Perhaps in Paul's conscious thoughts that was the case, but reading the lyrics with an eye on their subliminal impact shows the real effect all that drugging had on McCartney's mind. He'll never admit it but ALL the *Beatles* were pawns of Satan, willing guests at his loaded banquet table.

What about Paul's solo music after the *Beatles* break-up? Here are some lyrics to his 1972 song "Hi, Hi, Hi:"

"We're gonna get high, high, high
With the music on
Won't say bye by, bye by, bye by, bye by
Til the night is gone . . .
Well, well take off your face
Recover from the trip you've been on
I want you to lie on the bed
Gettin' ready for my polygon
I'm gonna do it to you, gonna do ya
Sweet banana, you've never been done
Yes, and like a rabbit, gonna grab it
Gonna do it till the night is done. . . "

This song was banned in Britain. Squinting through
drug-fogged eyes, Paul thought he could pull a fast one:

"I thought the 'Hi, Hi, Hi' thing could
easily be taken as a natural high, could be
taken as a booze high and everything. It
doesn't have to be drugs, you know, so I'd
kind of get away with it. Well, the first
thing they saw was drugs, so I didn't get
away with that . . . "[11]

As usual, dope was only the first step in Paul's perversion. McCartney and *Wings'* 1973 "Red Rose Speed-
way" album contained photographs of half naked, bare
breasted women in their underwear pasted to the
inner sleeve. And people call this stuff "safe?"

The song, "Letting Go," appeared on McCartney's 1975
"Venus And Mars" LP:

"Ah, she tastes like wine
Such a human being so divine
Oh she feels like sun
Mother Nature look at what you've done

76

Ah, she looks like snow
I want to put her in a Broadway show
Ah, she'll dance and dine
Like a lucifer she'll always shine. . ."

Here's a subtle clue as to who McCartney really serves. But he should do a little Bible study before he starts tackling theological issues. Lucifer will NOT always shine. He will one day be cast into the lake of fire and will burn there forever. Jesus Christ is the One who lives in unapproachable light. (See I Timothy 6:14-16.) Sounds like Paulie has been spreading some satanic lies. That doesn't sound "safe" to me.

"Venus And Mars - Reprise"

"A good friend of mine
Studies the stars
Sold me her sign
Reach for the stars
Venus and Mars
Are alright tonight . . . "

Now he's singing about occult-drenched astrology. Safe? Another song on the record is called "Spirits Of Ancient Egypt." Why is mild and mellow Paul McCartney singing about ancient spirits of the Egyptian occult? Lucifer, astrology, demonic Egyptian spirits, that's not supposed to be a part of Paul's squeaky clean, scrubbed-behind-the-ears image. What devil-inspired dope dreams led him to write those songs?

We need to wake up and realize that for over twenty years, McCartney's life has been a carefully planned master stroke of public relations. Though society adores him, his life and music tell a different story:

77

"Wino Junko"

"Doctor Tom is getting on, All he does is
    sign his name
I get things, my brainbox sings, But I'll go
    down again
Play with fire, Getting higher
Higher than a moth aflame
My soul is spinning, So's the room
But I'll go down again
Wino Junko, can't say no, Wino Junko,
    eyes aglow
Pill freak, spring a leak
Can't say no
Till you go down again . . . "

This song appeared on McCartney's 1976 "At The
Speed Of Sound" album. *Wings* guitarist Jimmy
McCulloch wrote and sang the tune, a junkie's funeral
dirge if ever there was one. Birds of a feather flock
together. But Paulie and his friends don't want to go
down alone, they want to take millions with them. As
part of this self-fulfilling musical prophecy, McCulloch
died of a morphine overdose in September, 1979.

The only reason any of this offends people is because of
the lingering, sweet-smelling image still clinging to
this ex-*Beatle*. See how sweet-smelling this quote
sounds to you:

> "I saw a show the other night on television
> which . . . I was not offended by – I mean,
> it doesn't really bug me – but it made me
> start to wonder whether people were going
> slightly far out. It was a gay thing, and a
> couple of guys were really gettin' to it.
> Now, I have no objection to anyone getting

their rocks off in any way they want. But maybe public telly isn't the forum for it."

Paul McCartney[12]

So homosexuality "doesn't really bug" sweet, unspoiled Paul. It's no wonder after the mountains of shameful sexual perversity he saw during his *Beatle* years! When on the road, even Fab Four flunkies Mal Evans and Neil Aspinall lived just like the rest of the "boys:"

"So anyway, I'd been dying to tell her about the raving on tour for years, you know, because I just wanted people to know what a scene it was ... and that's why people like Neil, they were living like kings, you know. They were having more fun than us. We were locked in our rooms all the time. They were going to the whore houses and ordering up the class whores. We were locked in our #@%! room and we couldn't go out ... "

John Lennon[13]

An unrepentant agnostic, convicted drug smuggler, pro-homo dopehead, and powerful prophet of a generation's immorality, Paul McCartney doesn't deserve hero worship. Despite his millions of bucks, world-wide adoration and a perfectly maintained clean-cut image, he and his music are anything but safe. Careful examination of McCartney's life shows that his real master is God's enemy. The power behind Paul McCartney is none other than Satan.

TINA TURNER

Tina Turner is one of the most successful and respected women in rock today. She has been put on a musical pedestal by a huge audience of teens and not-so-young

79

adults. A Grammy Award winning performer, her recent string of smash records, videos and concert tours have firmly established her as a gold-plated, black superstar.

Women respect her for escaping from years of physical and mental abuse at the hands of her ex-husband, musician Ike Turner. Men love her for the heart-thumping frenzy of her live shows and videos – as well as her shapely legs. If you see Tina Turner as a whole-some alternative to other rock stars, read on.

She was born Anna Mae Bullock in November of 1939, in Nutbush, Tennessee. Her older sister Alline was an illegitimate child. Though her parents were married by the time Anna was born, she was unwanted as well. She spent her early years in lonely isolation, wondering why she was ignored and rejected by her family.

In 1942, her parents pushed the children off on relatives as they moved away to seek better jobs. Tina was left in her grandmother's care. Roxanna Bullock was a strict and straight-laced Christian who forced Tina to attend the local Baptist church every Sunday.

After World War II, Anna Mae and Alline were reunited with their parents and Anna began to exercise her singing voice for anyone who would listen. Church songs and anything from the radio were her favorites. She was exposed at an early age to barrooms, the blues and "Boogie Woogie." She also joined the church choir:

> "I wasn't aware that I was singing about God, and how good he was; I just liked the songs. And I would always take the lead on the very upbeat ones – you know, the real shouters . . . "[14]

80

By 1952, Tina's parents called their marriage quits and abandoned their children. The girls were taken in by cousins. Tina gave up her virginity at age 15 to a high school sweetheart named Harry:

> "Naturally I lost my virginity in the back seat of a car: This was the fifties; right? I think he had it planned, the little devil - he told me there was nothing playing at the movies that night. I guess he knew by then that he could get . . . But I did it for love. The pain was excruciating; but I loved him and he loved me, and that made the pain less. I was really stimulated by Harry, and he was a good lover, too. Everything was right. So it was beautiful."[15]

> "I was protected by the gods. To actually have sex when you are in love is the best way. I hadn't fooled around before Harry, and I didn't afterward, because I'm a very faithful woman."[16]

Two years later, the Bullock girls moved to St. Louis, Missouri, where they once again took up residence with their runaway mother. Like homeless ping pong balls, they just kept bouncing back and forth between family members. The sisters spent their evenings and weekends visiting "clubs" (bars). It was at one of these lush lounges that Tina first met Rhythm & Blues band leader Ike Turner. His mesmerizing musical stage presence and complete control of the booze-happy crowd left her weak in the knees.

Ike's father was a Baptist minister who was beaten to death for having an affair with a white girl. Like his dad, Ike Turner was a nonstop womanizer. He had already been married twice when Tina crossed his path. Booze, guns, fornication and music were the basic ingredients of his lifestyle. Ike's band, "The Kings Of Rhythm," followed their leader's example. It was not unusual for forty women to be involved with all the band members at once. Under Ike's iron fist and cold-eyed discipline, the group became one of the most popular in St. Louis. Work hard, play harder, was Turner's motto. Into this maze of sweat, sin and hysteria walked 17-year-old Anna Mae Bullock.

She wrangled her way into a singing audition and Ike was knocked off his chair. With her mother's permission, Anna began traveling with the band. The sins of such a loose lifestyle inevitably took their toll, and she became pregnant by one of the Rhythm Kings while still in high school. The baby was born, the father drifted away and Ike moved in on Tina.

She gave in to Ike's advances and became his "main squeeze." Ike's other multiple affairs (he was still married) were going on simultaneously, producing even more illegitimate children. Anna Bullock once again became pregnant, this time by Ike. Like a bolt out of the blue, he renamed her Tina Turner and made her the singing centerpiece of his stage show. Other girls were hired to back up Tina. Wearing long, straight-haired wigs and dressed in spangly, hip hugging miniskirts, they gyrated while Tina sang. This latest addition to Turner's harem became "The Ikettes."

Hit records were released and by 1962 "The Ike & Tina Turner Revue" was hot stuff all over the country. Much of the act was outright filth. Tina recalls:

"When we started doing 'I've Been Loving

You' on stage, it was Jimmy Thomas who sang it . . . Then when Jimmy left, I started singing the song because it was a very good show song, and I started mimicking Jimmy, but putting my own female thing into it. I was really involved with that song in the beginning. Then I became bored with it, but Ike wouldn't let me stop. He started making those noises in the background, and it became really pornographic. Embarrassing. But the people loved it."[17]

Fired up on cocaine and other drugs, Ike became a madman. As the money and touring pressures mounted, he began brutally beating Tina. She was often left bruised and bloodied from his no-warning rages. She grew to hate him, and even underwent an abortion rather than bear another of his children.

Tina tried marijuana, speed, and even attempted suicide in 1967 by taking 50 Valiums. A stomach pumping at a Los Angeles hospital put her back on her feet, but Ike forced her to immediately resume performing. Desperately searching for a way out of her miserable marriage, she started consulting fortune tellers:

"The only things that kept me going in those years was the readers. Whatever cities we played – here, in Europe, wherever – I would always try to find a reader to go to . . . Then I'd tell Ike I was going shop-ping and I'd head straight for that reader. Some of these people read cards, some read palms, some read the stars. Some read tea leaves and coffee sediments . . . I was exploring my soul, for the first time. I had always held onto the Bible and the things I'd learned as a little girl – the Lord's Prayer, the Ten Commandments. And I prayed every night, you can believe that. But now I was really seeking a change . . . I'm not talking about fortune-telling or witchcraft. I was looking for the truth of a future I could feel inside of me."[18]

I've got bad news for Tina – fortune-telling **IS** witchcraft! (See Isaiah 47:12-15.) No matter what objects are used to give off the "vibrations," whether cards, palms, or crystal balls, it is still the "reader's" familiar spirits (demons) that give the information.

In the early seventies, Tina turned on to Buddhism. She chanted a special incantation every day, a cycle which eventually lasted up to four hours! Suddenly, her smallest wishes were miraculously granted. She plunged into this pagan religion wholeheartedly and bought a "butsudan," or prayer altar:

> "The butsudan looks like a little altar; but the idea is not that you're WORSHIPING this piece of paper or anything. These things allow you to focus, to be in the right frame of mind to RECEIVE, and they are a form of respect."   Tina Turner[19]

Tina's right. She isn't worshiping the butsudan. But she is worshiping the power behind it . . . Satan. And she was receiving, all right, but it was demons who were doing the sending.

> " . . . The chant brings you into harmony with the hum of the universe, that kind of subtle buzz at the center of all being. Close

your eyes and you can hear it all around
you . . . "   Tina Turner[20]

A new "soul reader" explained to Tina the Egyptian
after-lives and the revenge of Karmic mistakes she had
made in ages past. In a previous incarnation, she was
supposedly a female Pharaoh. Ike was her evil half-
brother/husband who was out to destroy their kingdom. Tina completely accepted this absurd occult
garbage without question.

Her autobiography, "I, Tina," reveals the depth of her
bondage to things forbidden by God, including astrology. In a photo on page 177, she stands before a huge
wheel emblazoned with every sign of the zodiac. This
pagan symbol hung above a fireplace in the home she
shared with Ike. A fiery representation of the sun fills
the center of the thing. In the Bible, "Baal" was the god
of the sun. The Bible names astrology and divining the
future as foul, forbidden works of darkness. (Leviticus
19:31, Deuteronomy 18:10-12 and Jeremiah 14:14).

By 1978, divorced from Ike, Tina was musically on her
own. Her solo career went nowhere for almost six
years, until her smash hit album, "Private Dancer,"
was released. Ten million copies were sold worldwide,
spinning off three Top 10 American singles. The song
that put her back on top was a cynical and jaded look
at sex called, "What's Love Got To Do With It:"

> "You must understand, Though the touch
>   of your hand
> Makes my pulse react
> That it's only the thrill of boy meeting girl
> Opposites attract
> It's physical, Only logical
> You must try to ignore that it means

85

> more than that
> Oh, what's love, Got to do, Got to do
>   with it
> What's love, but a second-hand emotion. . .
> But a sweet, old-fashioned notion . . . "

Several months later, Turner won four Grammys for "Private Dancer." She immediately began work on "Mad Max – Beyond Thunderdome," a futuristic film about life after nuclear war. Her character was called "Aunty Entity." In the movie, Tina wore a huge ring on her index finger shaped like an ankh, the Egyptian symbol of sun worship and reincarnation. To those in the occult, wearing an ankh shows that you have given up your virginity and take part in sexual orgies.

Tina's movie acting debut had come a decade earlier as the "Acid Queen," one of many perverse characters in the violent Ken Russell film, "Tommy." In her single heart-stopping scene, Tina injects *Who* singer Roger Daltrey with enough LSD to keep him flying high for life. As he trips out of the picture, she screams and howls with wicked delight, her eyes bulging out of her head, every muscle in her body convulsing with an uncontrollable trembling seizure.

Turnermania did not end in 1986. A new album entitled, "Break Every Rule" hit the record stores and immediately shot up the charts. (See Figure 2.) With the help of pop superstar friends David Bowie and Phil Collins, Tina sang songs like:

"What You Get Is What You See:"

> "Some guys got lips that you can't help
>   kissing
> Some guys got a smile that you can't

resist
Some guys gotta build a reputation
They just wanna add you to the list
You got a lot of physical attraction I can't
deny
But can you guarantee me satisfaction
Well I'm still waiting, waiting, waiting. . ."

"Paradise Is Here"

"Tonight I need your love
Don't talk about tomorrow
Right now I need your loving
Right now give it to me
Right now I want your loving
Right now . . ."

"Till The Right Man Comes Along"

"Oh baby you're the best thing in my life
But a one track mind is what you got
Oh baby you're my best bet here tonight
I've got no good reason to believe we'll last
for long
But that's good enough for me till the right
man
Comes along . . . "

These songs are examples of the sleazy themes of
casual sex so common in Tina's music. Because the
beat is subdued on a few of her songs, parents heave a
big sigh of relief when their kids bring home Tina
Turner instead of *Motley Crue*. But watch out Mom
and Dad, the message is the same: get your sex hot and
fast before it's too late. This kind of music is similar to
an old pornography trick – substitute the word "love"
for "sex" and no one will ever complain.

Figure 2

Tina Turner's image has always been that of a heavy breathing, steamy sexual lust baby barely under control. That hasn't changed since she's gone pop. The inner sleeve of "Break Every Rule" features a full length photo of Tina wearing a slitted mini-dress which barely covers her backside. The entire picture is bathed in red, the color of harlotry. And don't think there's no Rock & Roll on this record. Those breathy ballads may get her on MTV, but it's the slam-bang crunch of ripped-off rock for which she is best known.

How close are those songs to the "real" Tina?

"I've had a few love affairs, but nothing important."[21]

" . . . Sure, I get horny, I need a touch, but that's not as important as what I'm trying to achieve for this girl who's been struggling all these years . . . "[22]

"I've never sung anything I couldn't relate to . . . My music is about my life, my religion, and my friends."[23]

Tina Turner's life has included premarital sex, illegitimate birth, drug abuse, occult involvement, abortion and attempted suicide. Her religion is Buddhism, a totally anti-Christian pagan cult. Some of her best friends include bisexual coke-head David Bowie, as well as Mick Jagger and his *Rolling Stones*, the most infamous band of doped-up Black Magic rock monsters of all time. And she readily admits that this is what her music is about! The only question I have is how can this mess possibly fit into the "safe" category.

Beware, parents and young people. Just because pop stars like Tina Turner come in a pretty package and win lots of Grammys doesn't mean their music is safe, by any means. People like Tina Turner are just as dangerous as Ozzy Osbourne, and a lot more deceptive.

DARYL HALL

For many people, nothing seems safer than the music of one of the most famous pop duos of all time – *Hall & Oates*. They were the darlings of the 1984 American Music awards and have consistently hit the Top 40 charts for a dozen years. Daryl Hall is the lean and lanky, long-haired blond counterpart to his dark, curly headed song writing sidekick, John Oates.

Big, chart busting, sugary pop hits like "Rich Girl,"
"Kiss On My List," "I Can't Go For That," "Private
Eyes" and "Method Of Love" have made them millions.
Their audience consists of rabid pop fans and star-
struck teenage girls. Parents give *Hall & Oates* the
green light to enter their homes because they are a re-
spectable "safe" group, as opposed to some of the other
rock monstrosities. What could possibly be wrong with
idolizing Daryl and Johnny?

Homosexuality and satanism are the two main reasons you should burn any *Hall & Oates* records and
tapes you might own. Details?

Daryl Franklin Hohl was born in Pennsylvania in
1949. The hereditary witchcraft of his family dates
back at least three generations:

> "Benjamin, my great-great grandfather
> was a warlock, a mojo man ... People went
> to Benjamin Hohl for everything from
> curing cattle, dowsing for water, and ban-
> ishing warts to matters concerning
> curses. My grandfather was equally
> gifted at removing AND putting curses
> on people ... "[24]

Demonic spirits are often passed down from generation to generation. They pass their evil on from
parents to children through the opened doorways of
unrepented sins. (See Exodus 34:6,7, Jeremiah 32:18,
16:10-13 and Matthew 23:29-33.) Daryl Hall freely
admits possessing this "force:"

> "And just as I got my musical gifts from my

90

mom and dad . . . so I also inherited this personal FORCE from my earlier fore-bears. All my life I've had these unusual things occur in my head and happen to me, things I'm still not ready to discuss freely. I've had to learn more about these things that I feel are innate in everybody but more pronounced in me, to focus this power and make the best use of it."[25]

"When I'm singing and in touch with the energy I'm generating, I sometimes liter-ally have no awareness of where I am. The ego disappears, and me and my surround-ings with it. I've learned how to be able to do that in public, but I do it in private, too. And frankly, that's the reason I'm in music – to achieve that feeling."[26]

This sensation of losing touch with reality while sub-merging into a different world through music is a common testimony of big name rockers. Many have expressed these feelings of surrendering control of their will, mind and spirit to a force more powerful than themselves as they perform for their adoring masses. Daryl may think he is generating the energy, but he's just the fuse box. SATAN flips the switch!

The other half of the *Hall & Oates* team, John Oates, is completely dominated by his alter ego in every way – musically, professionally and personally. In their songs, videos and interviews, Hall is always the center of attention. Prideful and haughty, with a cold and revengeful spirit, Hall's intense desire to completely control and manipulate those around him is the hall-mark of a practicing satanist.

In the May, 1981 issue of "16" Magazine, Hall openly bragged of his involvement with the occult. In an October 13, 1977 "Circus" article, he revealed that his song, "Winged Bull," was dedicated to the "ancient Celtic religion" (witchcraft). Hall is also a devoted disciple of master satanist Aleister Crowley, one of the most evil Black Magicians of all time. Crowley is the patron saint of rock, having indirectly influenced the *Beatles*, the *Rolling Stones, Led Zeppelin,* Ozzy Osbourne, and of course, Daryl Hall:

> "Around 1974, I graduated into the occult, and spent a solid six or seven years immersed in the Kabala and the Chaldean, Celtic, and druidic traditions, (and) ancient techniques for focusing the inner flame, the will that can create unimagined things and truly transform your individual universe. I also became fascinated with Aleister Crowley, the nineteenth-century British magician who shared these beliefs . . . But I was fascinated by him because his personality was the late nineteenth-century equivalent of mine – a person brought up in a conventionally religious family who did everything he could to outrage the people around him as well as himself."[27]

Crowley was a bisexual, heroin addict, demonologist and satanist who detailed the proper way to perform a human sacrifice in his book, "Magick." What a great role model!

Their 1975 untitled album featured the two men cheek to cheek on the cover, their faces made up with lipstick, eyeliner and blush. Hall is wearing a small human skull as a necklace. (See Figure 3.)

Figure 3

An inner sleeve color photo shows Oates reclining naked under pink lights. His buddy Daryl is sporting an unzipped jumpsuit and pyramid jewelry. (The pyramid is greatly revered in the occult.) When asked about the obvious homosexuality of these pictures, Hall boldly replied:

> "The idea of sex with a man doesn't turn me off, but I don't express it. I satisfied my curiosity about that years ago. I had lots of

93

sex between the ages of three or four and the time I was fourteen or fifteen. Strange experiences with older boys. But men don't particularly turn me on. And no, John and I have never been lovers. He's not my type. Too short and dark."[28]

How does Daryl look at himself?:

"I grew up around that 'seein'-the-light' kind of thing. And now I'm a secular version of it. In my uncles' time, you were a minister. Two generations before that you were a warlock. Now you're me. It's just a current. I believe in the ability to change reality through will, and that is the definition of magic. I feel I have done that."[29]

"Do as thou wilt shall be the whole of the law."   Aleister Crowley

Daryl Hall's philosophy about himself and his music is summed up in these words:

"Because, if I have a religion, it's the religion of the self. I don't follow anybody. And that scares people, but I like the idea of scaring people. I wish I scared people more. I don't know if I scared anyone on this new album, but I'm better at scaring people in my personal life. I change quickly. I go from nice to not nice. I'm like a snake. Don't back me into a corner or I'll bite hard. Deadly hard."[30]

This "safe" stuff is getting more dangerous all the

time. Remember that the next time you hear *Hall &*
Oates on the radio.

MADONNA

Louise Veronica Ciccone, better known as Madonna, is
the idol of tens of thousands of young girls everywhere.
She is also a steamy sex object to hordes of drooling
young men across America, Canada and Europe. Her
soulful, heart-piercing ballads about the adolescent
pains of falling in and out of love have sky-rocketed her
to superstar status in just a few short years. As a
watered-down Marilyn Monroe clone, her movie roles
have made her much more than just an immensely
popular recording and video star. She has become
larger than life, thanks in no small part to her crass
"bad girl made good" image.

Most parents don't think twice about letting Madonna's
music into their home. After all, she is one of the most
popular female vocalists in the world. Is her music
dangerous? To answer that, we must dig through the
sleazy past of Ms. Ciccone, a woman with no shame.

Born in a large Catholic family in Bay City, Michigan
on August 16, 1959, her father was an executive in the
Detroit auto industry. Her mother is deceased. Like
multitudes of young midwestern girls with more guts
than sense, the big bucks hunger for bright lights and
movie stardom hit her right between the eyes before
she was out of her teens:

> "When you grow up in some hick town in
> Michigan, there's nothing that you can do
> that will make you feel like a movie star. I
> wanted to be a movie star."[31]

95

Establishing a pattern she was to use throughout her career, Madonna picked up and discarded men like used handkerchiefs. Each illicit relationship became just another rung in her frantic climb up the slippery ladder to success. When each of her lovers could no longer contribute anything to further her ambition, she dumped them and moved on to the next pigeon:

> "I used to borrow money from people, let some poor sucker take me out for dinner and then I'd go 'Can I borrow a hundred?' ' "[32]

Even before her high school graduation, Louise and her ballet teacher were hitting Detroit's homosexual nightspots together:

> "He used to take me to all the gay discotheques in downtown Detroit. Men were doing poppers (amyl nitrate) and going crazy. They were all dressed really well and were more free about themselves than all the blockhead football players I met in high school."[33]

While taking a short stab at studying dance at the University of Michigan, she met a musician named Steve Bray who taught her the basics of song writing. Thoroughly disgusted by the midwest, Louise packed her bags and headed for New York City in 1978.

She arrived there through a series of shameful circumstances. She lived for a year in an abandoned building in Queens with her first live-in lover, musician Dan Gilroy. Their band was called *The Breakfast Club*, but the group didn't last past lunch. Meanwhile, Steve Bray had followed Louise all the way from Michigan and was helping her make demo tapes to peddle at local discos. She moved in with him, and they lived together until she met disc jockey Mark Kamins. It was around this time that Louise became known as Madonna.

During this period she appeared in her first film – "A Certain Sacrifice," which featured a Madonna rape scene. She topped that later with a group sex orgy including herself, a man, another woman and a transvestite. Little Louise Ciccone, the star-struck teenager from Michigan, was finally a "movie star." (Needless to say, she did not win an Oscar for this film.)

Her "romance" with Kamins lasted just long enough for him to help market her first single and video, "Everybody." On the strength of this tune, Kamins bulldozed Sire Records into signing her to a contract, then ate Madonna's dust as she shot off to stardom.

After dumping Kamins, Ciccone took up with artist Jean Michel Basquiat. I'm sure it was a coincidence that Basquiat's close friend was the most powerful name in New York's underground art community – Andy Warhol. (Warhol's claim to fame was his 60's portrait of a can of Campbell's soup.)

After Madonna gave Basquiat the boot, next up to bat was famous New York disc jockey, John "Jellybean" Benitez. He produced her song, "Holiday," which became a big hit. Her self-titled debut album nudged her one step closer to the megastardom she so desperately craved, but her 1984 "Like A Virgin" album put her over the top. (See Figure 4.)

The runaway success of this record, (over 6 million sold) combined with her "Virgin" video, which played on MTV every hour for weeks, thrust her into the blinding spotlight of big bucks and superstardom. The eyes of the world soon were firmly glued to Madonna's bare belly button as hit after hit from the album cracked the Top 10.

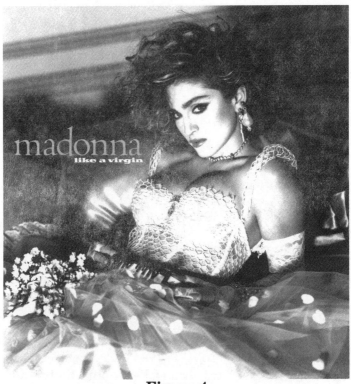

Figure 4

As part of her follow-up concert tour, she wore a white wedding gown and veil on stage. A new phrase was coined to describe this sleazy, oversexed superstar, taken from the belt she wore on "Like A Virgin's" cover – "Boy Toy." Liner notes on the album's inner sleeve read, "This album is dedicated to the virgins of the world." Very funny, Louise.

A cynical mockery of chastity had become Madonna's calling card to fame and fortune. She played it for all it was worth:

> "They say,'Well, I have to do a video now, and a pop star has to come on sexually, so how do I do that?' instead of being in touch with that part of their self to begin with. I've been in touch with that aspect of my personality since I was five."[34]

> "I couldn't be a success without also being a sex symbol. I'm sexy. People associate a girl who's successful with a bimbo or an airhead. I think people want to see me as a little tart bimbo who sells records because I'm cute and record companies push 'em because they know they can make a fast buck on my image."[35]

Our society has gotten so desperately sick that soft-core porn has become the order of the day in all forms of media entertainment. The smeared, brazen picture of a street-wise harlot now passes for "sexiness." What would have been rightly labeled as plain old smut 30 years ago is now disguised as "art." Several tunes from "Like A Virgin" are perfect examples of this:

"Like A Virgin"

> "I was beat, incomplete
> I'd been had, I was sad and blue
> But you made me feel
> Yeah, you made me feel shiny and new
> Like a virgin
> Touched for the very first time
> Like a virgin

When your heart beats next to mine
Gonna give you all my love, boy . . . "

"Dress You Up"

"You've got style
That's what all the girls say
Satin sheets . . .
I've got something that you'll really like
Gonna dress you up in my love . . .
All over your body
Feel the silky touch of my caresses . . . "

"Shoo-Bee-Doo"

"I can make it on my own, baby
But I'd rather share all the love that's
    there
I don't want to be alone and maybe
You will see the light
Baby, spend the night . . . "

"Pretender"

"I like the way he moved across the floor
And when he danced with me I know
    he wanted more
But in the dark things happen much too
    fast
I should've stopped him then, I knew it
    wouldn't last . . ."

No matter what kind of heart-thumping, lip-pouting,
wide-eyed innocent image Louise Ciccone may be trying
to project, a short dig into her background shows that
the whole concept of virginity is a joke to her. As she
sang "Touched for the very first time" on stage, her

miniskirt went north while her blouse went south. Draped in crosses, beads, bracelets and studs, her make-up an inch thick, her bouncing backside barely covered and her filmy see-through top hiked above her chest, Madonna's "Virgin" tour was in reality nothing more than a cheap traveling peep show.

> "As a jewel of gold in a swine's snout, so is
> a fair woman which is without discretion."
>   Proverbs 11:22

In 1985, Madonna starred in her second movie and first major role, "Desperately Seeking Susan." She played a dope-smoking, street-walking New York nomad who spent her time stealing from the men she slept with. In one scene, Madonna and her boyfriend are surprised by a stranger as they begin to have sex on top of a pinball machine. Talk about typecasting!

When the video, "Material Girl," was unveiled on MTV in 1985, Louise's image had undergone a drastic change. The mud-caked hair, biker's leather and too-tight stretch pants were gone. In their place was a jewel and fur bedecked blonde clad in expensive evening gowns - the kind of woman who gets her cigarette lit by tuxedoed gents as she steps out of her Rolls Royce. It was hard to imagine that anyone would take a second rate imitation of Marilyn Monroe seriously, yet this video became one of MTV's most requested. Madonna now had artistic credibility to match her multi-million record sales, all because of a bath and a new hairdo. The song lyrics reflect the cold shamelessness of a woman who will do anything to get what she wants:

"Material Girl"

"They can beg and they can plead

101

But they can't see the light, that's right
'Cause the boy with the cold hard cash
Is always Mister Right
Cause we're living in a material world
And I am a material girl . . . "

On August 16, 1985 Louise Ciccone married actor Sean Penn in a private ceremony that had all of Hollywood banging at their door. Muckraking journalists from the national scandal sheets hovered overhead in helicopters, while other nosy newsmen crawled through the underbrush, intent on capturing this earthshaking event on film. (Sean Penn is best known for his portrayal of tough-as-nails psychotic "bad boys" in his many movies. In June of 1987 he was sentenced to two months in jail for parole violation and battery.)

A month before the wedding, Madonna performed at Philadelphia's gigantic Live Aid festival, a massive production seen worldwide by almost 2 billion people. She also plunked down $800,000 for a swank New York apartment and co-starred with her new hubby in "Shanghai Surprise," a film backed by ex-*Beatle* George Harrison. Madonna played a missionary. (Wishful thinking never hurt anyone.)

Divorce came as easy as blowing one's nose when poor Sean Penn found himself the last hankie in Madonna's box. The "Material Girl" served him papers in January, 1988, then abruptly changed her mind. Married? Divorced? Separated? Only Madonna knows for sure.

Flushed with success beyond anyone's wildest dreams, idolized by millions, her foul-smelling past washed away by the sweet scent of teetering piles of green dollars, Louise Veronica Ciccone could have gone in a more positive direction with her next album and video.

Instead, she chose to return to the pig pen.

The album, "True Blue," hit the record stores in 1986. One of its most popular songs, "Papa Don't Preach," was hailed as a stirring, positive, right-to-life message, since the girl elected to keep her illegitimate baby rather than turn it over to the toilet bowl local abortion clinic.   Before you pat Louise on the back for her admirable stand, remember it's illicit sex that produces unwanted children in the first place.   Has she changed her position on such relations?   No.   She's just mad because her father might object.   This song isn't pointing teenagers toward a better way, it's simply reinforcing the "rightness" of premarital sex.   The result will be hundreds and thousands more unwanted pregnancies.   Somehow I know Louise could care less.

"Papa Don't Preach"

> "He says that he's going to marry me
> We can raise a little family
> Maybe we'll be all right
> It's a sacrifice . . .
> Papa don't preach, I'm in trouble deep
> Papa don't preach, I've been losing sleep
> But I made up my mind, I'm keeping my
>   baby . . . "

Late in the fall of 1986, MTV went nuts over Madonna's "Open Your Heart" video, taken from the "True Blue" album.   Every half hour for many weeks, they ran and re-ran this disgusting piece of soft-core porn.   Madonna is a porno palace peep show performer in this mini movie.   Her straggly blonde mane is butched close to her head.   Her only clothes are a leather S&M bondage corset, black fishnet stockings, elbow length gloves and heels.   She sits on a littered and dirty stage, surrounded by windows, bathed in purple light, while bug-eyed men with sweating foreheads sit behind the glass and watch her "perform." Outside, a boy about twelve tries unsuccessfully to get past the ticket taker.

Subliminal witchcraft sign language is all over this video, from the strange, stilted movements of the onlookers as they pass their hands and forearms across their unblinking eyes, to Madonna's wild "dancing." Like intertwining snakes, her hands whip back and forth, clasp and release.

Her clothes changed, and her shift over, Madonna the "working girl" meets the boy waiting outside, and plants a sensuous kiss full on his lips. They dance off into the sunset together - innocence and harlotry hand in hand. Here are some lyrics to "Open Your Heart:"

> "I've had to work much harder than this
> But some things I want, Don't try to resist
>   me
> Open your heart to me baby
> I hold the lock and you hold the key
> Open your heart to me darling
> I'll give you love if you'll, You'll turn the
>   key . . . "

Put Satan in those words instead of just boy/girl "love," and you'll get the true meaning behind the message.

Madonna Ciccone's influence on teens everywhere (especially young girls) is staggering. Her music, movies and videos are an accurate reflection of her life, an existence dedicated to the three S's – Sex, Smut and Shock. After her initial wave of mind-boggling triumph had crested in 1985, the pornographic magazines "Penthouse" and "Playboy" both printed nude photos of

Madonna that she had posed for years earlier. The pictures cost them close to a million bucks.

Her super-successful 1987 concert tour splashed Madonna's picture all over supermarket mags and rock fanzines alike. Clad in leather, fishnet, and little else, she bellowed into stage microphones across the country, "Are ya ready to paaaarrrty?"

With a glossy sheen of superstar slickness hiding the ugly reality beneath, Madonna has become a widely imitated role model. She sells sexuality on a silver platter. She sings about trash and she lives what she sings. A life and career like hers deserves shame, not support. Her opinion?

"I never #@%! anyone to get anywhere."[36]

That's not what your music says, Madonna.

STEVIE NICKS

If Stevie Nicks is not a witch, then my mother wears army boots.

For 13 years, the musical career of this wild-haired, chiffon-draped gypsy from the West Coast has been full of fantastic successes and record breaking musical milestones. But the eerie weirdness of her songs, videos, interviews and personal life leave little doubt as to where the real source of her fame and fortune comes from. With a husky laugh and a careless shrug of her thin shoulders, she denies being a part of the "dark side," yet stops just short of openly admitting her interlock with the occult. While being questioned by MTV veejay Mark Goodman in 1984, Nicks was asked:

"**MTV:** You've written so much about visions.
Do you feel you have connections . . .
elsewhere?
NICKS: Not bad connections.
MTV: You once said you were a witch.
NICKS: I lied. Or just in the funny sense . . . like
the silly witch that crashes into your
window on the broom.
MTV: We once talked about the fact that you
DO believe in reincarnation. Do you
ever try to contact other people?
NICKS: No. I think . . . You can summon things
that you shouldn't mess with. There
are mischievous spirits around, and I
don't . . . I don't even watch scary movies anymore . . . "[37]

So poor little Stevie wants us to believe she is a harmless white magic crusader, in tune with the "good"
forces of the universe, huh? Kind of like a bumbling but
well-meaning Samantha from the old "Bewitched"
T.V. show. She may fool the millions who worship the
ground she walks on, but two short words stand out in
the above interview like glaring neon lights – "I LIED."

Just who is this woman who has helped sell over 20
million *Fleetwood Mac* albums, as well as plenty of
platinum records and tapes during her own phenome-
nal solo career? How black is the darkness she moves
in? And what clues can be gleaned from her music,
videos and interviews? Let's shine some light on the
performer Rolling Stone magazine called "*Fleetwood
Mac's* blond priestess of the occult."[38]

Stephanie Nicks was born in Phoenix, Arizona on May
26, 1948. Her father was a high level business executive for Greyhound, Armour Meats and General Brew-

106

ing. As a result of his constant job-related travel, the Nicks family moved often. Though she was barely a toddler, Stevie was greatly influenced by her grandfather A.J., a strange and eccentric traveling musician who lived in the Arizona mountains. He would take his five-year-old granddaughter into dark barrooms where she sang and danced while A.J. played guitar.

By the time she was sixteen, Stevie had lived in half a dozen states, finally settling in California during the mid sixties. When the Summer of Love hit San Francisco with a multi-colored, psychedelic bang in 1967, she had already been infected with the Rock & Roll bug. While still in high school, Stevie was singing in an Acid Rock quartet cloned after *The Mamas and Papas* called *Changing Times*.

The times changed and the rock got harder when Lindsey Buckingham entered the scene. A California boy with a burning desire to make it big in the music business, Buckingham fronted a Bay area band called *Fritz*. When Lindsey met Stevie, sparks flew. They lived together for the next seven years. *Fritz* eventually folded, leaving the two love birds poised between starvation and the unemployment line. They produced one album during this period, 1972's "Buckingham Nicks." It was a dismal commercial flop.

While Stevie waited tables and Buckingham played with his tapes, a washed up trio of British blues musicians arrived in California. As part of a group called *Fleetwood Mac*, in eight years they had watched six guitarists come and go. With few hit singles and no musical future worth mentioning, the three remaining Macs scoured LA studios for up-and-coming talent. It was there that drummer Mick Fleetwood first heard the Buckingham-Nicks album. Stevie and Lindsey accepted the band's offer to join, and by January 1975, a new *Fleetwood Mac* record was being made.

Though the other members contributed greatly to this LP, it was Stevie Nicks' "Rhiannon" which pushed the record to the top of the popularity polls. This song became one of the biggest hit singles of 1975. "Rhiannon" not only gave the group their first taste of real superstar success, it also opened a window for Stevie's musical explorations into blatant occultism. The song is based on the legend of the Nightmare Witch of Wales, the Dark Rhiannon:

> "Rhiannon rings like a prayer through the
>   night
> And wouldn't you love to love her
> Takes to the sky like a bird in flight
> And who will be her lover
> All your life you've never seen
> Woman taken by the wind . . .
> She is like a cat in the dark
> And then she is the darkness . . . "

When "Rumours" was released in 1977, almost over-night *Fleetwood Mac* became the most popular group in America. The album sold over 15 million copies as single after single spun its way into the Top 10. On one of the songs, Nicks' "Gold Dust Woman," as the final chorus winds down with one last keening wail from Stevie's sandpapery throat, something very strange takes place. Mick Fleetwood's drumming abruptly changes. Instead of the laid back, unforced style maintained throughout the song, he instantly double times until the tom-toms throb with a tribal beat like something straight out of the jungles of Haiti. Her voice shimmery and distant, Stevie very slowly and deliberately recites a witchcraft incantation:

"Great shadow of demon
Black widow
Hail shadow of dragon . . . "

In the occult, the word "hail" means "come forth." So
Stevie has just called up demons on this record. And
every time you play your copy of "Rumours," those
same demons are called into your room with you. Burn
that cursed junk!

More *Fleetwood Mac* albums followed in the wake of
"Rumours," including the monolithic "Tusk," which
took more than a year to make. (What were they doing
in the studio all that time, "hailing" black shadows?)

The 1982 "Mirage" album was recorded in a spirit-
haunted French chateau. While working there, Nicks
experienced direct demonic manifestations:

> "If ghosts are friendly and willing to talk,
> I am ready to sit down at any time . . . "[39]

Some other facts which tie Stevie to her master, Satan
include: Halloween is her favorite night of the year.
She would like to build her own pyramid, and someday
retire to a "little witch house" by the sea. Her publishing company is, "Welsh Witch Music." She has been
photographed wearing occult jewelry like the crescent,
pyramid and crescent/star necklaces. She believes in
reincarnation and says she was a monk in a former life.

> "I can't believe that the next life couldn't be
> better than this. If it isn't, I don't want to
> know about it. I think that if you're rein-
> carnated, you're probably reincarnated as
> many times as you want to come back."[40]

Plus, she cannot stand the light of day:

> "I'm only UP at night. I don't know any-
> thing ABOUT the day – so I can't write
> about it. When the sun comes up, you'll
> never see a girl move around so fast to close
> up this room! I've always liked the night,
> ever since I was real little . . . And a lot of
> people are asleep, so there's a lot of energy
> running around. So I hang around and
> wait for it . . . "[41]

It's interesting to compare Stevie's lifestyle with the
Word of God:

> "And this is the condemnation, that light is
> come into the world, and men loved dark-
> ness rather than light, because their deeds
> were evil. For every one that doeth evil
> hateth the light, neither cometh to the
> light, lest his deeds should be reproved.
> But he that doeth truth cometh to the
> light, that his deeds may be made mani-
> fest, that they are wrought in God."
> John 3:19-21

It's also an interesting coincidence that the Greek
goddess NYX (as in Nicks?) was synonymous with
night. She had power over sleep and death. Another
fascinating tidbit can be found in a 1985 Stevie Nicks
calendar made available to her most devoted fans:
Every major holiday of the year is listed on the calendar's
pages, except for one – Christmas!

Let's see how some of the things just mentioned relate
to the devil. Halloween, contrary to popular belief, is
not a jolly holiday made to scare us silly while the kids

gorge themselves on free candy. In witchcraft, Halloween is known as Samhain, a high holy day for devil worshipers world-wide. Ritual animal and human sacrifices are performed across the country on Halloween night. Combined with the carefully planned mutilations and poisonings of young trick-or-treaters, October 31st has been a time of torture, death and demon raising since the days of the Druids. And this is Stevie's "favorite night of the year."

Pyramids hold great significance in the occult, as they are supposed to focus the psychic energies all around us into a concentrated blast of spiritual power. They are also symbols of humans becoming gods, depending on which way they are pointed. Every serious occultist would love to meditate within the confines of a pyramid. No wonder Stevie wants to build her own!

Personal jewelry is also very important to those in witchcraft, since they receive it during ritual ceremonies, having had it "blessed" (cursed) with clinging demons. Since such things are worn close to the body, the witch or warlock always has his or her familiar spirits "on call." The symbols on this jewelry are very important; they are never accidental or harmless. The crescent or crescent and star are two of the most common symbols representing the Queen of Heaven and the "bright morning star" – Lucifer.

The devil-inspired doctrines of Hinduism and reincarnation are favorites with occultists, since the sins of their present lives can be put on hold for a few thousand years while they continue working their wickedness in the here and now. But Hebrews 9:27 says:

> "And as it is appointed unto men once to die, but after this the judgment:"

111

Nicks also uses Hindu symbolism on her first solo album, 1981's "Bella Donna." (See Figure 5.) The crystal ball endorses divination (knowing the future). The tambourine represents the porthole of perception into the spirit world, and the three roses indicate the power of the pyramid.[42]

Are there deeper meanings here as well? Listen to what Herbert Worthington, the man who photographed both "Rumours" and "Bella Donna" had to say:

> "I like to say something with a photo. I love to use symbolism – crystal balls, the juxtaposition of the big and small on those covers, the mighty and the weak, the yin and yang."[43]

"Yin and yang" is more occult jargon for the delicate balance between male and female and good and evil.

The Hindu term "maya" also sticks closely to Stevie Nicks, since both her clothes and custom made boots are turned out by the Maya Design Studios and Maia Custom Shoe Salon, respectively. What is maya? In the Eastern religions, the goddess Devi is also known as Maya. She represents the sensory illusion of the world. In other words, what we see is not necessarily what is really there.

Finally, the title, "Bella Donna," itself has satanic significance. Not only is this wild plant a deadly poison, it is also burned at devil worship ceremonies to put the witches into a proper state of mindlessness![44] In Italian, bella donna means "Beautiful Lady." On the flip side of the album is the following message: "Come in – Out of the darkness." No one can say that Stevie doesn't have a sense of humor, though warped. This beautiful lady, whose music is full of deadly poison, is trying to recruit people to enter into her dark and satanic lifestyle.

Figure 5

In 1983, she released a record titled, "The Wild Heart," whose cover featured Nicks dressed in a hooded robe, her hands held out in a strange form of "signing." The album was dedicated to her childhood friend, Robin Anderson. Robin died of leukemia in 1982, giving birth to a child one week before she passed away. Stevie was

113

the baby's godmother. Within a year, Nicks married Robin's husband, Kim Anderson! Kim was a member of a charismatic Christian group called the Hiding Place Church. He and Stevie were divorced several months later. Something very, very weird is going on here.

In 1985 Nicks produced one of her witchiest videos ever. To support her new "Rock A Little" album, Stevie's minifilm, "I Can't Wait," was plastered all over MTV, much to the fans' delight. Several disturbing things stand out about this video. As the film progresses, Stevie's costume alternates between spotless white and jet black. In witchcraft, white is the symbol of purity and innocence, indicating great power. Black, of course, signifies evil.

Spiritual imprisonment is also pictured. In lightning quick flashes from an overhead camera, Nicks is seen trapped in a closet-like room without a door. Pounding frantically on the stone walls, there is no way out. Strobing scenes of her dancing wildly mix with the strange, wrist-snapping hand movements so prevalent in many MTV videos. This is not choreographed rock dancing; she is again "signing," or calling forth demons. Added to the utter hatred of her unblinking stare, the reality of her evil soul is both sinister and chilling.

Stevie Nicks may be a rich and famous Bella Donna, but her involvement and enslavement to the occult becomes more obvious with every album she releases. There are flashing spiritual danger signs in all her music and videos, but few listen as they blindly follow their favorite rock goddess down the dark and bloody path of the Highway to Hell.

Please don't continue to tag along with Stevie as she tumbles to certain destruction. There's nothing "safe" about anything she's involved with, especially her music. Unless she repents of her wicked ways and trusts Jesus Christ as her Savior, she will one day realize that Satan deceived her too, and she'll be thrown into an eternal lake of burning fire.

DON'T FOLLOW HER THERE.

CONCLUSION

These five people are only the tip of the musical iceberg. Many, many more could easily be added. It is a sad fact that virtually nothing in popular music today is worth your support, ESPECIALLY if you are a Christian. If you think your favorite groups are "not that bad," then you need to rethink your devotion to them. NO ONE makes it big in secular music today without selling out to Satan. Study the lifestyles of your favorite rock stars. Research their lyrics and see what they're really saying. The same goes for your favorite "Christian" rock gods. Then, once you've discovered the truth for yourself, do what you know you should . . . dump that vile garbage right in the trash.

The only "safe" place in this world is standing hand in hand with the Lord Jesus Christ. The further we stretch toward the world, no matter how harmless it seems, the deeper we plunge into deception, error and sin. The only way to truly play it safe with Satan is to completely reject everything he offers you, including the beautiful, sexy, talented stars of popular music. Their clean cut faces and rich false fronts mask a world of dirt, disease and darkness.

Today, like never before, the devil is using many different forms of music, including "Christian," to deceive millions and lead them to their destruction.

Which will it be for you – the beauty and peace of the Lord . . . or the deceptive and destructive filth of the world?

I pray you'll make the right decision.

4

THE BEAT AS BAIT

" . . . their works are works of iniquity, and
the act of violence is in their hands. Their
feet run to evil, and they make haste to
shed innocent blood: their thoughts are
thoughts of iniquity; wasting and destruction are in their paths."   Isaiah 59:6,7

"My mind projects, And I'll inject
Into your ears a new concept
Consume in silence, To be unveiled
To the Cool J phenomena
All must hail!
I'm dangerous . . ."   LL Cool J[1]

"Rap" music is Heavy Metal's ugly young cousin come
to call. For kids who are worn out and turned off by the

incredible, brain-damaged boredom of today's Metal mush, the hypnotic, street-wise chanting of rap fills the gap. A popular misconception is that rap belongs only to blacks. While it may have begun on the hot, crumbling streets of inner city ghettoes, in just a few short years rap has spread throughout all areas of the country. Regardless of race or economics, young people of all ages have embraced "hip hop" as their own. The break dancing and skate boarding craze has also helped draw younger and younger kids into rap's orbit.

"Rap" is street slang for a long winded, loud mouthed, lotta talk about nothing, set to rhyme. In recording studios and live concerts, an electronic drum machine is used to keep time. With his sophisticated stereo setup, an "MC" (Master of Ceremonies) "scratches the cuts" by putting his hand on the record as it plays, starting and stopping the song in order to create a variety of two-second sounds. A one-note bass line rounds out the noise.

Over this "music" (or lack of it), the rappers do their thing, barely pausing for breath as they talk, talk, talk, talk, talk. Listening to the average rap record is like spending 45 minutes with a stuck stereo needle. Pretty soon the mindless monotony either mesmerizes you or drives you out of the house.

An entire culture has sprung up around this noise, and it's not pretty. The head rappers like *Run-DMC* and LL Cool J wear $1500 gold chains (rope) around their necks. And they're never seen without their expensive and spotlessly fresh Adidas and Fila basketball shoes (unlaced). Jogging suits and floppy Kangol hats round out their costumes. They drive brand new Lincoln Continentals and Cadillacs, creating a "ghetto chic" image that has thousands of poor minority kids drooling at their feet. Their music is filled with sex, violence and greed, backed with the same relentless beat that powers all of rock.

To street gangs in every major metropolis, rap is the rallying cry for bloody combat. The base elements of personal revenge, lustful greed and blood-boiling violence are central to most of this music – a simmering match set to the short fuse of urban unrest. Premier rap kings *Run-DMC* have taken the brunt of the blame for creating such chaos.

Run-DMC

On August 17, 1986, 14,500 fans streamed into the Long Beach Arena in Los Angeles to hear LL Cool J and *Run-DMC*. Swept into a frenzy by the music, several hundred members of the "Crips" and the "Bloods" (rival "gang-bangers") lashed out at each other with fists, clubs and other weapons, catching the rest of the crowd in the middle. Three hours of wholesale destruction and blood-letting followed, with LAPD riot police finally called in to restore order. The final tally – one stabbing and 45 injuries.

Long Beach wasn't the only scene of such episodes during *Run-DMC's* cross country tour. In response to their rapping beats, gang violence also occurred in Pittsburgh, New York City, St. Louis, Cleveland, Atlanta and Cincinnati. Ironically, the name of their tour was "RAISING HELL." It is no coincidence; their rap brought Satan to the surface through a voodooish mix of gut-stomping rhythm and vain repetition.

Here are some rock magazine reports on the concert chaos that followed:

119

"I knew there was going to be trouble, there had to be. We were just sitting there, listening to LL Cool J, and these Crips started to show their colors under their jackets. That wasn't right, man. Then they started snatching gold chains and breaking chairs, you know, to use the legs as clubs. We had to do the same #@%!"

"Raising Hell" concert-goer[2]

"You could see them walking through the crowd like a herd of elephants stomping on a crowd of ants. It was like a stampede – chairs coming up in the air, panicked kids in the crowd, knowing the gangs were coming their way and couldn't get out."

Jason Mizell, of *Run-DMC*[3]

"You could see 300 people all moving against one section, beating and robbing them. I was really scared for our fans out there."   Joseph Simmons, of *Run-DMC*[4]

Like a hundred rock stars before them, *Run-DMC* denied any responsibility for the actions their music provoked. Joseph Simmons ("*Run*") said in Time magazine:

"Rap music has nothing to do with Crack or crime. Check my lyrics. I'm a role model for kids, and I go out of my way to give them a positive image."[5]

Months later, he expanded on those comments:

"They say we're putting out bad messages to kids. ALL – you hear? – ALL our messages are good . . . Our image is clean, man. Kids beat each other's heads every day. They are fighting because they were fighting before I was born. I'm no sociologist, but we're role models, man, big-time role models . . . I get bigger and bigger, and I don't care what people think."[6]

If Joseph Simmons wants us to take a look at his lyrics, that's just what we'll do:

"Rock Box"

"So listen to this, Because it can't be missed
And you can't leave till you're dismissed
You can do anything that you want to
But you can't leave until we're through
So relax your body and your mind
And listen to us say this rhyme
And you might think that you have waited
Long enough till the rhyme was stated
But that's not where it's at, It would be
    crazy
Agree – Let's not debate it
Nothing too deep and nothing dense
And all our rhymes make a lot of sense
So shake your butt to the cut . . . "

So Joe says that ALL – you hear? – ALL his songs have good messages, huh? In this one tune alone we see:

1) An order to relax the body and mind through concentration on the music, which is nothing less than hypnotism, which is an essential requirement for demonic infestation.

2) The revelation that the rhyming is NOT the

121

real purpose behind the rap, because that "would be crazy." Evidently, there is another, more sinister purpose for rap music. No matter how evil and destructive it is, Joe wants the fans to blindly "agree" and not "debate it." Sorry Joe, we're going to dig a little deeper. I'm afraid your cover's blown, "man."

Just who is *Run-DMC*, anyway?

Joseph (*Run*) Simmons (a former mortuary science student) and Daryll (*DMC*) McDaniels are childhood friends from Hollis, New York. They grew up in a middle class neighborhood of Queens, practicing their raps together while still in their teens. When they hooked up with fellow beat boy Jason (Jam Master Jay) Mizell, the three immediately hit it off and stuck together like glue, all bound up in rap. The disco craze was dying while Jason was busy experimenting with new sounds on his disc jockey turntable. He still provides the weird stop-start "cut creations" that back Simmons and McDaniels' motor mouthings.

Joe's older brother, Russell, is a pioneer in producing and promoting rap artists and their records. An ex-street gang member and dope pusher as a teenager, he is also the manager of Joe's group, as well as LL Cool J and *The Beastie Boys* (more about them later). *Run-DMC* owe much of their success to Russell Simmons. Under his guidance, their 1984 debut album became the first rap record to spawn an MTV video.

The turning point for McDaniels, Simmons and Mizell came with the 1986 release of their third album, "Raising Hell." They teamed up with Heavy Metal drug-rock legends *Aerosmith* to produce a video of the song, "Walk This Way." Thanks to *Aerosmith*, the "Raising Hell" album shot up the charts and *Run-DMC* were suddenly very, very rich and famous young men. As for setting a "clean" example to their fans, both Joseph Simmons and Jason Mizell lived with their girlfriends before hitting it big. Each relationship produced a child. Some "role models."[7]

Appearances on TV talk shows and a short stint at the massive Live Aid festival quickly followed. Then came the violence at seven major cities on the "Raising Hell" tour. As future concerts were quickly canceled by nervous promoters and city councils, Simmons and McDaniels called press conferences to contend that it wasn't their fault. They blamed "poor security." Their long-faced excuses fell flat, though, when they made these comments several months later about a *Run-DMC* movie project called, "Tougher Than Leather:"

> "('Tougher Than) Leather' is going to be much more violent, a LOT more violent."
>
> Jason Mizell[8]

> "('Leather' will be) the best movie in the world. At the end, we're all heroes. You're happy we're kicking their butts. It has to be violent because it has to be violent. Sometimes violence is needed."
>
> Joseph Simmons[9]

> "We can't go to Heaven to perform. We out here with the bad people. We got to put as much positive message behind it as we can, but we can't stop the devils."
>
> Joseph Simmons[10]

Whoa! Hold on a minute. Which devils is *"Run"* talking about here? Does he mean the teenage gang soldiers who have ruined his concerts, or is he describing the spiritual demons that are unleashed through their music? THERE is the real purpose behind the blood-beats of Simmons and his friends. Violent riots and stabbings occur at one concert. *Run-DMC* deny responsibility. More beatings and blood-letting take place at the next concert; again they play innocent. On and on it goes, city after city. Busted heads, bloodied faces, broken ribs and even gunshots. And every time, they deny being responsible. I believe Joe is trying to tell us that it's the demons who are causing all the violence, not the band.

We must wake up and realize that there is something IN THE MUSIC that is provoking those deadly concert rampages. This is only common sense. We are dealing with a SPIRITUAL matter here. Some people recognized this fact over thirty years ago when rock first arrived. There is something in the BEAT of this music that fires up those who listen to it and releases primitive lusts within them. The spiritual power behind the music is from Satan, (Luke 4:5-7) NOT from God, (I Corinthians 14:33). The preachers who boldly stated in 1957 that rock's beat was demonic were hooted at and shouted down. But they were right then, and they're still right today.

If skeptics want proof, it can be found in the lyrics and lifestyles of the musicians. But it's also in the fruits from the Rock/Rap tree – the kids who listen to the music and attend the concerts. The "proof" is wailing ambulances, police paddy wagons, handcuffed teenagers and kids beaten bloody because they refuse to stop worshiping demons – the gods of rap and rock.

THE BEAT

The same beat that drives Rock & Roll like a thundering freight train also powers rap, but with one big difference. The rap beat is stripped down to the barest thumping bones – drums and bass. Rap is the basic, bottom-line essence of the beat, streamlined and amplified hundreds of times until it merges with the body, seeps into the soul and twists the mind and will like a curlicued pretzel. Simply put, the beat is the drums. The modern bass guitar greatly enhances rap drumming, thereby creating the foundation of a musical "rhythm section." Add more guitars and this would become rock. But in rap, only the thudding, hypnotic drums and bass are necessary.

There is a very special relationship that exists between drummers and bass players. Their minds merge through constant practice until they are two parts of the same whole. The drummer will leave "holes" for the bassist to drop notes into, and vice versa. The end result is a "punch," a staggering, piston-slapping steam engine of a beat that never stops grinding itself into the brain. Since rap has few or no other instruments to get in the way, the listener's entire concentration is on the beat, a beat that is rooted in voodoo.

Here's where our super-sophisticated minds recoil and deny the truth. VOODOO? Come on! That's plain old superstition, isn't it?

No, Voodoo is not a superstition, it's a religion. It is satanism and demon worship in the truest sense, involving blood drinking, animal sacrifice, sexual orgies and demonic possession. At the very root of the voodoo ceremony lies the pounding pulse of drums. The frenzy of the ritual would not be possible without them. Their beats and counter-rhythms play a vital role in getting demons into the bodies of the worshipers.

Rap music is just a highly refined form of voodoo. Our modern brains, weaned on decades of Grade B jungle pictures, deny this truth and look for answers elsewhere. But the cold, hard facts linking voodoo music with literal Satan worship are undeniable.

When it comes to using the satanic voodoo beat, rappers do not have a corner on the market. Some of the biggest names in rock have traveled to the ends of the earth seeking out the primitive tribal music of Africa, India and the Caribbean. Why do they soak up the atmospheres of these exotic places, record the local sounds of native musicians, then incorporate those beats and rhythms into their own tunes?

Because they know that the voodoo rhythms have a power that can be harnessed and transferred into their own music. Simply put, the voodoo beat is demonic, and the demons have power. Rockers who have sold out to Satan want that power, so they can control their fans and increase their own fame. That's why they'll span the globe searching for it. To reject these facts because of our own ignorance is unwise.

Many rock stars have made pilgrimages to the musical heart of Satan-country to recharge their spiritual batteries. Brian Jones of the *Rolling Stones* journeyed to Morocco, Africa in the mid-sixties to record demon conjuring ceremonies from the Joujouka tribe. The tapes were released under the title, "The Pipes of Pan." Much of the inspiration he received from these sessions was transferred to the next *Stones* album – coincidentally called, "Their Satanic Majesties Request."

John Phillips of *The Mamas and Papas* also spent time in Marrakesh, Morocco with his wife Michelle in 1967. He sampled African dope, tripped his brains out on

LSD and ate local delicacies like sheep eyeballs and stomach linings while the G'naoua drums incessant pounding sank into his stoned-out consciousness.

When Paul McCartney recorded his "Band On The Run" album in Lagos, Nigeria in 1973, the native musicians accused the ex-*Beatle* of stealing their music. Mick Fleetwood, drummer for the witchy pop super-group *Fleetwood Mac*, recorded his solo album, "The Visitor," in Ghana, using African musicians to get the sound and feel he wanted.

In 1972, *Led Zeppelin* giants Jimmy Page and Robert Plant journeyed to Bombay, India. With expensive sound equipment in hand, they walked the teeming and dusty streets, recording native performers. They rented a local studio and jammed for hours with Bombay's best. The tapes went back to England with them.

One of the *Rolling Stones'* most satanic albums, "Goat's Head Soup," was made in Jamaica. The Caribbean is full of transplanted African voodoo, and this record literally drips with demonic influence. Guitarist Keith Richards hung out with the local dope-smoking Rastas, learning their guitar riffs and hypnotic stop-start reggae rhythms, all of which were incorporated into the next few *Stones* albums.

These rockers and many others like them are constantly searching out literal voodoo music for their albums. Don't be fooled, they're seeking powerful witchcraft music . . . and finding it! Behind it all is their lord and master, Satan.

That powerful voodoo beat that rockers have searched world-wide for is the root of rap, and it's causing chaos all over the country. Don't let the wide-eyed innocence of Joseph Simmons or Daryll McDaniels deceive you. Since these guys wear gold crosses around their necks like good luck charms, fans automatically assume they're Christians! No way. Their music and lifestyles shout out the true message the devil they serve wants everyone to hear – "WORSHIP ME!"

Figure 6

Run-DMC show their true colors on the cover of their 1984 self-titled album. Joseph Simmons, with his left hand outstretched, is making the Il Cornuto devil sign of allegiance to Satan! (See Figure 6.) I spoke with a photographer to see if the fuzziness around Simmons' little finger was intentional doctoring, or just bad picture taking. His opinion was that a retouch had been done. If so, *Run-DMC*, obviously servants of Satan, were trying to obscure the proof just enough to throw Christians off the track. What a joke it must be to the devil! How he must split his sides with laughter at our expense! Look closely and you will see that Simmons' thumb, second and third fingers are in the classic Il Cornuto salute. (For a full explanation of the sign of allegiance to Satan, see **"The Devil's Disciples,"** by Chick Publications.)

Run-DMC are role models, all right, but for whom? The answer is obvious – LUCIFER.

LL COOL J

James Todd Smith, another Queens, New York native, is one of the most powerful names in rap music today. As LL Cool J, (Ladies Love Cool James) he has struck it rich by rapping out dirty ditties like "Dear Yvette:"

> " . . . They say you're a man eater
> During the full moon
> Mascot of the senior boys locker room
> They said Yvette walked in
> There wasn't too much rap
> Her reputation got bigger
> And so did her gap . . ."

His double platinum 1987 album "Bigger And Deffer," contained a warning sticker on its cover about the offensive lyrics inside. With songs like "My Rhyme Ain't Done," it's easy to see why:

129

"Tight leather pants that'll make you grunt
Two nice soft things right up front . . .
If you're kinda confused as to what a skeezer
  is
It's a girl who's on my jock
Cause I'm in show biz . . . ."

Cool J's music is chock full of such smut, and judging
from his 1987 arrest for public lewdness, so are his
concerts. During a live performance in Columbus,
Georgia, Smith simulated having sex on stage, while
the fans went wild. When the concert was over, "Cool"
James was led away in police handcuffs.

He's another great role model for kids to follow and
worship. Here are his priorities in life:

"I can't live without girls, money, or food.
The radio's pretty high on my list, but it
don't come before family. Family comes
first, and after family comes money, and
after money, girls."[11]

Smith's smash crossover album, "Can't Live Without
My Radio," made him a superstar long before he joined
Run-DMC's "Raising Hell" tour. His music was whip-
ping up violence in Baltimore, Maryland ghettoes
back in 1986. An average of two teens were murdered
every month for over a year in the black Baltimore
inner city. Children as young as 13 killed each other
with .45's, shotguns and even automatic weapons.
Pushing drugs like heroin and cocaine were the main
source of income for these kids. The music of LL Cool
J, *Run-DMC* and *Schooly D* fueled the fires of murder:

"P is for the people
Who can't understand

130

How one home boy became a man
S is for the way you scream and shout
One by one I'm knocking you out . . ."

These are lines from *Schooly D's* hit rap single, "P. S. K. – What Does It Mean?" (The initials stand for "Parkside Killers".) Other lyrics include:

"Put my pistol up against his head
Said, 'Sucka #@%! nigger
I should shoot you dead . . . "

Figure 7

Why all the violence? Why all the rage? The frightening reason for those Baltimore murders and in-concert uproars can now be exposed: James T. Smith is calling up demons of violence on the back of his "Radio" album. (See Figure 7.)

Look closely at Cool J's hands. They are in very odd positions. He is "signing," or calling up demons. Superstar Prince also uses signing on his 1986 "Parade" album cover. Most of today's rock videos are full of these manual incantations. I once sat through six hours of nonstop MTV. At least HALF the videos I watched contained witchcraft signing! This is NOT rock dancing; it's the literal calling up of demons.

Notice the lyrics from LL Cool J's song "Dangerous" at the beginning of this chapter. The word "hail" (come forth) is used. LL Cool J is calling forth demons. Are the demons the "new concept" he's injecting "into your ears?" I'm afraid so, LL fans. At least he tells the truth in the last line when he proclaims, I'm dangerous. If only his fans would heed his warning.

Demons are the devil's foot soldiers who do his dirty work. Part of those dark deeds include attaching themselves to the rock and rap star saps who see satanism as a free ticket to money, fame and sex. Many years are spent learning to "control" these spirits. (Actually, the joke is on the stars. The demons are the ones doing the controlling.)

Further confirmation of this comes from a woman named Elaine, who reached the highest levels in witchcraft during her seventeen years in the craft. She is now saved by the blood of Jesus, and a tireless and dedicated servant of the Lord Jesus Christ. She's got the scars to prove it. She identified LL Cool J's signing as a demand for demons of violence to appear to afflict, control and attack those listening to his music.

This should be no surprise to a true Christian. The Bible tells us that Satan is the god of this world (II Corinthians 4:4) and has been given much power (Ezekiel 28:12-16 and Isaiah 14:16, 17). He also gives that power to people, in return for their worship (Luke 4:6, 7). What Satan NEVER tells his servants is that the eternal flames of hell await them when they die.

When we finally realize that rap stars like LL Cool J are directing unclean spirits of violence at their audiences, we get a much clearer picture of why teenage blood is being spilled from one end of the country to the other. LL says it best in these lines from "You'll Rock:"

> "The momentum of this party can only
> increase
> The design of this rhyme is a masterpiece
> You'll want to kick steps to the musical
> feast
> And witness the force I'm about to
> release . . .
> A promoter of recordings that I call my
> own
> And I'd love to take one of you ladies home
> I'm complete and clear
> Infiltrating your ear . . . "

Are the lyrics beginning to make more sense now? The "force" Cool J is "about to release" is an army of demons. The "promoter of recordings that I call my own" are his own demons that are called up on his records. They are the ones who have caused his astronomical success. The demons "infiltrate your ears" and cause fans to do whatever they're told.

Hence, the incredible violence and destruction that surrounds rap music wherever it's played. And Satan is well pleased, because no one loves violence and destruction more than Satan.

Run-DMC and LL Cool J are bad enough, but they look like little kids playing in a sandbox compared to the most disgusting group in rap:

THE BEASTIE BOYS

In a very short time, these three loud-mouthed New Yorkers have carved out a huge chunk of the rap empire for themselves. A trio of white Jewish kids from upper middle class families, Adam (King-Ad-Rock) Horovitz, Adam (MCA) Yauch and Michael (Mike D) Diamond, got their first big break by performing with Madonna on her "Like A Virgin" tour. When that was over, they jumped onto *Run-DMC*'s "Raising Hell" road show and shot straight to the top of rap's rat-infested garbage dump.

Beer soaked, drug drenched and sexually perverse songs are the backbone of their smash 1986 album, "Licensed To Ill." (See Figure 8.) Several alarming facts about the record reveal the group's ties to their wicked task master, Satan. On the clear band of vinyl surrounding the label, a message has been inscribed on both sides of the record. Side 1 states: "GET OFF MY BACK 666." The message on side 2 reads, "WATCH YOUR BACK."

The song, "No Sleep Till Brooklyn," features a special guest guitarist named Kerry King, who is a member of one of the most bloodthirsty and grisly Satan-Rock groups around – California-based *Slayer*.

"No Sleep Till Brooklyn"

"Our manager's crazy, He always smokes
   dust
He's got his own room at the back of the bus
Goin' round the world, You rock around
   the clock
Play to hotels, Girls on the job
Trashin' hotels like it's goin' outta style
Gettin' paid along the way, Cause it's worth
   your while
Four on the floor, And rocks out the door
MCA's in the back
Cause he's #@%! with a whore . . ."

Figure 8

On the inner sleeve of "Licensed To Ill," the following

words are stuck between the pictures of the in-concert *Beastie Boys* taking a booze bath: "SPECIAL KNOWLEDGE TO *RUN-DMC* & JAM-MASTER JAY."

Why did they use the word "knowledge" instead of "acknowledgment?" The *Beasties* are paying homage to Joseph Simmons, Daryll McDaniels and Jason Mizell for some shared knowledge. What secrets passed between the two groups, and why be so mysterious about it? I think the secret's just been let out of the bag.

The *Beasties* are the first group to successfully weld traditional Heavy Metal music to rap. The result is a doubly dangerous dose of the absolute worst of both worlds:

> "We're playing black music to a white audience on rock stations that might never hear it otherwise. We're breaking ground for other rap groups just like 'Walk This Way' broke ground for us."
> Michael Diamond[12]

Here are some more examples of *Beastie Boy* ground breaking:

"The New Style"

> "I got money in the bank
> I can still get high . . .
> Twin sisters in my bed
> Their father had envy
> So I shot him in the head
> If I played guitar, I'd be Jimmy Page
> The girlies I like are under age . . . "

In a few short lines, the *Beasties* promote drug use,

illicit and perverted sex, murder, idolizing a famous Satan worshiper and sex with underage girls. From there, it just keeps getting worse:

"Slowride"

"I got money, I got juice
I got to the party, And I got loose
I got rhythms, I got rhymes
I got the girlies with the best behinds
I got ill, I got busted
I've got dust, and I got dusted . . .
All the fine ladies are makin' a fuss
But I can't pay attention
Cause I'm on that dust . . ."

"Angel Dust" is a very popular drug with both rockers and rappers alike. A powdered form of PCP, (Phencyclidine) this corrosive chemical was used to tranquilize hogs until kids began snorting and smoking it several years ago. PCP has been found to cause brain lesions, along with many other horrible side effects. What does it feel like to be "dusted" and why is it so hard for the *Beasties* to "pay attention" when they're "on that dust?" Witness these comments from some teenage drug abusers, taken from a Rolling Stone magazine article on satanic killing:

"You don't feel anything. You feel like you could rip your gut open and not even know it . . . Dust is the ultimate. The end. Complete hallucinations. You sit down, totally numbed out, and you start sinking into it. People can put out cigarettes on you and you don't even care. You can experience yourself sinking into a cinder-block wall . . . the dust high was great, but the

137

after effects make your brain feel like a pile of #@%! You can't function, can't think for #@%!. When you're on it, it's like you're drunk, stoned, tripping. When you walk, it feels like you're walking on water. You feel like a feather. And you feel pressure start building in your skull . . . "[13]

This is the kind of "fun" the *Beastie Boys* are encouraging - smoking "dust" until your brain explodes. With friends like this, who needs enemies?

Though their songs paint a sickening picture of the non-stop sexual debauchery that accompanies their tours, those poor *Beasties* still have to contend with the same curse as all the rest who spit at God's laws for human sexual behavior – AIDS. Witness these comments from People magazine:

"The *Beastie Boys* have demanded a special rider to their contract with Columbia Records; awaiting them on each stop of their current U.S. tour is a protective assortment of condoms . . . "[14]

(This was the same tour on which a huge mechanical replica of the male sex organ was unveiled as part of their show.)

Everywhere I speak (including churches and Christian youth groups), I take a survey of the teens to find out who their favorite groups are. Believe it or not, our families and churches are in such a mess that the *Beastie Boys* are often listed as the top choice of teens. NO ONE, especially Christians, should have anything to do with a satanic group that endorses murder, sexual perversion, drug abuse and alcoholism, like these monsters. What do Mike D, MCA, and King Ad-Rock really think of the fans who worship them?

> "Basically, our philosophy is, the middle finger for all."[15]

Really makes you want to run out and buy one of their records, doesn't it?

Ear infiltration and dust-headed death is not all that the rappers are after. They and their demonic troops are going soul-hunting in concert halls and teenage bedrooms everywhere. These groups are servants of Satan and they are recruiting converts for hell. Don't fall into their deceptive traps.

Parents, what are your kids listening to? Do you know for sure? Young people, please don't be the next easy mark for hell raisers like *Run-DMC*, LL Cool J and the *Beastie Boys*. Please put the lid on rap.

The lid of the garbage can.

5

TRICKS IN THE DARK

"The thief cometh not, but for to steal, and
to kill, and to destroy: I am come that they
might have life, and that they might have
it more abundantly."   John 10:10

"Be true to your heroes, or they might turn
on you."   Sammi Curr[1]

Thanks to videos, movies and MTV, Satan-rock is no
longer confined to mere ear assault. In **"The Devil's
Disciples - The Truth About Rock,"** we examined
indepth many MTV videos and rock movies, both old
and new. Things are much worse now. As a prime
example, let's look at a rock film that perfectly showcases the sneering satanism and anti-Christian hatred
that is being ground into young minds everywhere.

This movie is typical of a slick new breed of occult brain-washer. It featured big name rock performers like Gene Simmons of *KISS* and madman Ozzy Osbourne to suck kids into the box office. Once there, the children were at the mercy of their musical masters.

"TRICK OR TREAT" was released in late October, 1986, just in time for Halloween. Though advertised as a fun-filled rock fantasy, it was really a crash course in Heavy-Metal-meets-Witchcraft. Brain bashing noise, violence, backmasked messages, filthy sexual smut and actual Satanic ceremonies formed the backbone of this film. Here are some highlights:

Eddie Winebauer (played by Marc Price, "Skippy" to fans of the T.V. sitcom "Family Ties") is a high school "Metal head" who worships ALL Heavy Metal, especially a perverted and demonic rock monster named Sammi Curr. Curr literally "French kisses" a writhing, four foot long snake as part of his concert act. He then chews the snake in half with his teeth, the spurting blood spraying into his opened mouth. Next he smears and rubs great gouts of it all over his chest.

The scene where Sammi Curr dies in a hotel fire sent chills rippling through my spirit. It felt like an icy blow to the heart. Awash in flames, he sits calmly on the floor, eyes rolled up as his head turns and wobbles while he chants a guttural stream of words BACK-WARDS! Backmasked messages fill this movie. Some are deciphered for the audience; many are not. It's anybody's guess what satanic commands entered the hearts and minds of the unknowing theater-goers.

With the death of his rock god, Eddie plunges into an almost suicidal depression. Every square inch of his bedroom is decorated with skulls, posters, rock books, magazines, records and tapes. It becomes a literal altar to Satan as he begins lighting candles in the dark and exploring backmasked messages on Sammi's album, "Songs In The Key of Death." The record was given to the troubled teen by a disc jockey friend (played by Gene Simmons). Gene's appearance in the film is his little joke on all Christians, since *KISS'* binding ties to satanism are obvious. Before you know it, demons start speaking to Eddie through the music.

Teen sex/smut is soon played for all its worth when a sleazy young girl who is under the spell of Eddie's cursed cassette tape has sex with a demon, an act that takes place frequently in Satan worship circles.

The demons gain more and more control over Eddie until he finally realizes he's playing with fire and attempts to bail out. Too late. An incredibly powerful demon manifesting as Sammi Curr appears in Eddie's room. His words strike fear into the teenager's heart. "BE TRUE TO YOUR HEROES, OR THEY MIGHT TURN ON YOU!"

At midnight on Halloween, all Sammi's hellish powers break loose. Nothing can stop this son of Satan as he blasts three authority figures into oblivion, including a trembling policeman, a gray haired grandmother who heads a PTA "Stamp Out Rock" crusade, and an anti-rock preacher (played by real life Metal madman, Ozzy Osbourne). Ozzy makes men of God who are doing their moral duty look like limp-wristed whiners afraid of their own shadows. With one swipe of his studded fist, Sammi strikes the preacher dead of a brain hemorrhage.

The message in all these killings rings out loud and

clear: "Rock surrenders authority to NO ONE. Mess with rock, you <u>die</u>!"

It's no coincidence that this movie was tied to Halloween. "All Hallows Eve" is thought by many to be a harmless kiddie holiday. Actually it is a high time for devil worshipers worldwide, a day of human sacrifice and special service to Lucifer. The young trick-or-treaters who tragically die each year from eating tainted candy are really well-planned and highly organized witchcraft human sacrifices. (See **"The Trick,"** by Chick Publications.)

The movie, "Trick Or Treat" is itself a form of poisoned candy. After coming out of the theater, I felt like my spirit had been shoved through a wringer. The first hour contains an intense level of demonic attack that is designed to break down any of the viewers' spiritual defenses. The satanic rock music, the many backmasks, the subliminal assault and the shocking, vulgar cruelty of the flick's fictitious hero, Sammi Curr, all drive home the same message . . . this is Satan's movie, from beginning to end.

Much of the film is a brutal spiritual attack on whoever is watching. For example: Before the first scene begins, a genuine demonic incantation is spoken in the darkness, setting the stage for everything to follow. Part of the chant involves serving Lucifer in return for the destruction of enemies. The evil, booming voice offers his soul in return for "whatever I demand."

"Trick Or Treat" hits VERY close to home for so many people. Eddie is typical of thousands of teens today. He's a member of a one-parent family. His mother worries about her son's rock obsession, but can do nothing about it. The rock stars speak a rebellious language this isolated teenage misfit understands. They feed his hurting ego with a message of hate, rage and revenge. And he eats it all up, never realizing he is plunging deeper and deeper into their world of devilish darkness. Young viewers have no idea how painfully accurate this film really is. Eddie's horrible fate is exactly the same as the one that awaits any who persist in worshiping Satan through rock music.

Three basic truths about Rock & Roll are revealed in this movie. The devil is giving us fair warning:

1) Satanism and Heavy Metal rock music are the same thing.

2) There is a demonic power behind this music.

3) The goal of rock music makers is the cold-blooded destruction of any who oppose them (especially Christians).

Other more subtle facts are also brought out:

1) Demon power increases its hold through "familiar" objects, which are anything made by, used for or dedicated to Satan (objects like rock posters, magazines, tapes and records). "Familiars" serve as a power base from which demonic spirits operate. Their express purpose is to maintain spiritual control over the people who own them.

2) Backmasks in rock are some of Satan's favorite tools to gain that initial control over the listener.

3) Rock magazines are a big part of the plan. In Eddie's room is a copy of "Hit Parader" magazine, with Sammi Curr's picture and name splashed on the cover. "Hit Parader" really exists. Sammi Curr does not. How did the makers of this occult movie get to use "Hit Parader's" logo and format?

Figure 9

To get demons into the homes of millions of teenagers after the movie had ended, a sound track album was

145

released on Columbia records. (See Figure 9.) The music was written and performed by *Fastway*, a rag tag bunch of *AC-DC* clones. Their founder, Fast Eddie Clarke, was formerly in the English power trio *Motorhead*. (Two of *Motorhead's* best known songs are, "Don't Need Religion" and "Orgasmatron.")

Here are some lyrics from the title cut, "TRICK OR TREAT":

> "Knock, Knock, Knockin'; for a sweet
>   surprise
> It's a Trick Or Treat
> See my face through a thin disguise
> If ever we should meet
> Maybe you'll see
> Someone has put a spell on me
> Rock & Roll, Rockin' on all midnight
> Steal your soul . . .
> Take control . . ."

Some other songs from that same album include:

"After Midnight"

> "You got it, I want it
> Pretty soon he's gonna change his tune,
>   now
> So keep a knockin', Keep on Rockin'
> I gotta, I gotta hear you scream
> I'm gonna get you, Get you after midnight
> Shock you, Shock you till the sparks
>   fly . . ."

"Get Tough"

> "Devils they are schemin', Evil meaning

You're in their sights, You'd better beware
No holdin' back, They're on your tracks
Now you're the one giving them Hell
Does anybody know what's going on?
Does anybody care? . . . "

On the album's label, a triangle within a circle is
printed as a logo. It is NOT the traditional Columbia
Records trademark. This is very similar to marks of
satanic "blessing" found on many other rock records,
tapes and album covers. The point of the triangle is
facing downward, which represents black magic, or
evil. When the point faces up, it's supposedly "good" or
so-called white magic. The triangle/pyramid has always
been one of the most revered symbols in the occult.

A brother who corresponds with The Rock Ministries
told me this topic is discussed in the book, "Occult
Theocrasy," by Edith Starr Miller. When a mark of
blessing is placed on things like the "Trick Or Treat"
sound track album, demons have been ordered to cling
to them through witchcraft spells. Their goal is to gain
control over the listener's mind, just as in Eddie's case.

Whoever brings such satanic filth into a home curses
not only themselves but everyone in the home! (See
Deuteronomy 7:26 and Joshua 6:18.) The scriptural
thing to do is BURN those records, tapes, posters,
jewelry, rock books, magazines and other things that
have been dedicated to the devil (Acts 19:13-20).

Parents, you've got double trouble. Today's popular
music is straight from the devil. Now he is the mastermind behind a growing number of movies and videos.
Steeped in witchcraft, yet widely accepted because of
the music and stars who are involved in them, kids are
falling by the thousands. YOUR kids are falling.

147

Like the sneaky criminal he is, Satan will do anything he can to keep his evil deeds hidden. He does not want you finding out what your kids are watching. He and his slaves cannot stand to have their evil works exposed to the light. (See John 3:17-21.) Like slimy bugs living under rocks, these cowardly monsters run for cover when their hiding place is removed. When a bright ray of sunlight hits them, they fearfully flee back to the darkness.

Movies like "Trick Or Treat" are made for the dark, shown in the dark and appeal to the blackness within all hardened hearts. The ruthless and merciless power of rock to smash to pieces all religious and civil authority is the centerpiece of this movie. The only way to expose such degenerate trash is by continually flooding our youth with the intense light of the gospel of Jesus Christ - His life, death, burial and resurrection. Let Gene Simmons and Ozzy Osbourne continue to wallow in the dirt and crawl around in the dark. Young people, please don't let their filth infect you. Damnation is the price you will pay to have the power of darkness, and they know it!

Parents, find out what your kids are watching, as well as what they're listening to. What they're watching just might be even more dangerous.

6

BOWING TO BAAL

"And have no fellowship with the unfruit-
ful works of darkness, but rather reprove
them." Ephesians 5:11

"I feel your fire in my soul
You got the fever
Cause you were born to rock an' roll
Don't run for cover
I'm gonna show you what I've learned
Just come a little closer
Come on an' get your fingers burned . . . "
Whitesnake[1]

Our Christian young people are in big trouble. When
giving rock seminars at Christian churches and youth
groups, I always survey those present for their favorite

performers. It's bad enough that these youth are naming stars like *Stryper*, Amy Grant, *Petra*, and others of that ilk. But I stand in utter amazement, shocked and sickened, at the new lows to which Christian teens have sunk regarding secular rock.

Whenever I speak in the Christian community, the young people I meet are consistently listing secular rock performers like Madonna, *Poison*, *AC-DC*, *Whitesnake*, *Heart* and *Motley Crue* as part of their Top 5 favorites. Please keep in mind we're talking about CHRISTIAN youth.

But two especially rotten secular outfits are named at almost EVERY church and youth group I go to. And these two are not even close to resembling anything Christian. As we discuss these two groups, please keep in mind, we're talking about CHRISTIAN youth here.

Not only does this prove the utter failure of "Christian" rock as an alternative to the worldly garbage, it also illustrates a far greater problem – absolutely no holiness in the lives of our kids. With a few wonderful exceptions, the majority of young Christians are wallowing in carnal worldliness and loving every minute of it. What a slap in the face of Jesus Christ.

Let's take a closer look at two secular groups often named in church youth group surveys as "the best."

Christian parent, read the evidence, then you decide if such music belongs in your home. Christian teen, read the facts, then compare what God has to say in this matter. The Lord minces no words:

> "No man can serve two masters: for either
> he will hate the one, and love the other; or

else he will hold to the one, and despise the other. Ye cannot serve God and mammon."   Matthew 6:24

"And Jesus said unto him, No man, having put his hand to the plough, and looking back, is fit for the kingdom of God."
                                  Luke 9:62

"Can two walk together, except they be agreed?"   Amos 3:3

The following information is meant to wake and shake you parents into realizing that as long as Satan's rock is in your house, your kids are NOT in a right relationship with God.

WHITESNAKE

Floating through the sludge to the very top of rock's slimy cesspool is a group named *Whitesnake*. Even though musical filth is their calling card, hundreds of thousands of supposedly saved kids have pledged their unfailing allegiance to "The Snake."

In the winter of 1987-88 *Whitesnake* sold over 3 million records, had three hit singles, a barrage of dirty MTV videos, a Top 5 album and a smash concert tour. They have been called the *"Led Zeppelin* of the 80's." Now you're going to read the behind the scenes story of David Coverdale and his band. You can reject it if you choose, but when you stand before the Lord on Judgment Day, don't say you weren't warned.

Whitesnake was born in 1978 from the ashes of one of the biggest supergroups in rock – *Deep Purple*. The primary originators of Heavy Metal music, the *Purps*

151

had a real revolving door policy in their personnel department. Full of pride, arrogance and overwhelming ego, eight different musicians came and went through *Deep Purple's* ranks before the group finally called it quits in 1976. (They mounted a massive comeback tour nine years later, and made millions.)

One of the eight who passed through the *Deep Purple* parade was an English singer named David Coverdale, a former Redcar boutique store clerk who hit the big time by getting drunk. In 1973, boozed up and cocky, he responded to an ad in the music newspaper, "Melody Maker" by recording a demo tape for *Deep Purple's* vacant vocalist slot. Much to his surprise, he was hired instantly. Five days later, instead of ringing a cash register, he was on stage, singing to 20,000 screaming teeny-boppers. Dave was a real "overnight sensation."

What kind of a band was *Deep Purple*? Having seen them in concert twice while Coverdale sang for them, I can tell you they were one of the loudest, most obnoxious and destructive groups of their time. Guitarist Ritchie Blackmore (who wears all black outfits on stage) climaxed his shows by smashing his guitar to smithereens while towering stacks of expensive Marshall amplifiers exploded behind him. One of his favorite tricks was to bayonet speakers with the jagged shell of his splintered Stratocaster, then toss the remains into the audience. Pity the poor stoned headbanger in the front row who caught that five pound mass of wood and wires in the face!

Blackmore is a devoted occultist who claims to "astral project" his spirit around the concert hall as he plays.[2] He has recorded music in a castle haunted by a demon "servant of Baal."[3] Ritchie also loves to attend seances, as evidenced by the following from "Circus" magazine,

"We rehearsed in a castle in Wales for two or three weeks, but we had more seances and games of football than we rehearsed."
Ritchie Blackmore[4]

The following interview in "Circus" magazine also proved very revealing:

CIRCUS: Is there a connection between *Deep Purple* and your interest in the supernatural?

BLACKMORE: When we formed *Purple*, we had a bassist called Nic Simper. He used to do all these seances. I was totally opposed to all that, till I saw what was going on. I got intrigued with it all out of curiosity. I believe more in religion because I see what goes down in an evil sense. I don't practice evil stuff, but I see how effective it is . . .

CIRCUS: What happens if a participant doesn't believe?

BLACKMORE: A friend of mine, a guitarist, said, 'Ah, I don't believe in all this rubbish. I'm not scared of you ghosts; I'm stronger than you are.' The next moment, he was knocked out of his chair and was foaming at the mouth – he was unconscious . . . "[5]

Together, "Witchy Ritchie" and David Coverdale produced some absolutely disgusting music while they were a team. Writing the words to this occult trash was the singer's primary responsibility. *Whitesnake* fans might be shocked to know what good old David was into fifteen years ago. Witness the following lyrics from two *Deep Purple* tunes that Coverdale helped write:

"Burn" (1974)

" . . . People say that the woman is damned
She makes you burn with a wave of her
hand . . .
I didn't believe she was Devil's sperm
She said, 'Curse you all, you'll never learn'
When I leave, there's no return
The people laughed when she said,
'BURN!' . . . "

"Stormbringer" (1976)

"Comin' out of nowhere, Drivin' like rain
Stormbringer dance on the thunder again
Dark cloud gatherin,' Breakin' the day
No point in running cause he's comin' your
way
Ride the rainbow, Crack the sky
Stormbringer's comin'
Time to die . . .
He's got nothin' you need, He's gonna make
you bleed
You know he's gonna get ya . . . "

Just who is the Stormbringer, anyway? Could it be the same monster revealed in a chilling slice of demon-inspired Satan-Rock which appeared four years later? Compare the words in *AC-DC*'s Metal-monger anthem, "Hell's Bells," to Coverdale's devil-prose, and draw your own conclusions:

154

"Hell's Bells" (1980)

" . . . I'm comin' on like a hurricane
My lightning's flashin' across the sky
You're only young
But you're gonna die
Don't take no prisoners,
Won't spare no lives
Nobody's puttin' up a fight
I've got my bell, I'm gonna take you to
  Hell
I'm gonna get ya, Satan get ya
Hell's Bells . . ."

Demons, directed by Satan, have been moving through ALL rock music and the people who make it from the beginning! They have blatantly warned of their evil intent in song after song after song. Today Coverdale and his crew produce sexy, steamed-up videos and # 1 hits about "love" (sex). Though that is satanic as well, a glimpse at his earlier days makes the picture crystal clear. Dave's songs with *Deep Purple* reveal the true spirit behind the man – Lucifer.

In a 1988 interview in "Rip" magazine, Coverdale dropped the mask a few inches more. Blinded by their own idolatry, it's unlikely that the fans caught on:

> **RIP:** Do you feel as though God shines on you and guides your path?

> **DAVID:** Oh, yes, without a doubt. I make music for the glory of God and the recreation of the mind and body.

> **RIP:** Do you practice any religion?

155

DAVID: No, and whatever I do is intensely private. It's very important to do what I do and to share it, but I've never used the stage as a political or religious platform . . . "[6]

Whoa! Hold it right there. At first, sweet innocent Davie claims he doesn't practice any religion, but in the next breath he admits he does but insists it's "intensely private." He also says that he makes his music "for the glory of God," but says he would never use that music to spread his religion. The man seems to have a problem figuring out what he believes. Either that or he can't keep all his lies straight. What kind of a person can lie like that?

> "Ye are of your father the devil, and the lusts of your father ye will do . . . When he speaketh a lie, he speaketh of his own: for he is a liar, and the father of it." John 8:44

When *Deep Purple* cracked apart at the seams in 1976, David Coverdale went solo. His first record was titled "White Snake." (It flopped.) Realizing he wasn't cut out to be a crooner, Coverdale surrounded himself with eager, unemployed unknowns. The *Whitesnake* concept was hatched and sent slithering. Records were made and moderate success was achieved in Europe, but due to Dave's mammoth ego, musicians were hired and fired in rapid succession.

Once, Coverdale was quite miffed to see two of his sidemen LAUGHING behind his back as he sang! Needless to say, they joined the growing ranks of ex-*Whitesnakes*. Eventually, out-of-work *Deep Purple* ear-pounders Jon Lord (keyboards) and Ian Paice (drums) joined Dave's serpentine crew. They flew the

156

coop months later. When Coverdale hired pretty-boy guitarist John Sykes, the girls started flocking backstage at *Whitesnake* concerts. This pleased Dave.

Mom and Dad, read these quotes from lover-boy David and see if you want your teenage daughter going to one of his concerts:

> "But there's no question that many more pretty young girls started coming to the shows once John joined us. Even my mother called me up one day and told me how silly I was for having him in the band. She told me I'd be frustrated because he'd get all the girls. He gets his share, but I get to play belly bump often enough . . . "
>
> David Coverdale[7]

> "Isn't sex what rock and roll is all about? . . . That's what *Whitesnake* has that so many younger bands are missing. They bash at rock and roll like two teen-agers in the back seat of a car. It takes the experienced hand to know how to take it slow and easy – how to build the excitement until there's a great climax . . ."
>
> David Coverdale[8]

I wonder how many parents who bought *Whitesnake's* latest album for their kids for Christmas know that a favorite Coverdale concert stunt is to hold his microphone between his legs as the girls in the audience scream. His comments about touring with Devil-Rockers *Motley Crue* are as follows:

> " . . . We were gonna call it the 'Suitcase Full of Rubbers' tour, but we settled on

157

'Invasion of the Snatch Magnets' . . ."[9]

(He is talking about fast and loose backstage sex, as well as fears about contracting AIDS.)

The pornographic cover of *Whitesnake's* 1979 "Love Hunter" album shows a naked woman in a state of sexual ecstasy riding a loathsome serpent, which is really a dragon! (Revelation 20:1,2) This record is on public display at shopping malls everywhere. How about the one in your home town?

The cover of *Whitesnake's* million selling "Slide It In" album features a glistening snake slithering down the front of a woman's dress. What parent would want their kids singing these lyrics from the album's title cut?:

"Slide It In" (1984)

" . . . I know what you want
I can see what you're looking for
I know what you want from me
And I'm gonna give you more . . .
I'm gonna slide it in . . . "

"Oh, but their 1987 album is different," some fans will say. "It's all about love." Wrong! Songs like "Still Of The Night," "Give Me All Your Love" and "Don't Turn Away" are nothing more than crude, graphic, lust-filled animal sex tunes. Although multitudes of star-struck fans don't seem to care, Coverdale and his group of *Snakes* are plumbing the same old seedy depths of fornication they've always pursued. This time, though, it's draped in a shimmery, fake romantic smokescreen where animal lust magically becomes "making love."

158

Although radio hoopla and nonstop rock magazine hype helped, it was a series of MTV videos that made this album a "triple platinum" seller. So what's wrong with *Whitesnake's* videos? Anyone who has seen "Is This Love" on MTV shouldn't even ask.

The minifilm opens with Dave and his lover (actress Tawny Kitaen) in the middle of an argument. She is about to walk out on him. As the light and fog machines do their thing, Coverdale and the band put his inner turmoil to music. We see flashbacks of David and his girl as they shared happier times together. The viewer's heartstrings are tugged and manipulated. David is SO handsome. Tawny is SO beautiful. The song is SO sad. NOW comes the smut. (And that's putting it kindly.) As the camera retraces their relationship, Tawny Kitaen's backside is the main focus of the shots. She wears next to nothing, just a series of super-short mini skirts that wouldn't even cover a car seat. As the camera zooms in, David pulls her onto his bed where they begin passionately kissing. There's a good word for this stuff, and it's called PORN!

This is the true secret of *Whitesnake's* success – firing up the hormones of their drooling fans. Coverdale and Kitaen began a real-life, off-screen romance as a result of their work together. David's assessment of the first time they met is typical:

> "(We met) in a charming restaurant in the City of the Lost Angels (Los Angeles). Our eyes locked, and then our limbs . . . "[10]

What a "coincidence" that Kitaen has also appeared in an occult film called "Witchboard" about demonic manifestations called up through a Ouija board. Her sex-soaked "acting" has lust-witch written all over it.

A 1987 "USA Today" article tells how she was picked to star in the *Snake* videos:

> "Coverdale was on his way to director Marty Callner's house to discuss the concept for the upcoming *Whitesnake* videos, and Callner said, 'That's her! I knew I wanted to have a sexy woman in it,' Callner says. 'Sex is a part of rock 'n' roll and the song was about sex ...' "[11]

Figure 10

160

Sex isn't the only reason for *Whitesnake's* success. The occult plays a major role as well. For example, there are several strange things about their 1987 album cover. (See Figure 10.) The centerpiece of the picture is a seal. Before modern methods of documentation existed, seals were very important. Two things are worth remembering:

1) Anything bearing a seal was authentic.
2) Anything bearing a seal declares its ownership.

Take a close look at the picture and you will see serpents, strange symbols and two Latin words. Three snake heads are visible, but there are really four serpents there. Two are facing each other and one has swallowed the head of another. This implies that even though all the snakes are intertwined together, one is the most powerful of all. As interwoven parts of the same whole, these vipers form the outer boundary protecting the inner circle where we find *Whitesnake*, represented by the WS. In other words, to get to *Whitesnake*, you have to get through the serpents first.

Between these two areas is a thin ring filled with occult signs. Some are from the zodiac, including Aquarius, Leo, two Virgos and Capricorn. In my opinion these represent the five band members: David Coverdale, Vivian Campbell, (guitar) Adrian Vandenberg, (guitar) Rudy Sarzo, (bass) and Tommy Aldridge (drums). Five other symbols remain, some astrological, the rest unknown. The circle with a dot in the center stands for the sun (Sol) in astrology. (Baal was the sun god of ancient Babylon.) The crescent depicts the moon, (Luna) known in witchcraft as Diana, Queen of Heaven.

At the bottom are two words – "SERPENS ALBUS." In

Latin, "SERPENS" means "snake," while "ALBUS" means "white." Thus, "White Snake." But there are other meanings to these words as well. "SERPENS" can also mean "Dragon," and "ALBUS" isn't just white. It's "dead white," like a bloated, rotting carcass of a dead animal.

Here's the bottom line. This seal declares the stamp of its master's ownership and authority. It should be obvious by now that the owner, manager and director of *Whitesnake* is the serpent/dragon, Satan.

Let's take a quick look at the boys in the band. The current video and touring lineup of *Whitesnake* is composed of well known, big name members of the rock community. The group in the videos is NOT the same musicians that made the record. Having fired his old crew, *Snake* singer Dave decided to debut a new gang of Metal-makers once the cameras started rolling. Please note the backgrounds of David's video vipers:

VIVIAN CAMPBELL – Formerly a member of *DIO*, one of the most blatant Black Magic bands in Heavy Metal. Dio actually means "God" in Italian. These guys called themselves God!

RUDY SARZO – Rudy played bass for a head crunching group called *Quiet Riot* before joining *Whitesnake*. (One of *Quiet Riot's* home videos is titled "Bang Thy Head.") Sarzo also has recorded and toured with bat-biting bozo Ozzy Osbourne.

TOMMY ALDRIDGE – got his start eighteen years ago with *Black Oak Arkansas*, one of the originators of modern Satan-Rock. (One of their records was titled "X-Rated.") A *Black Oak* song called "When Electricity Came to Arkansas" contains a backmask stating:

"Satan! Satan! Satan! He is god, he is god, he is god!"
Like Sarzo, Aldridge has also drummed for Ozzy
Osbourne on stage and in the studio. In fact, both men
were in Ozzy's band at the same time.

These guys are "all-stars," alright. They shine like
Lucifer when he pours his power on them. But in the
end, without repentance, they'll join their master in
the pit of hell (Isaiah 14:12-15, Revelation 20:15).

Parents, there is more about David Coverdale and
Whitesnake that could be exposed, but it cannot be
printed. What you've read should be more than enough
to prove to you that your kids are being pounded,
beaten, brainwashed, and burnt alive by groups like
Whitesnake. You have the knowledge now. Only one
more question needs to be asked: Why have you got
this stuff in your house? Burn it!

HEART

Like a steam-belching freight train, the Heavy Metal
music machine called *Heart* has been bulldozing its
way up the come-back trail for quite some time. Not too
many years ago, *Heart* was a bad joke in the recording
industry. Their albums didn't sell and their image as
a streamlined, steel-smacking version of *Led Zeppelin*
Jr. went down the tubes.

Headed by two sisters from Seattle (Ann and Nancy
Wilson), it seemed like only a matter of time until the
band would collapse from terminal *Heart* failure. On
stage, burly Ann bellowed out tunes like a rampaging
bull elephant while her kid sister Nancy stood motion-
less like a frozen telephone pole. Guitarist Howard
Leese usually appeared to be falling asleep. Record
buyers and concert-goers spent their money elsewhere,

and *Heart's* days seemed numbered. This was a far cry from their early years, when they were the undisputed rulers of FM radio.

When their career couldn't go much lower, the Wilsons gave their entire band the boot (except for "Howie") and completely changed their image. Raw sex and satanism became the theme and the new *Heart* plunged headlong into darkness. As expected, they hit a nerve in Metal-head rock fans across the country and the money came pouring in. A handful of Top 10 MTV videos and hit singles put them back on top of the rock heap. Queens of the garbage dump once more, by 1988 they could look smugly out over their personal Heavy Metal battleground of reclaimed souls. What sneering joy they must have felt to see masses of Christian youth gathered in the midst of that mob.

Though shameless sex, devilish doings, and songs hinting at pornographic perversion have played a part in their work over the years, the 1980's *Heart* has pulled out all the stops and pushed the pedal to the Metal. Doing business with (and for) the devil is bad enough, but when millions of teenagers are being sucked in as well, it's time to blow the whistle and expose them for what they are. Let's turn on the lights and probe into *Heart's* dark corners.

Ann and Nancy Wilson are by-products of the sixties generation. They hit their teens just as the flag burning, dope smoking, Acid-Rocking blast of the Vietnam era was peaking. Since their father was in the Marines, the Wilson clan moved frequently, eventually settling in Seattle, Washington. Painfully shy and awkward, in high school Ann turned to drugs and music for escape:

" . . . In my case it was because I was this incredibly ugly duckling – 40 pounds over-weight, braces, bad complexion, you name it – and a real bad stutterer from being shy and uptight and nervous . . . It was proba-bly my fault because I was a real bad influence by the time (Nancy) was in high school. I was in college and it was the drug era – and in my day I really did a lot of acid and speed . . . When you're high, food just becomes matter – you don't want to eat – so the excess weight just fell away . . ."

Ann Wilson[12]

Like millions of other teenagers at that time, Ann and Nan found fulfillment in life by becoming *Beatle-maniacs*. Making Rock & Roll music suddenly was their never ending obsession. Where big sis led, Nancy followed. The girls got guitars and spent hours singing and playing along with the records of their rock gods. What did their parents think of all this? According to an article in "Hit Parader" magazine, the elder Wilsons smoked dope with their daughters and did everything possible to encourage them in their rock "career."[13]

Meanwhile, a Seattle bar band was slogging its way through the dark, smoky, booze-soaked taverns of the Pacific Northwest. Founded by brothers Mike and Roger Fisher, along with bass player Steve Fossen, this early version of *Heart* was playing Heavy Metal for hippies long before head-banging came into style.

At 22, Ann Wilson met Mike Fisher, and sparks flew. By the early 70's they were lovers and Ann was front-ing their band called *Hocus Pocus*. Always one to repay a favor, she talked the boys into letting kid sister, Nancy, step onto the stage as well. The younger Wilson immediately took a shine to Roger Fisher and the two wasted no time setting up house together. The nucleus of *Heart* was complete.

After 1974, Mike Fisher took a back seat to the band, becoming their production assistant. Two more musicians were drafted to take his place – drummer Michael Derosier and guitar whiz Howard Leese. This lineup sold millions of *Heart* records for nearly a decade. The group's first big commercial break came with 1976's "Dreamboat Annie" album (over 5 million copies were sold). The seeds of witchcraft, sexual sin and drug abuse in the music were sown from the very beginning. These lyrics from *Heart's* first big hit tells the story:

"Magic Man" (1976)

" . . . Come on home, girl
He said with a smile
You don't have to love me
And let's get high awhile
But try to understand . . . I'm a magic man

Winter nights we sang in tune
Played inside the months of moon
Never think of never, Let the spell last
    forever . . . "

Though the "Dreamboat Annie" album contained some soft sounds and cloud-driven vocals, one tune in particular exposed the depraved side of *Heart* which would grow progressively darker as the years went by:

"White Lightning And Wine" (1976)

" . . . I bring them in with the eyes of sin
It's a down drinkin,' freaky crowd. . .

> Watching you chew on the bones
> In the morning light you didn't look so
>   nice . . . "

In a "Circus" magazine interview shortly after "Dreamboat Annie's" release, Ann Wilson had this to say:

> "There's too much down music being made.
> There are too many kids who are influenced by music, and I can see it hurting
> them. Too much decadence, and sometimes, if you go too far, enjoy yourself too
> hard, it can kill you. We're trying to make
> music that is constructive – like Paul and
> Linda McCartney . . ."[14]

So "constructive" music to *Heart* is getting high on drugs, casting spells that last forever and bringing them in with the eyes of sin? Even Ann admits how rotten she and her crew are:

> "Sometimes it strikes me funny how wholesome people think we are . . . "
>   Ann Wilson[15]

When their next record, "Little Queen," was released in 1977, the Wilsons revealed even more of their witchy character. On the cover, the band is dressed like 19th century gypsies. Ann holds a crystal ball in her outstretched hand, and a goat (international symbol of satanism) is tied nearby. Glaring at the camera, Ann and Nancy stand cheek to cheek, their dead eyes burning like glass marbles.

When *Heart's* "Magazine" album hit the record racks a year later, there was no longer any doubt about which side of the fence they were on:

"Devil Delight" (1978)

" . . . Darkness dancers get down –Heavily
  hoping
Stroking the stone soul – Loving, drinking,
  and doping . . .
You might feel me burning all night
Like a dirty demon daughter – Don't put
  up no fight
I dance in the spotlight – I'm all right
It's just my Devil – Lord, it's my Devil
  Delight . . . "

As the song reaches its climax, electronic effects shoot
Ann Wilson's shrill screams back and forth through
the speakers as she shouts out in a phased-in shriek:

"I've seen my Devil!
The Devil! The Devil! The Devil!. . .
You'd better hear me, baby
I've seen the Devil!
You'd better help me . . .
The Devil!"

Another tune from the "Magazine" album showcases
what it's really like to sell your soul to Satan. (*Heart*
ought to know.)

"Just The Wine" (1987)

"Do you recall my friend
We never thought we'd ever fall
When the salesman came to call
Selling our soul to buy
Sometimes it ain't no deal at all
Jai tant rêvè du toi . . ."

The last line of that verse is in French, and means, "I have dreamt so much of you."

On their next album, 1978's "Dog & Butterfly," *Heart* inscribed a short secret message to their fans. On the clear band of vinyl surrounding the middle of the record, four words are engraved: "LOVE FROM HONNA LEE." If that leaves you scratching your head, it's probably because you're not a drug abuser, 1960's style. Stretch your memory and recall the words to Peter, Paul and Mary's "Puff The Magic Dragon." Remember Little Jackie Paper and Puff, who "lived by the sea," and "frolicked in the autumn mists in a land called Honna Lee?" To druggies, those lyrics meant rolling your own joints and puffing away until you reached oblivion. Only true dopers would understand the hidden meaning contained in a message like that. Dopers like *Heart*.

As the eighties dawned, the Wilson sisters did some *Heart*-felt house cleaning and booted both Fisher brothers out of their lives for good. A double record set of their biggest hits was also issued in 1980. This marked a milestone for the group – four years of mega-hits and worldwide worship.

Pull out the inner sleeves of the "Greatest Hits/Live" album and you will find a collage of dozens of photographs, some dating back many years. One of these color snapshots shows a VERY young Heart waiting to go onstage at some high school or college. In the picture, bass player Steve Fossen, with his right hand, which is resting on drummer Michael Derosier's shoulder, is making the Il Cornuto devil-sign of satanic allegiance! This proves that at least one member of *Heart* was into witchcraft from the beginning.

At the end of the song, "Strange Euphoria," on side 3 of "Greatest Hits/Live," Ann Wilson admits that she is high on LSD. As the song fades out, Ann yodels in a long, keening wail, "I'm tripping . . . I'm tripping . . . " Looks like the drugs didn't stop with her teen years.

As if any further proof of their ties to Satan was needed, *Heart's* 1982 "Private Audition" album shows BOTH Ann and Nancy Wilson making the Il Cornuto sign of "The Horn." In devil worship, this signals two things: The head of the goat (Satan), and the defeat of the Father, Son and Holy Spirit to Satan/antichrist.

After seven years at the top, the Wilson women and their bombed-out band buddies started slipping out of the public's good graces. They slid back down that greasy mountain of Rock & Roll success, scrambling to hold on. The critics booed, and the fans yawned. *Heart* was learning the hard way that sooner or later, Satan ALWAYS double-crosses his servants.

There was only one thing left to do.

In 1985, *Heart* returned to the rock scene with a crashing blast of fire and smoke. Instead of the Chinese robes, flowers, scarves and lacy outfits of the past, Ann and Nan hit MTV like a blazing fireball – two mean, hard-rockin' mamas decked out in enough leather and studs to fill a furniture factory. The bombs blew up and the flame pots belched while the girls pounced, leaped and wailed, wild witch-hair flying in the wind. Petite little Nancy Wilson, Ann's shy, quiet sister, now sported a nail-spiked dog collar and leather corset. Her bosom bared and backside wiggling, she sent men and boys at her concerts into a sex-steamed frenzy.

The rest of the band looked different too. Long time

170

member Howie Leese lost weight and clipped his wavy locks into a spiked and mousse-gobbed hairdo. No fat hippies in THIS group! Fossen and Derosier were replaced by two new pretty boys, Mark Andes (bass) and Denny Carmassi on drums. (Denny got his start 12 years earlier, pounding tom-toms for some metal-masters named *Montrose*. One of their records, "Jump On It" bore a full cover shot of female body parts.)

Figure 11

Figure 11 shows the record that rejuvenated *Heart's*

life-blood. Hit singles shot off this album like shells out of an M16 machine gun. Over a million copies were sold in its first four months. Why such a drastic change from washed-up wimps to Top 10 superstars in two short years? Satan's toy box called MTV was the key.

For the first time in their career, *Heart* mined the hypnotic medium of rock video to its fullest potential. Sex and the occult, always sure-fire big sellers, were employed to the maximum in these minifilms. If watching two lust-soaked sisters in chest-baring, skin-tight spandex didn't get you, then the eerie subliminal spookiness of their dark dreams put to film surely would. The plan worked. *Heart* made millions, and Satan was glorified. Their renewed allegiance to the devil had paid off. (For the moment.)

Let's examine some of those videos to pinpoint the power that put *Heart* back on top. "What About Love" was the single that launched the new album. In the video, Ann Wilson enters, under the banner of the Nazi eagle, with sledgehammer in hand. Lit by plumes of flame, the band plays before masses of hypnotized slaves whose arms are all outstretched in the "Sieg Heil" salute. The setting is a smoke filled foundry where dirt-caked people clothed in rags and sweat are producing gold bars for the band. Kneeling in sacrifice, Nancy lifts up her arms and offers her guitar to the god of the flames.

The message of this video is very simple. The multitudes of unthinking captives represent *Heart's* fans, who are making tons of money (gold bars, in the video) for their rock gods. *Heart* has gotten rich off the loot from millions of teenagers around the world. Their music (as shown by Nancy's Gibson guitar) belongs totally to Satan.

Their "Nothing At All" video opens a Pandora's box of evil about the physical relationship the Wilson sisters share. Both Ann and Nancy are lounging on the same rumpled bed together. Dressed only in silky robes and slips, their hair mussed, Ann shares a glass of wine as she croons the following words to her SISTER:

> "It was nothing at all
> Like anything I had felt before
> No nothing at all
> Like I thought, no it's so much more
> No one else has ever made me feel
>   this way
> When I asked you how you did it, you just
>   say
> It was nothing at all . . . "

The looks these two women exchange are not only unnatural (especially in THAT setting) but are down-right perverse. Few Christians know it, but sins like lesbianism and homosexuality are highly encouraged in satanism.

Does this shock you? It should! If you have MTV in your home, the same kind of filth is available to your kids 24 hours a day, seven days a week. If you still question the Wilsons' perversion, the lyrics to this tune from the 1985 "*Heart*" album will remove all doubt:

"What He Don't Know" (1985)

> "He don't know that you been coming
>   around
> He don't know that we been out of
>   bounds
> Things we do are better left unsaid
> You and me can never keep our heads

173

What he don't know will never hurt
   him
What he don't know
Is I have changed . . . "

Having regained their lost witch-throne through the
power of Satan, these queens of corruption and their
jungle-rock beat boys refused to rest. "Bad Animals,"
Heart's 10th album in a dozen years was released in
1987. Since the ground had already been broken with
the previous record, "Bad Animals" continued plowing
the same old rotten trench. Weird cave drawings of
half-human creatures adorn the outer sleeve. Each of
the five beasts pictured has its own occult symbol
which can be matched with the band members' photos
inside. Howard Leese explains:

> "On the album there are the five figures in
> different colors, and on the inside each of
> the figures has a symbol on it, so you can
> decipher who's who. But you have to do
> that yourself . . . "[16]

"Bad Animals" (1987)

> "They're bad animals – bad animals
> Got to swim upstream got a rebel seed . . .
> Out here on the frontline
> Our territory is nighttime
> We walk the jungle line
> We stay alive . . . "

Who are the "Bad Animals?" Ann Wilson gives the
answer with a laugh and a sneer:

> "WE'RE the bad animals. It's just some-
> thing we call ourselves among ourselves."[17]

Christian parents, if after reading all this you still allow your children to keep *Whitesnake* and *Heart* albums, tapes, posters, etc. in your home, you deserve the heartbreak you will surely get. When those wicked groups and the devil behind them are finished with your kids, you won't even recognize them.

Christian young person, if you can still enjoy these groups knowing what you do now, then you need to check your salvation. No true child of God can idolize bands that openly promote satanism. If you are a genuine Christian, when you start listening to such evil and pornographic filth, the Holy Spirit of God will convict your heart immediately. If you really enjoy this trash and have never felt any conviction at all, you need to accept Jesus Christ as your personal Savior. With far too many teens, it's not a matter of being backslidden or fallen away from God; it's a matter of not being saved at all.

When supposed Christians listen to this kind of muck, buy the records, attend the concerts, and support groups that actively worship Satan, they too are help-ing recruit multitudes of kids into literal Satan wor-ship. No real Christian could continue doing that.

Christian teen, if this has opened your eyes and you want to repent, here's a good first step: Since every-thing on this earth is going to be utterly consumed with fire anyway (II Peter 3:10-14), give those *Heart* and *Whitesnake* albums, tapes and videos a head start. Then burn everything else you have that glorifies the devil as well.

Jesus wanted NO part of anything that belonged to Satan. Do you?

7

THE LUNATIC FRINGE

"Finally, brethren, whatsoever things are true, whatsoever things are honest, whatsoever things are just, whatsoever things are pure, whatsoever things are lovely, whatsoever things are of good report; if there be any virtue,and if there be any praise, think on these things."

Philippians 4:8

"We have all these ideas for the videos. You'll see one of the gruesomest videos ever! We'd cut someone's head off, poke their eyes out, cut their ears off, pull their teeth out, tear their nails out . . . I like it because it scares people. If you can scare someone, you know you have some control over them."   Tom Araya, of *Slayer*[1]

Eating dead bodies is rocks latest obsession.

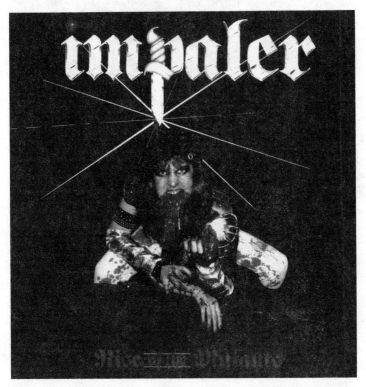

Figure 12. *Impaler* "Rise Of The Mutants" (1985)

This member of *Impaler* is having a little lunch –
fresh from a coffin. Such sickening madness has
become an exploding industry in modern rock.
The multitudes of kids who follow such groups
don't realize that cannibalism is a very basic
part of Satan worship. *Impaler* understands,
though.

Land of the damned – our kids' future home?

Figure 13. *Diamond Rexx* "Land Of The Damned" (1986)

With members named Nasti Habits and St. Lust, *Diamond Rexx* sounds like a bad joke until you take a closer look at their album cover. A hexagram (witchcraft curse) is being formed by combining the lighting with the music. (See Luke 10:18.) The "Lunatic Fringe" has now become rock's mainstream.

The serpent speaks through Alice's mouth.

Figure 14. *Alice Cooper* "Constrictor" (1986)

Nearly twenty years ago, a preacher's boy from Arizona named Vincent Furnier contacted a spirit while using a Ouija board. Vince took the demon's name as his own and became Alice Cooper. His concerts feature chopped off heads and front row bloodbaths.

Servants of Satan saluting their master.

Figure 15. *The Mentors* "Up The Dose" (1986)

The filthiest group in rock, the *Mentors* also hold part-time jobs in the porno industry. Their hand signals are good examples of witchcraft "runeing," a means of calling up demons. The same crossed X guitar appears on an album by so-called "Christian" Rockers, *Barren Cross*. "Birds of a feather . . ."

In hell the "party" never stops.

Figure 16. *Slayer* "Hell Awaits" (1985)

These demons are ripping the insides out of new
arrivals in hell. Too bad the members of *Slayer*
don't realize they have just pictured their own
fate. Unless they repent of their devil worship,
Slayer will soon meet their master face to face,
and get their "rewards," eternal flames in hell.

Beauty and the Beast

Figure 17. Ozzy Osbourne "The Ultimate Sin" (1986)

Ozzy began his solo career by chewing the head off a live dove, and eating a live bat during a concert. He claims nuclear war is the Ultimate Sin, but I believe allowing this human geek to continue selling his satanism is a much greater abomination.

Pretty girls, aren't they? Look again. They're men! (I think.)

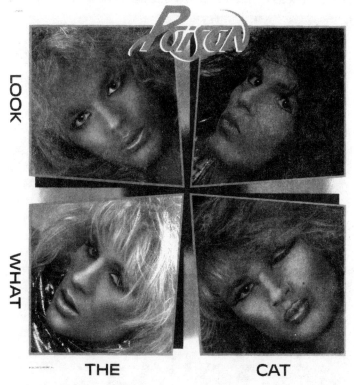

Figure 18. *Poison* "Look What The Cat Dragged In" (1986)

Poison lives up to their name. Full of smut, filth and perversion, the music made by these four men (?) is even enjoyed by supposed Christians! Is it because they share the same record label as fellow pretty-boys, *Stryper*?

183

"The show of their countenance doth witness against them; and they declare their sin as Sodom, they hide it not. Woe unto their soul! For they have rewarded evil unto themselves." Isaiah 3:9

Figure 19. "Christian" Rockers *Stryken* "First Strike" (1987)

The following is on the inner sleeve: "CAUTION: Subliminal messages appear throughout this recording beneath the audible level of consciousness which exalt Jesus Christ as God Almighty! Listen America!" This group is cursed for doing the work of the Lord deceitfully. Jeremiah 48:10.

8

THE FUTURE IS NOW

"And then shall that Wicked be revealed, whom the Lord shall consume with the spirit of his mouth, and shall destroy with the brightness of his coming: Even him, whose coming is after the working of Satan with all power and signs and lying wonders. And with all deceivableness of unrighteousness in them that perish; because they received not the love of the truth, that they might be saved. And for this cause God shall send them strong delusion, that they should believe a lie: That they all might be damned who believed not the truth, but had pleasure in unrighteousness." II Thessalonians 2:8-12

" . . . Harmony and understanding
Sympathy and trust abounding . . .
Mystic Crystal Revelation
And the mind's true liberation
Aquarius . . .
This is the dawning of the
Age of Aquarius . . ."
                    The 5th Dimension (1968)[1]

The New Age Movement is coming at us like an unstoppable, monstrous, bone-crushing steamroller. Its intent is to wipe Bible-believing Christianity off the face of the earth and replace it with a Satanically-controlled one world government, one world money system, one world dictator and one world religion. Its public relations department consists of every major rock music star in the world.

Not surprisingly, New Agers have twisted and perverted the very term "Christian." Today, Christians are pictured as wild-eyed anti-love, anti-women, anti-freedom and anti-fun religious nuts. They are portrayed as being intent on turning back the clock to a Dark Age of superstitious religious hokum, forcing everyone to join their narrow-minded bigotry.

The people behind the New Age Movement conveniently follow in the footsteps of such disgusting monsters as Nero, Karl Marx and Adolph Hitler. They have put into practice what these men taught – when covering your tracks and hiding your evil works from the eyes of men, blame the Christians.

In her book, "The Hidden Dangers Of The Rainbow," New Age expert Constance Cumbey says Nazism and New Ageism are one and the same thing. Hitler's program for the cold blooded extermination of the

186

Jewish race was only the beginning of a larger agenda; Christians were next on his list. Every despotic, tyrannical, devil-worshiping dictatorship in history has sought to erase Bible-believing Christianity.

Why?

Because Satan cannot gain the all-out worship he desires from every living human being until the last steadfast and uncompromising Christian has been executed. The New Agers have a delightful euphemism for such murderous genocide. They call it "releasing from physical embodiment."[2] The founders of the movement readily admit that Lucifer is the primary power behind the New Age.[3]

New Agers have successfully infiltrated every modern business, institution and government in the world. For many years they have been busily spreading their philosophical poison of godless globalism, using the Bible as a smokescreen. "Love your neighbor as yourself" and "You are your brother's keeper" are mottoes of the movement, but world control and satanic domination are its goals.

Since the New Age Movement fulfills all the prophetic scriptures about the antichrist system ushering in the end of the world, it is obvious why genuine Christians are such a stumbling block to this plan:

1) They refuse to worship anyone but the Lord Jesus Christ.

2) They cling to the Word of God as the one unshakeable source of truth in a wicked world which denies all absolutes.

According to New Age thinking, the gods and goddesses of Hinduism and the Eastern religions (demons) are equal with Jesus. They claim that Christ is within every man and woman and that you can find your own personal godhood through hallucinatory drugs, hypnosis regression, transcendental meditation or any of the other popular mind control disciplines. Old fashioned Bible doctrines and moralities have to go for the "power" to flourish.

Throughout history, these things have rightly been labeled, "occult sorcery." Today they are called, "paranormal psychology." By using these methods, New Agers claim you will eventually see that YOU ARE GOD! Don't worry if you don't get it right in this life – reincarnation and the inevitable law of Karma will make it good next time around. (They conveniently fail to mention that according to the strict principles of reincarnation you just might miss the boat altogether and come back as a rock or a cockroach.) Can't you hear it now, "Don't swat that fly, it might be Grandma!"

The concept that eternal godhood is an attainable reality through individual human willpower is the oldest lie Satan has ever used. He fed the same line to Eve in the garden of Eden in Genesis 3:4-5:

> "And the serpent said unto the woman, Ye shall not surely die: For God doth know that in the day ye eat thereof, then your eyes shall be opened, and ye shall be as gods, knowing good and evil."

How did this massive New Age system take root in America? It was ushered in through rock music, especially through the influence of the *Beatles*. Yes, Satan used the Fab Four and their music to introduce the world to the antichrist. Their influence in preparing millions for the advent of Lucifer's takeover can never be fully calculated.

How did the *Beatles* lay out the musical welcome mat for the New Age Movement?

1) They were the first big rock group to popularize and whole-heartedly endorse the use of drugs like marijuana and LSD. They threw their incredibly powerful appeal behind the take-dope lifestyle. Others jumped on the bandwagon, but the *Beatles* blazed the trail.

2) They pioneered bringing Hinduism, Eastern thought and Transcendental Meditation (TM) to millions of young would-be initiates in the West. They opened the floodgates for the demons of Asia to run wild throughout Europe, America, Canada and the rest of the civilized world. *Beatle* George Harrison was a prime spokesman for these anti-Christian philosophies.

3) Through songs like "All You Need Is Love," which was broadcast live via satellite to over 400 million in 1967, the *Beatles* single-handedly molded the entire world into the New Age model. They branded into the minds of a large portion of the earth's population the basic New Age philosophies . . . one world thinking, the brotherhood of man, eternal peace, etc. This kind of "Instant Karma" (a Lennon tune) had never been done before.

> "We had been told we'd be seen recording it by the whole world at the same time. So we had one message for the world – Love . . . " Paul McCartney[4]

After the *Beatles'* well publicized break-up in 1970,

John Lennon carried on the Aquarian goals his group had begun. He was an outspoken and proud secular humanist/globalist/agnostic, as evidenced by his songs, interviews and wild, hare-brained media events for world peace. He was the perfect New Age Aquarian P.R. man, and his songs are perfect showcases for the New Age religion. They are stuffed with Aquarian terms and concepts.

Let's look at some of Lennon's most famous tunes to prove that point:

"Instant Karma" (1970)

"Instant Karma's gonna get you
Gonna knock you off your feet
Better recognize your brothers
Everyone you meet
Why in the world are we here
Surely not to live in pain and fear
Why on Earth are you there
When you're everywhere, Come and get
    your share
Well we all shine on
Like the moon and the stars and the sun
On and on and on and on . . . "

The Buddhist-Hindu law of "KARMA" says that your actions in this life determine your rewards and/or punishments in the next. Reincarnation is central to New Age teaching. If you've been a good boy or girl through all your lives, you'll eventually hit the bull's eye of Nirvana (Heaven) and be absorbed into the great spiritual over-soul. To the Aquarians, that over-soul is Lucifer. This belief contains two false doctrines – reincarnation (Hebrews 9:27) and works for salvation (Ephesians 2:8,9 and II Timothy 1:9).

190

"Mind Games" (1973)

"We're playin' those mind games together
Pushing the barriers, Planting seeds
Chanting the Mantra, 'Peace on Earth'...
Some kind of Druid dudes, Lifting the veil
Some call it magic, The search for the Grail
Taking the future out of the Now...
Projecting our images in space and in time
Doin' the ritual dance in the sun
Millions of mind guerillas
Putting their soul power to the Karmic
   wheel..."

A "MANTRA" is a word or phrase a guru gives his TM (Transcendental Meditation) students. (The *Beatles'* guru was named Maharishi Mahesh Yogi.) The meditator is to repeat the mantra non-stop until inner peace comes. In reality, the mantra is usually the title of a demon who is only too glad to make his home in your body as you continually chant his name. This is part of the "vain repetitions" Jesus warned us about in Matthew 6:7. In 1968, the *Beatles* spent over two months meditating with the Maharishi in his remote ashram near Delhi, India. Thanks to their famous example, untold numbers of *Beatle* fans opened themselves up to demonic affliction through TM.

"DRUIDS" were celtic devil-worshipers of ancient England, France and Ireland who used rhythmic music as part of their human sacrificial rites. Adolph Hitler was obsessed with the "SEARCH FOR THE GRAIL," supposedly a way of attaining higher consciousness. New Age disciples feel the same way.[5]

"PROJECTING IMAGES IN SPACE AND TIME" another Aquarian concept, involves visualizing and

191

sending out images from the demonized mind of a transcendental meditator to change things around them. The projection of these thoughts is a complex act only advanced TM'ers are capable of.[6]

"Bring On The Lucie (Freeda Peeple)" (1973)

"We don't care what flag you're wavin'
We don't even want to know your name
We don't care where you're from or where
   you're going
All we know is that you came . . .
We understand your paranoia
And we don't want to play your game
You think you're cool and know what you
   are doing
666 is your name . . .
Free the people now, Do it, Do it, Do it now
Bring on the lucie . . . "

"BRING ON THE LUCIE," I believe, stands for Lucifer, (Satan) the god of the New Age Movement. The main publishing arm of the New Age Conspiracy is called Lucis Publishing Company (formerly Lucifer Publishing Co.).[7]

The number "666" is sacred to the founders of New Ageism.[8] In "Lucie," Lennon seems to be anti - 666 and up for bringing on Lucifer to "free the people." How sad that the ex-*Beatle* apparently didn't know that 666 and Lucifer were both part of the same antichrist system he so wholeheartedly promoted.

"Instant Karma" and another Lennon biggie, "Give Peace A Chance" (1969) both taught doctrines near and dear to a New Ager's heart – world-wide oneness, wholeness and interdependence. The purpose of Aquarinaism is to make the world one big "global village."

John Lennon's most masterful stroke in this area came in 1971 when he released his hit song, "Imagine." It pictured Utopia as a planet without any countries, religion, Heaven or Hell, where people had no possessions – a brotherhood of man. For a New Age Christhater, I suppose that's about as perfect as perfect gets:

> "Imagine there's no Heaven, It's easy if
>   you try
> No Hell below us, Above us only sky
> Imagine all the people, Sharing all the
>   world
> You may say I'm a dreamer; But I'm not
>   the only one
> I hope someday you'll join us
> And the world will live as one . . . "

Several die-hard Lennon fans I know will be frothing at the mouth as they read this. They'll say, "Lennon was a great man, the *Beatles* were a great group, and together they made some great music . . . "

John Lennon was a long way from "great." He was a drug abuser, a wife beater, a heroin addict, a Communist sympathizer, a habitual liar and a drunkard, not to mention being an adulterer and an arrogant, foulmouthed blasphemer of Jesus Christ:

> "Christ, you know it ain't easy
> You know how hard it can be
> The way things are goin'
> They're gonna crucify me . . . "[9]

> "And these #@%! #@%! there just sucking
> us to death, that's about all that we can do,

193

is do it like circus animals. I resent being an artist, in that respect. I resent performing for #@%! idiots who don't know anything. They can't feel; I'm the one that's feeling, because I'm the one expressing. "[10]

"So Paul (McCartney) was always like that. And I was always saying, 'Face up to your Dad, tell him to #@%! off. He can't hit you. You can kill him, he's an old man.' I used to say, 'Don't take that #@%! off him . . .' "[11]

"I was so afraid of the outcome, of nearly killing Wooler (a disc jockey friend). Because I nearly killed him. He'd insinuated that me and Brian (the *Beatles'* homosexual manager) had had an affair in Spain. I was out of me mind with drink . . . And obviously I must have been frightened of the fag in me to get so angry . . . So I was beating the #@%! out of him, and hitting him with a big stick, too, and it was the first time I thought, 'I can kill this guy.' "[12]

"So where do people get off saying that the *Beatles* should give $200 million to South America? You know, America has poured billions into places like that. It doesn't mean a thing . . . We would have to dedicate the rest of our lives to one world concert tour, and I'm not ready for it. Not in this lifetime, anyway."[13]

" . . . For those who didn't understand the *Beatles* and the sixties in the first place, what the #@%! are we going to do for them now? Do we have to divide the fish and the

loaves for the multitudes again? Do we
have to get crucified AGAIN? Do we have
to do the walking on water AGAIN because
a whole pile of dummies didn't SEE it the
first time or didn't believe it when they saw
it . . . "[14]

Judging from these comments, John Lennon loathed
his fans. His mouth was always full of slogans about
world brotherhood, peace and love, but his interviews
dripped with bitter resentment and hatred for the
masses who blindly followed him. This is the essence
of New Ageism in action. On the outside, the Aquarian
philosophy sounds SO good – a rational, balanced, fair
and prosperous world where all men and women share
equally. But beneath that rosy false front lies a grim
and well-planned future of blackness, control, enslavement and the delusion of personal godhood.

John Lennon was a perfect mirror of the New Age lie.
While he could spit out the glossy New Age slogans
with the best of them, his wretched existence told a
completely different story. He also had a Christ complex that wouldn't quit. He began his blasphemy in
1966 by saying the *Beatles* were "bigger than Jesus,"
and continued insulting the Lord right up until his
death in December of 1980. Early in his *Beatle* career,
he drew a cartoon of Christ on the cross with bedroom
slippers at the base.[15]

Here's how he described the Lord:

" . . . A garlic eating stinking little yellow
greasy fascist bastard Catholic Spaniard."[16]

His final interview with "Playboy" magazine was finished just weeks before he was gunned down. It was

one of the most exhaustive he had ever done, producing so many thousands of words it eventually was released in book form. The pages were full of comparisons between Christ, himself, and the *Beatles* as a group. He saw Jesus as merely a wise philosopher on a par with Buddha and Confucius, nothing more than a sign-pointer to the paths of happiness and peace. (But most assuredly NOT the only begotten son of God, Savior of lost mankind.) Christianity was a definite downer to Lennon because it "proselytized" (actively tried to convert). Buddhism was better, in his opinion, because "There is no one answer to anything."[17]

That's not what John 14:6 says:

> "Jesus saith unto him, I am the way, the truth, and the life: no man cometh unto the Father, but by me."

This verse would have been a joke to the ex-*Beatle*, just as it is to all New Aquarians. According to their philosophy, only a narrow-minded bigot would deny the equality of Vishnu, Mohammed and Buddha with Christ. Though this philosophy was boldly preached by Lennon for over ten years, it is a lie straight from the pit of Hell. Thanks in no small part to Lennon and his *Beatles*, it has now spread through much of the civilized world.

The Bible plainly tells us that the earth will never become a Utopia through mankind's efforts (Matthew 24:21-25 and II Timothy 3:12-13). It will take the second coming of our Lord to usher in universal peace and harmony (Revelation 19:11-16; 21:1-4). This is not to say that we should stop doing good and sit back, lazily waiting for Jesus to return. The church at Thessalonica adopted this attitude and was chastised for it by the Apostle Paul (I Thessalonians 4:9-12; 5:1-6, II Thessalonians 3:10-13). We should continue binding up the world's wounds (Galatians 6:9, Hebrews 10:23-25). But to think that we as individuals or a "global community" have the power to transform our sick planet into a perfect showplace is sheer nonsense. Only a "god" could do that.

And that's just what the New Agers say we are, you and I – gods. Kind of appeals to our pride a little, doesn't it? Gee, I'M A GOD! I can do anything, even save the world! Unfortunately, the one true God doesn't agree:

> "I am the Lord thy God, which have brought thee out of the land of Egypt, out of the house of bondage. Thou shalt have no other gods before me."   Exodus 20:2-3

John Lennon and his *Beatle* brothers were the best public relations team Satan could have had for his New Age Movement. They left a legacy that has been absorbed by millions. Eventually, McCartney, Harrison and Ringo Starr will follow Lennon in the way of all flesh – to their graves. But their one-world ideals will live on as long as their records and interviews exist. As long as ageing *Beatle* fans still lovingly listen to those dusty old albums, New Ageism will still have a foothold in hearts and minds everywhere.

Introduction of the evil system through which the antichrist will rule the world is what the *Beatles* were all about. Satan used these four saps more than any other group of morons to rewrite history. THERE is the final testament of *Beatle*-mania – the endorsement of Lucifer as god.

Mind control is another occult area Lennon plunged

into. Having whetted his psychic appetite with TM, he also opened himself up to all manner of demonic indwelling through more advanced brain bondage.

In 1970 both he and wife Yoko Ono underwent "Primal Scream" therapy in England and California. By regressing to a childhood state within the confines of complete isolation, the person taking part in this "therapy" can supposedly face his own naked soul head on. Such trauma usually causes uncontrollable screaming and weeping. A record came out of this titled, "John Lennon/Plastic Ono Band." On some songs Lennon screams until his shredded voice gives out. One tune is called, "God." Here are some of the lyrics:

> "I don't believe in Jesus . . .
> I just believe in me
> Yoko and me
> And that's reality . . . "

Primal Screams were not the last stop on Lennon's psychic merry-go-round, however. His song lyrics plus a very eerie part of an 1980 interview hint that the ex-*Beatle* may also have been involved in Silva Mind Control or even Scientology. (Scientology was also used by that well known sweetie, Charles Manson.):

> "Psychedelic vision is reality to me and always was. When I looked at myself in the mirror at twelve, thirteen . . . I used to, literally, trance out into alpha. I didn't know what it was called then. I only found out years later that there is a name for those conditions. But I would find myself seeing these hallucinatory images of my face changing, becoming cosmic and complete. I would start trancing out and the

198

eyes would get bigger and the room would vanish . . ."   John Lennon[18]

Lennon is describing the demons within him manifesting and forcibly submerging his own personality. Since this was years before he started taking LSD, he must have been demon possessed from his youth.

An interesting part of his statement is the word "Alpha," a term used in Silva Mind Control. "Alpha" designates a certain altered state of consciousness. Beta, Theta and Delta are other levels of spiritual awareness. (Charles Manson claimed to be a "Theta Clear," the highest point possible.)[19]

In her book, "The Beautiful Side Of Evil," ex-occultic psychic healer Johanna Michaelsen details the mind bondage system she was involved in. She reveals how it actually brought her into close contact with demons. She describes the terms "Alpha," "Theta," "Beta" and "Delta" as signifying the progressive emptying of her mind, dropping her spirit into lower and lower levels of conscious awareness. The process was similar to self-hypnosis. The leader of her group induced these altered states and physically "counted her down" to lower levels. Once there, "spirit guides" came and talked with her. One looked exactly like Jesus Christ. These beings turned out to be demons who nearly drove her insane, and tried to kill her before she was set free by the blood of Jesus Christ.

What has this got to do with John Lennon? His wife Yoko Ono often "counted him down" at night to help him relax. Another clue that Lennon was involved with Scientology comes from the lyrics, "Out of the Future/Into the Now" from his song "Mind Games." "Coming to Now" is a Scientology term.[20]

The tie-in here is that New Agers aggressively encourage mind expansion to reach higher states of consciousness. That's a fancy way of saying, "demon possession." Lennon found out the hard way that "mind control" meant just what it said. The real shocker must have come when he realized that HE wasn't the one doing the controlling!

John Green, who was at one time the Lennons' official Tarot reader and occult consultant, said in his book "Dakota Days" that Lennon attended a seance, often had his future read with Tarot cards and practically flipped when he saw a UFO fly by. May Pang, one of Lennon's sexual companions, pictures the ex-*Beatle* in her book "Loving John" as a paranoid schizo who flew into violent rages at the drop of a hat. His entire personality changed in the wink of an eye.

THIS jerk was the prophet of global peace and brotherhood? THIS was the New Age model man? If that's the best the New Aquarians can come up with, their philosophy is in a boatload of trouble!

The founders of the New Age antichrist system wrote most of their books while under the influence of their "spirit guides." Sometimes, "automatic writing" took over. This happens when demons have such strength and control of a human being, they literally dictate their evil thoughts nonstop onto paper, using the hand of their "host body." The bedrock laws and beliefs of the New Age Movement were produced in just this way. There is a positively chilling connection here. Lennon and the *Beatles* made their music while under the same type of influences!

> "More than anything it was the time and
> the place when the *Beatles* came up.

Something did happen there . . . It was as
if several people gathered around a table
and a ghost appeared. It was that kind of
communication. So they were like mediums in a way. It was more than four people
. . . As I said, they were like mediums. They
weren't conscious of all they were saying
but it was coming through them . . ."

Yoko Ono[21]

"But my joy is when you're like possessed,
like a medium, you know. I'll be sitting
around and it'll come in the middle of the
night or at the time when you don't want to
do it - that's the exciting part . . . I don't
know who the #@%! wrote it − I'm just
sitting here and the whole #@%! song comes
out. So it, you're like driven and you find
yourself over on a piano or guitar and you
put it down because it's been given to you
or whatever it is that you tune into."

John Lennon[22]

"Drop out, Tune in, and Turn on" was one of the most
popular catch-phrases of the sixties − the "*Beatle
decade.*" But what were they and their millions of followers "tuning in" to? The evidence indicates that the
Beatles' greatest "contribution" to mankind was the
unleashing of demons, NOT the beginning of universal
world brotherhood. John Lennon and his three partners in crime opened wide the door to a New Age of
Barbarism which is now sweeping the globe.

The following lyrics from the famous "White Album"
show just how deeply Lennon was involved in witchcraft.

"Yer Blues" (1968)

" . . . Black cloud crossed my mind
Blue mist round my soul
Feel so suicidal
Even hate my Rock & Roll
Wanna die, Yeah, wanna die
If I ain't dead already
Ooh, girl, you know the reason why . . . "

The "Blue mist" around Lennon's soul refers to REGE', a demon who appears in witchcraft meetings as a ghostly, bluish fog. This major demon is used frequently to "bless" (curse) records and tapes when called up by satanists in rock recording studios.[23]

If you don't think *Beatle* John's works, goals and philosophies had that much of an impact on the world, consider this. Lennon worship was so strong in July of 1985 that rumors of a *Beatle* reunion at the upcoming "Live Aid" concert spread hysterically throughout Europe and America. Multitudes of rock worshipers were in an absolute frenzy at the thought of seeing the *Beatles* on stage again. It didn't seem to matter that John had been dead and in his grave for five years.

Even without John around, rock music is still blazing the New Age trail. The best example is the gigantic Live Aid Rock Festival which was held simultaneously in Philadelphia, Pennsylvania and London, England on July 13, 1985. Like Lennon's life, it was a masterpiece of New Age public relations. More than 1.5 BILLION people in 100 countries saw the televised concert via satellite. "Instant Karma," indeed! Over 60 of the biggest names in rock appeared on stage during the 16 hour marathon event, including ex-*Beatle* Paul McCartney, Tina Turner, Madonna, Mick

202

Jagger, Elton John, Keith Richards, Bob Dylan, David Bowie, Daryl Hall, *Run-DMC* and Phil Collins. Four groups, long ago disbanded, temporarily reformed for the concert – *Led Zeppelin, Crosby, Stills Nash & Young,* The *Who* and *Black Sabbath.* MTV carried the entire show nonstop.

With that single smashing blast of musical merchandising, two things happened:

1) The idea of a "global community" took several giant steps forward.

2) The rock stars became humanitarian saviors of the starving overnight.

Live Aid was the brain-child of an Englishman named Bob Geldolf. In late 1984, he saw a British T.V. special about the famine that was ravaging the African nation of Ethiopia. A third-string rock star himself, he knew many of the big time rock stars personally. His own band was called *The Boomtown Rats.* As the head *Rat*, he had sung their only big single – "I Don't Like Mondays." The tune, based on a true incident, described a 16-year-old San Diego girl who took a rifle and opened fire on a crowded childrens' playground. As kids and teachers fell, mortally wounded, her only excuse for murder was, "I don't like Mondays."

After the initial success of this grisly song, the *Rats* sank like a stone in the deep waters of the mass musical market place.

His sensibilities deeply disturbed by the scenes of starvation he had witnessed, Geldolf started rounding up rockers and formed a one-time group called "Band-Aid." Over thirty stars showed up to record the song,

"Do They Know It's Christmas?" The $10 million generated as a result of that best-selling single was donated to Ethiopian famine relief. Global support and contributions quickly snowballed. The Band-Aid Trust fund was set up to oversee acceptance and distribution of incoming millions.

Overnight, Rock & Rollers were perceived to be generous, kind-hearted souls willing to help at the drop of a hat. Never mind the on-going perversity of their private lives and music. If they gave time and money to help feed the hungry, they must be A-OK.

> "Take heed that ye do not your alms before men, to be seen of them: otherwise ye have no reward of your Father which is in heaven. Therefore when thou doest thine alms, do not sound a trumpet before thee, as the hypocrites do in the synagogues and in the streets, that they may have glory of men. Verily I say unto you, They have their reward. But when thou doest alms, let not thy left hand know what thy right hand doeth: That thine alms may be in secret: and thy Father which seeth in secret himself shall reward thee openly."
>
> Matthew 6:1-4

About the same time, yet another Hunger-Rock event took place. This one was so big it blew Band-Aid right out of the water. This event included stars of every type. Black artists Ray Charles, Michael Jackson, Diana Ross, Harry Belafonte and Stevie Wonder mingled with country greats Kenny Rogers, Waylon Jennings and Willie Nelson. Rockin' superstar Bruce Springsteen chimed in, as did pop idols Cyndi Lauper and Kenny Loggins. If John Lennon had been alive, he would have been there with bells on. This was "Imagine" reincarnated, a "Global Jukebox" of music makers. The song they produced, "We Are The World," was one of the best-selling singles of the last decade, and a masterpiece of New Age "oneness" put to music:

> "There comes a time when we heed a
>   certain call
> When the world must come together
>   as one . . .
> We are all a part of God's great big family
> And the truth, you know, Love is all we
>   need . . .
> As God has shown us, By turning stone to
>   bread
> So we all must lend a helping hand . . .
> We are the world, We are the children
> We are the ones to make a brighter day
> So let's start giving
> There's a choice we're making
> We're saving our own lives . . . "

Now please read those lyrics again carefully.

That "CERTAIN CALL" we are to heed is not the cry of the hungry, but rather the command of the New Agers that "the world must come together as one." Jesus never taught that. Our Lord said just the opposite:

> "Suppose ye that I am come to give peace
> on earth? I tell you, Nay; but rather
> division:"   Luke 12:51

"GOD'S GREAT BIG FAMILY" sounds so comforting and so religious to unrepentant mankind, but the scriptures tell a different story. When talking to the religious leaders of his day, Jesus said:

"Ye are of your father the devil . . . "
John 8:44

It doesn't sound like Jesus was claiming them as part of the family. The Bible also plainly states that those without Christ at His return will not be welcomed into Heaven but will be punished in everlasting fire. (See Matthew 13:36-43 and Revelation 14:9-11.) What happened to God's great big family? I guess God never heard about it!

"LOVE IS ALL WE NEED" is the lyric of an old *Beatles* song and the creed for the New Age. It was a lie 20 years ago, and it's a lie today. JESUS CHRIST is what the world needs. Only through Him will anyone know true happiness and everlasting peace (John 15:1-5).

The line about God "TURNING STONE TO BREAD" is the dead give-away that this song comes straight from Satan. Nowhere in the Bible did God ever turn stone to bread. The only one who ever talked about that was the devil, when he tried to persuade Jesus to do so in Matthew 4:3. Our Lord's reply?:

> "It is written, Man shall not live by bread alone, but by every word that proceedeth out of the mouth of God."
> Matthew 4:4 and Deuteronomy 8:3

"TO MAKE A BRIGHTER DAY" is referring to Lucifer, the "Light Bearer" – Aquarian god of the New Age.

"THERE'S A CHOICE WE'RE MAKING, WE'RE SAVING OUR OWN LIVES . . ." These are the most disturbing lines in the whole song, for they mean exactly what they say. Those who refuse to bow down to the New Age antichrist will be brutally executed.

The Bible says:

> "And he (the antichrist) had power to give
> life unto the image of the beast, that the
> image of the beast should both speak, and
> cause that as many as would not worship
> the image of the beast should be killed."
> Revelation 13: 15

MTV re-ran the "We Are The World" video so many
times the tape must have worn out. Just a few
viewings of it were enough to burn the words and the
message behind it into my brain. Many multitudes
eagerly inhaled this New Age teaching and philosophy
without even knowing it.

There is nothing wrong with being concerned about
helping the hungry and hurting; that's a very noble
and honorable cause. But the leaders of the New Age
are not concerned about helping starving people, just
as John Lennon wasn't sincere when he talked about
loving everybody. He clearly despised his millions of
fans. New Age spokesmen are interested in one thing
and one thing only: ushering in antichrist. This is
Luciferian cunning at its worst and most deceptive.

In his "Last Trumpet Ministries" newsletter, David J.
Meyer states that every member of the "We Are The
World" recording session was hand-picked by one of
the heads of the Aquarian conspiracy.[24] This project
was no accident, and the fruits are obvious – a drastic
change in our perception of our planet, and a glowing
halo over the heads of today's music stars.

Like the carefully constructed steps of a master stair-
case, "Band-Aid" and "We Are The World" set the stage
for the ultimate New Age blowout – "Live Aid."

After months of intense negotiations in both the U.S. and England, Bob Geldolf's dream of a massive global rock concert bigger than anything the world had ever seen began to take shape. The rallying point was again the starving in Ethiopia. Two huge stadiums on opposite sides of the Atlantic were secured and a world-wide network of sponsors was nailed down. Satellite transmission was developed and all systems were go. Geldolf worked with promoters, government officials, network communications bigwigs and preening rock stars who were already measuring the jump in their popularity percentage points:

> "I would think that there's ulterior motives for over 75% of the acts," said Roger Forrester, manager of rock superstar guitarist Eric Clapton. "They forget what the cause is about – 'I want prime-time viewing. I want this. I'm not playing with him. I'm not following that person. I've got to be on between 8 and 11 for the ABC Network.' Forget it all, just do it!"[25]

Sounds like their hearts were really broken for the starving people in Ethiopia. Veteran promoter Bill Graham has been a pioneer in staging rock concerts since the mid-sixties. Even he was awed by the potential audience for Live Aid:

> "There is a general awareness now of the power of Rock & Roll and how far-reaching it is. This is the first show that's going to challenge the all-time record of viewing audience, which was for the 1982 world soccer cup (about 1.2 billion viewers). And what's challenging it? A Rock & Roll show . . . "[26]

208

On Saturday, July 13th, the biggest rock concert of all time began. Live Aid made 1969's massive Woodstock Festival look like a corner block party. The highlights of the day-long event included Mick Jagger and Tina Turner on stage together, gyrating wildly in a smutty sexual embrace. Their eyes rolled, their tongues stuck out and their hands groped at each other. When Tina lost her dress, she wrapped her legs around Mick's thigh. Almost two billion people were treated to hour after hour of this kind of "entertainment."

When the last light snapped off and the show was finally over, Live Aid had grossed over $100,000,000, supposedly for African famine relief. Head *Rat* Bob Geldolf was even nominated for a Nobel Peace Prize! Suddenly, the Kings and Queens of rock could do no wrong. Years of bad press simply melted away in the warm glow of Live Aid's overwhelming success.

At the end of the concert, Bob Geldolf was hoisted onto the shoulders of ex-*Beatle* Paul McCartney and former *Who* member Pete Townshend, while the crowds roared; a modern day "saint" basking in the light of a job well done. Back slapping and cork popping champagne parties were everywhere, and still the millions continued to pour in. There is just one question that still needs an answer:

Where did all the money go?

In a July, 1986 article in "Spin" magazine, writer Robert Keating tells the sickening truth behind the Live Aid lie. Dr. Claude Malhuret headed a medical relief agency that operated inside Ethiopia. According to him:

"Western governments and humanitarian

groups like Live Aid are fueling an opera-
tion that will be described with hindsight
in a few years time as one of the greatest
slaughters in the history of the 20th century."[27]

The Communist government, whose iron fist controls
Ethiopia, took those millions of dollars and hundreds
of thousands of tons of food and intentionally withheld
them from the starving masses. Embroiled in civil
war, whole sections of Ethiopia were denied any kind
of aid as punishment for sympathizing with rebel
forces. Much of the tons of foodstuffs shipped to
Ethiopia simply rotted in the blistering African sun.
The only transportation system to move it belonged to
the military, and the government wasn't about to use
troops to help feed their internal enemies. Instead,
Live Aid food and money went to strengthen the army
and to buy weapons from the Russians.

In the meantime, the starving multitudes of Ethiopian
farmers and peasants were shot, burned, tortured and
forced into concentration camps as the government
grew ever richer from the bounty of Live Aid and other
relief organizations. According to the "Spin" article,
those organizations are well aware of what's going on
but are too heavily involved at this point to back out.

Were they honestly duped? If so, the aid would surely
come to a grinding halt. Or is there another purpose
behind all this? The answer came when Bob Geldolf
announced that he is forming still other ways to continue financing the destruction of starving human
beings. His latest venture is called "School Aid:"

"Part of School Aid is a package that school
children receive which tells them about

the causes of famine, the world's interdependence, and how the future will be brighter for the children of Africa."[28]

Within the entire Ethiopia/Live Aid mess, we see New Ageism in action. Gullible people, dazzled by the rich and famous royalty of Rock & Roll, blindly follow where their musical gods lead. Lies on a scale that make Hitler look like a boy scout are boldly stated as fact. The rich masses are manipulated and fleeced to the bone, never knowing their money is going to finance the furtherance of Satan's New Age movement. Meanwhile starving Africans, merely pawns in the game, continue to die miserable deaths. THIS is the New Age of Aquarius . . . and it's here!

The only winners in this hellish scheme are the heads of the antichrist movement. They have proven that entire nations can be manipulated like mice in a maze. The method? Rock & Roll.

What a cunning deception Live Aid created! Rock's image under the warm, bright glow of these various relief projects is light-years from reality. If only the cameras had followed the stars off the stage and back to their luxury hotel suites and private limousines. What a different world we'd behold as these master deceivers smoke, snort and shoot dope, while gulping down booze and bouncing prostitutes on their knees. The results of Live Aid soon spawned a whole slew of Aid imitators, most notably "Hear 'N' Aid," and "Farm Aid." Again, rock stars were the drawing card. Though it was supposed to benefit African famine victims, Hear 'N' Aid was a cheap and cynical imitation of "We Are The World," featuring only Heavy Metal stars. David St. Hubbins of the Heavy Metal group *Spinal Tap* proved that his crowd is no more concerned about

211

the starving masses than the man in the moon:

> "It's like, people get the wrong idea about crazy headbanging people who don't give a twist about anyone else. I think that whether or not this feeds one person, it's gonna be good for the image of metal."[29]

Rob Halford, lead screamer for *Judas Priest*, echoed St. Hubbins' self-serving comments with his own mouthful of mush about Hear 'N' Aid:

> "There's still a very negative attitude by a lot of people towards metal, people who think that we're all sitting around black candles at night, jacking off over goat's heads. That isn't the way it is. Basically, we're just very normal, straightforward people who like to help other human beings. It's important that people see that we CARE!"[30]

The entire Hear 'N' Aid project was directed by master occultist Ronnie James Dio, former singer for witch-rocking Metal monsters *Black Sabbath*. (See Figure 26.) His motives?:

> "However, if it doesn't help the Heavy Metal image, I think people are stupid. If it does, then great. In any case, we've made another inroad for the kind of music we play. Let's hope that the jungle doesn't grow back over the road that we pave."[31]

Dio's caring and compassionate concern for the starving masses in Africa almost brings tears to my eyes.

"Farm Aid" was another example of media manipulation. John Cougar Mellencamp, *Van Halen*, Willie Nelson and Bob Dylan were some of the headliners who had their faces splashed across T.V. screens from one end of the country to the other. The publicity was great. Many undoubtedly thought, "Gee, isn't it wonderful that these big stars really care about the farmers." No, what they care about is selling ten times as many records as a result of the personal exposure.

After "Farm Aid" raised $50 million, one thing quickly became evident to everybody involved; $50 million wasn't enough to pay even one day's interest on the American farmers' debt.

Let's be realistic. Most of these rock stars are so rich that donating a few hours of their time is no big deal, especially when you consider those two or three hours will make them a few million dollars richer. They're not sacrificing anything; they're making money, big money. And they're boosting their popularity to boot. The starving multitudes are nothing more than a great public relations gimmick to them.

If these people are really interested in feeding the starving Ethiopians, why don't they each kick in a few million bucks of their own money and get the job done? Why? Because they aren't the least bit concerned about starving people. They want to make money, boost their own popularity and prolong their fame. The richer they get, the more frantically they try to hold onto their pile of ill-gotten loot.

If a famous multimillionaire rock star ever gets genuinely burdened to help starving people, he'll do more than "give" two hours of his time.

COUNTERFEIT SECOND COMING
OF CHRIST

One last area of the New Age/Rock & Roll overlap that must be exposed is the possibility of a counterfeit second coming of Jesus Christ to earth. Incredible as it may seem, the limitless money supply and demonic cunning of the top level Aquarians has given them the ability to manufacture an imitation of Christ's return. The success of such a hoax would depend on humanity's knowledge of the Bible. Since half the world spends most of its time watching television while the other half struggles to find enough food to stay alive, that shouldn't be much of an obstacle.

How could such a thing possibly be accomplished? In her stunning expose´ of the New Age Movement, author Constance Cumbey notes that New Agers have installed huge holographic projectors on top of a cathedral in New York City.[32]

A hologram is a three dimensional image which can be projected into the air. Though very weird in appearance, these images can even be made to speak. Cumbey believes that by beaming one of these projections off a satellite, a 3-D hologram big enough to fill the heavens could be produced. The image could even speak in the language of the culture it was aimed at. You think that wouldn't stop traffic at rush hour?

On March 9, 1987, I saw a report on "Today's Business" on WRTV, channel 6, in Indianapolis, Indiana, which stated that holograms are now being tested in supermarkets. Pity the poor housewife who is innocently consulting her shopping list when one of these images leaps out in the aisle and starts hawking peanut butter!

214

The New Agers are counting on people not being ready for such massive deception, for it will usher in their Aquarian nightmare of death, destruction and chaos. Even atheists would become instant believers if they saw the sky filled with a heavenly host of singing creatures, guiding huge motherships as they proclaimed the arrival of Christ to restore order to earth. Match this scenario with Scripture and judge for yourself:

> "And no marvel; for Satan himself is transformed into an angel of light. Therefore it is no great thing if his ministers also be transformed as the ministers of righteousness; whose end shall be according to their works." II Corinthians 11: 14, 15

> "And he doeth great wonders, so that he maketh fire come down from heaven on the earth in the sight of men. And deceiveth them that dwell on the earth by the means of those miracles which he had power to do in the sight of the beast; saying to them that dwell on the earth, that they should make an image to the beast, which had the wound by a sword, and did live. And he had power to give life unto the image of the beast, that the image of the beast should both speak, and cause that as many as would not worship the image of the beast should be killed." Revelation 13: 13-15

NEW AGE SATAN ROCKER – NINA HAGEN

How is Satan promoting his evil plans and preparing the masses to accept them when they come? How else?

Through rock music. A prime example is Nina Hagen, one of the most demonic stars in rock music. For the past six years, she has been singing about the very things we've been describing.

Though not a mainstream Rock & Roll artist, she is worshiped by untold thousands around the world. You will probably never hear her music on the local Top 40, yet she has successfully penetrated the discos of both American coasts, and Europe. Her heavily synthesized dance music has made her the underground queen of "electro-funk," providing a huge audience to her demonic preaching. Her international fame led her to perform at Brazil's gigantic 1985 "Rock in Rio" festival, which 175,000 rock-starved South Americans attended every day for a week and a half.

Hagen's 1982 album, "Nunsexmonkrock," is one of the most frightening examples of evil put to vinyl I have ever heard. Many, many voices come from Nina Hagen's throat as she and the legions of demons within her "sing." Some sound as sweet and pure as a rosy-cheeked choirboy; others could have come straight from the "Exorcist" – a string of deep gutteral rasps and hacks that scarcely sound human. (They're not!) ALL of the voices sing, howl, wail, mutter and simultaneously screech throughout the album. Some are male, some female; some are a combination of both. As soon as the needle hits the first groove of this record, it becomes horribly obvious that the gates of Hell have been opened WIDE.

The nightmarish cover of "Nunsexmonkrock" is a painting of Nina and her very young daughter. A bloody triangle is carved into the mother's forehead and a band of flowers encircles the baby's brow. Wearing a Hebrew headdress and holding her child in her arms, this picture is a disgusting blasphemy of the Virgin Mary and the baby Jesus. Nina's daughter is named Cosma Shiva. (In Hindu mythology, Shiva is the god of destruction.) Who or what fathered the child is a mystery, as Hagen is unmarried.

Nina was born over 30 years ago in Communist East Germany, the daughter of film star Eva Maria Hagen. Her experiences with witchcraft began at an early age:

> "I saw my first witch sitting under the table when I was about 3 years old."[33]

By the late 1970's, Nina had emigrated to the West and was making violent Heavy Metal rock records that drove European youth into a frenzy. One of these early German albums, "Unbehagen" (Ill At Ease) contained a song about chopping off her lover's head, impaling it on a pole and watching a rat eat the remains.

Hagen's belief in flying saucers stems from a "close encounter" she claims to have had in which beings from another world, a "master race," told her they are coming soon to impose peace and order on earth. She is their "chosen one," a prophetess who will pave the way for their entrance and acceptance by mankind.

This could all be written off as the byproduct of a bad LSD trip if not for the many similar stories of people around the globe who also claim to have been abducted by UFOs. In a majority of cases, the "master race" gave them the same instructions – saying they would return in force to bring about world peace when the time was right. The kidnapped victims were to help prepare the way by telling others.[34]

A demonic deception of mind-boggling proportions is

under way right now, designed to take our eyes off the Bible and put them on the starry host of a science fiction heaven. And rock star Nina Hagen is one of the New Age's most valuable and wickedly cunning tools in this project. Let's look at her ties to New Age Aquarianism by examining her music:

"Taitschi-Tarot"

"Kundalini yoga is so nice
Let's do meditation, don't think
   twice . . .
Reincarnation, Reincarnation
Reincarnation, Reincarnation . . . "

According to a prominent New Age author, Kundalini yoga is a spiritual "fire" in the form of a snake that is raised from the base of the spine through meditation. It is pulled upward through the seven chakras (nerve centers) of the body, resulting in a "new land of expanded consciousness" for the person meditating.[35]

"Dr. Art"

"First we change you, a revolution
You a believer
I am his prophet
I am the chosen one
I give you the message
You're gonna see it
All over the world . . ."

I don't recommend that anyone listen to the chilling, demonic prophecy, "Dr. Art," especially those unprotected by the blood of Jesus. I cannot describe in words just how evil this "music" is. There are so many voices weaving and moaning in and out of the mesmerizing

218

background buzz, it would be impossible to count and identify each one. They are Legion, in the most scriptural sense of the word.

In the song, "Cosma Shiva," Hagen slowly and deliberately counts from 1 to 9 as the deep, steam belching, jet engine bass drone of a synthesizer grows louder and louder until it reaches a peak that could rattle windows. Just before she reaches "10," a voice from the pit says, "MATERIALIZED." I believe she is "counting down" to another level of consciousness, a technique used in New Age mind control. The "song" ends with these words, "And my little baby I tell you, GOD IS YOUR FATHER."

"UFO"

> "Absolute concentration, Transcendental
>   meditation
> It's a totally different energy
> And you are not alone
> The UFOs are picking us up
> They give you the highest of all the spirits
> The Holy Spirit, The Holy Spirit . . ."

This utter blasphemy of the Holy Spirit of God is typical of Hagen's vile mix of Christianity and satanism. She is no different than the "Christian" rockers who conveniently hide behind a godly facade while doing the devil's work. With Nina, it's not hard to figure out which "god" she is talking about:

> "I'm with God all the time. He's sending me to the right places at the right time. I'm always in the here and now. So it's a birthday every day."[36]

This Bride of Satan may be with "God" all the time, but it's the god of this world! Her crafty use of Christian catch-phrases while spewing outright blasphemy against Jesus Christ is a typical New Age tactic.

NEW IMAGE

In 1983 Nina became a wild, red headed New Wave Space Child. Huge new teen and young adult audiences crowned her the "Queen of Funk." She became the darling of disco night spots everywhere. The blatant satanism of her previous records was submerged under a synthesized drum machine and the lush production of big name pop producer Giorgio Moroder, who directed her "Fearless" album.

Though her music was now much more acceptable to the masses, Nina's flying saucer fixation had not diminished one bit. On the back of "Fearless," she is dressed as a bride, standing amidst the vapor trail of a disappearing UFO. Check out these lyrics from the "Fearless" L.P. for a glimpse of demonic prophecy:

"Flying Saucers"

"Flying saucers everywhere, Say, did you
see one too?
One night they came to me, And they will
also come to you
Those flying saucers are my friends, Cause
they're so nice . . .
For flying saucers we are unbelievably important
Because they know the secret of life . . .
And we are observed in the name of the
light
And it's so funny when those scary mon-

sters try to shoot them
And when those bullets just go through
them through . . .
Close encounter third kind for the first
time
Then they wake up
Good morning America, Good morning
America
Good morning America, Good morning
America . . .
Zion's close
Be fearless"

Do you see what this prophetess of darkness is saying? A "close encounter of the third kind" is a face-to-face confrontation with UFOs. What would you think if you got up one day, turned on the early morning T.V. news program, "Good Morning America" and saw thousands of UFOs filling the skies? The toast and coffee would surely get cold while you sat watching in shock. Can you see the terrified looks on the faces of the newscasters as they report something beyond anyone's wildest dreams? Air Force planes try to shoot these things down, but the "bullets just go through them" BECAUSE THESE HOLOGRAPHIC IMAGES NEVER EXISTED IN THE FIRST PLACE. Great thunderous voices boom from the heavens and declare that "The Christ has come, and is now here . . ." Would that not fulfill this verse?:

> "For there shall arise false Christs, and false prophets, and shall shew great signs and wonders; insomuch that, if it were possible, they shall deceive the very elect."
> Matthew 24:24

Figure 20

The bottom line is this:

1) According to the foremost expert on the New Age Movement, the Aquarians/satanists have the technology to imitate the second coming of Christ, in whatever form they think most effective.

2) For over 40 years, they have been preparing our sick, bleeding and blasphemous world to accept a massive "close encounter of the third kind." When broadcast via global T.V. transmission, this would

deceive everyone on earth – except the few Bible-believing Christians who know better.

3) Nina Hagen is much, much more than some exotic variety of fruitcake. She prophesies the deep things of Satan, while throwing a dash of Christianity in for good measure. The sugar-coated evil of her musical obsessions is the perfect example of New Age witchcraft in action. For a closer look at the face of deception, see Figure 20.

Hagen's 1985 "Ekstasy" album threw out a few more clues about Satan's end-time "revival:"

"Gods Of Aquarius"

"The gods of Aquarius are coming with
  UFOs
They love me and they love you
And what they have to say is true
The good old communication with Holy
  Spirits
Of God's creation
Is true but our church denies it . . .
What I want is automatic writing
Oh my God, the Heavenly Host sends us
Down his Holy Ghost
The Golden Age of Aquarius the second
Coming of the glorious . . ."

Could it be any plainer? In line after line, song after song, rock star Nina Hagen is preaching the doctrines of antichrist. Her music and lyrics are wickedly deceptive and dangerously evil. At times she almost sounds like a Christian. But that is the very essence of deceit, making a good appearance to scatter evil abroad. The New Age Movement in a word is – DECEIT. Because of its caring and compassionate front, nobody notices that it's rotten to the core.

As these last days grow ever darker, Satan is making greater and greater use of his rock stars to fulfill his treacherous plans. Parents, young people, wake up! You are playing with fire. These rock chumps are all servants of Satan, and everything they say and do is well planned to further his evil kingdom. The Bible said it would happen, and now its unfolding before our very eyes. WAKE UP!

Since the Bible tells us how it ends for both sides, I want to be a part of God's Army all the way. You can join too – by making Jesus Christ your Lord, Master and Savior:

> "And he said unto me, It is done. I am Alpha and Omega, the beginning and the end. I will give unto him that is athirst of the fountain of the water of life freely. He that overcometh shall inherit all things; and I will be his God, and he shall be my son. But the fearful, and unbelieving and the abominable, and murderers, and whoremongers, and sorcerers, and idolaters, and all liars, shall have their part in the lake which burneth with fire and brimstone: which is the second death."
>
> Revelation 21: 6-8

9

IGNORANCE IS NO EXCUSE

"Now the Spirit speaketh expressly, that
in the latter times some shall depart from
the faith, giving heed to seducing spirits,
and doctrines of devils;"   I Timothy 4:1

"Give it a chance, Freedom at last
Yours for free, Take and receive
Better than pot, Jesus rocks
Come and believe . . .
You will find out joy will come to you
Take it, drink it, No fee, Come and believe
Smoke on his love - Believe . . . "
        "Christian" Rock group *Barren Cross*[1]

Today the church of Jesus Christ is being torn and
bloodied by a force more deadly than anything the New
Age Movement could ever throw at us – the false

doctrine of "Christian" Rock. The song lyrics above are the end result of Satan's 30 year master-plan for rock music – the destruction of all music that brings genuine praise and honor to Jesus Christ.

Awash in confusion, split by division, tight-lipped parents on one side and wildly celebrating teens on the other, C-Rock is Satan's trump card, the fulfillment of his master plan to bury the church. He knows that Christian youth are the key to a Christian future, and that popular music is the charm to spiritually destroy them. Stripped of discernment, an entire generation of young believers have fallen victim to the devil's delusion. Clothed in snappy Christian catch-phrases and guaranteed to set the flesh on fire, C-Rock has something for everybody – as long as they are willing to ignore the Bible.

An anti- "Christian" Rock stand is probably the most unpopular view any servant of God could take. Some of the most vocal and well-established anti-rock ministries in the country have openly endorsed C-Rock as a wholesome alternative to the secular garbage. This is just what young believers trapped in musical bondage love to hear. What they don't love to hear are verses like:

> "For the time will come when they will not endure sound doctrine; but after their own lusts shall they heap to themselves teachers, having itching ears; And they shall turn away their ears from the truth, and shall be turned unto fables."
>
> II Timothy 4:3,4

The excuses for soaking up this trash are endless. "Don't judge another's ministry." "The words are all that matter." "Nothing is good or evil in and of itself." "Praise Him with a LOUD noise!" These defenses and many others are put forward to show that "Christian" Rock is anointed of God.

Is it really?

All opinions are just that, opinions. All that matters is, what does the Bible say? That's the bottom line! We will, with the Lord's help, scripturally examine Christian music – its biblical definition, intended uses and limitations. We will also address 11 of the most popular reasons cited to show that rock music can and should be used to evangelize the lost and entertain the Christian. Feelings are sure to be hurt and tempers will rise, but I'll take the Word of God over man's opinions any day. All true believers should have no problem doing the same.

> "God forbid: yea, let God be true, but every man a liar; as it is written, That thou mightest be justified in thy sayings, and mightest overcome when thou art judged."
> Romans 3:4

> "I will worship toward thy holy temple, and praise thy name for thy lovingkindness and for thy truth: for thou hast magnified thy word above all thy name."
> Psalm 138:2

Without doubt, the devil is waging spiritual warfare through secular rock music, enslaving the souls of millions. To deny this reality is to call Peter, Paul and James liars. (See I Peter 5:8, Ephesians 6:12, and James 4:7.) Satan's spiritual attack against all Christians rages night and day. How then is it possible to take something as deeply drenched in evil as secular rock music and suddenly claim it for the glory of the Lord Jesus Christ? That would be like dragging a bloodstained stone altar used for satanic human sacrifice into a church sanctuary for Sunday morning worship! On the face of it, the very idea of "Christian" Rock music is not only absurd but borders on blasphemy. What does the Bible say?

> "This I say then, Walk in the Spirit, and ye shall not fulfil the lust of the flesh. For the flesh lusteth against the Spirit, and the Spirit against the flesh: and these are contrary the one to the other: so that ye cannot do the things that ye would."
> Galatians 5:16,17

The basic truth in these verses is just plain old common sense: The flesh and the spirit are in constant opposition to each other and produce only warring and confusion. In his excellent book, "Satan's Music Exposed," Lowell Hart tackles a fact most C-Rock defenders would rather ignore. At the bedrock of its foundation, "Christian" Rock and the Bible stand in direct opposition to each other. Why? Because C-Rock says that the flesh (worldly musical styles) when combined with the spirit (godly words of praise) will produce more spirit (people getting blessed and saved). This sounds so very noble and idealistic. Unfortunately, Galatians 5:16,17 says just the opposite. Before it even gets off the ground, C-Rock hasn't got a leg to stand on.

> "There is a way which seemeth right unto a man, but the end thereof are the ways of death."
> Proverbs 14:12

But what about all the scriptures and excuses used to

justify a musical C-Rock ministry? Does the Bible support converting the rotten rock scraps from Satan's bloody table to win souls to Christ? Let's see. You be the judge. But let's stick to the facts in light of the Word. It's not what you or I feel that counts; what the Bible says is all that really matters. Here are some excuses I've heard:

1.) NO ONE should judge another's ministry or music. One of their favorite proof texts for this is:

> "Judge not, that ye be not judged. For with what judgment ye judge, ye shall be judged: and with what measure ye mete, it shall be measured to you again."   Matthew 7:1,2

C-Rock defenders love these verses because they supposedly shut down any and all criticism of their pet groups and singers. No one wants to be judged because there is none righteous (See Romans 3:10-12), and that includes me. However, Christians are indeed to judge! Leviticus 19:15 says, "... in righteousness shalt thou JUDGE thy neighbor." John 7:24 instructs us to "JUDGE RIGHTEOUS JUDGMENT." Isaiah 61:8 says, "For I the Lord LOVE JUDGMENT ..." Proverbs 21:15 says, "It is joy to the just to do judgment ..."

There is more to judging than the two verses from Matthew quoted above. Please carefully study the third through fifth verses of Matthew 7 and you will see that it is the HYPOCRITE who is to refrain from judging, until he has cleaned up his own act. When the C-Rockers fracture this scripture, they have condemned themselves as hypocrites.

When someone exposes rock for what it is and warns others, he is not violating Matthew 7, he is doing

229

exactly what it says to do. When someone has gained victory over rock music through Christ's power, they have a responsibility to point out another's fault in the same area. They are not speaking in hypocrisy, but are obeying the direct commands of God's Word. If you are going to use Matthew 7, then use it all. Those still in bondage to rock ("Christian" or otherwise) should stay silent until they too overcome their addiction.

2.) The Bible says we can play our music loud, right? After all, doesn't it say in Psalm 33:1-3:

> "Rejoice in the Lord, O ye righteous: for praise is comely for the upright. Praise the Lord with harp: sing unto him with the psaltery and an instrument of ten strings. Sing unto him a new song; play skilfully with a loud noise."

There's a big difference between loud, as used in this passage, and ear-bleeding painful! The "Christian" Rock concerts I have attended were loud enough to vibrate my guts. What IS praise, anyway? Is it screaming, "JESUS IS THE WAY!" over the amplified roar of rock guitars? I've been to church services where the choir director instructed the congregation to sing their praises to the Lord with a loud voice. Even so, it was still praise to God. Psalm 33 isn't talking about blasting out your eardrums with the sound of a 747 jet dive-bombing through your brain. Only someone who is hopelessly addicted to such trash would ever make such a ludicrous statement. Can a 110 decibel guitar solo possibly bring praise to God?

Before you accuse me of being one of those old fogeys who "just don't like it loud," let me give you a little of my background. Before being saved, I attended some of the most awesome, ear-shattering secular rock concerts around, featuring some of the loudest bands in the world. I've seen groups like *The Who, ZZ Top, Deep Purple, KISS* and *Aerosmith*. C-Rockers *Petra, DeGarmo & Key, Stryper* and others are just as intensely painful to the eardrum in concert as any of their secular counterparts. I would like to ask devoted fans of live "Christian" Rock shows a question: Since groups that are openly praising and serving Satan play their devil - anthems at ear splitting levels for a specific reason, should humble servants of God use the same evil method to obtain a holy purpose? Using the devil's methods will bring the devil's results.

How do your ears feel after a night of such brain-busting racket? That burning buzz in your head should tell you something is very, very wrong. If you take I Corinthians 6:19,20 seriously, you know that the Christian's body is a temple of the Holy Spirit. How the Holy Spirit must grieve as He endures the turbo-scream of live C-Rock as He dwells within you! Glorify God with your body, and that includes your ears.

Are deafening C-Rock concerts justified by the following scripture?

> "But the wisdom that is from above is first pure, then peaceable, gentle, and easy to be entreated, full of mercy and good fruits, without partiality, and without hypocrisy. And the fruit of righteousness is sown in peace of them that make peace."
>
> James 3:17-18

A NEW SONG?

Is "Christian" Rock really a new song? No! For over

thirty years, rock music has been Satan's private playground. And now some poor C-Rocking fans think it's new because the words are religious? How sad. Many of these youngsters have inhaled such a steady diet of musical junk food for so long, they've lost all spiritual discernment. The only thing that's new is that kids are now getting their teaching from a C-Rock cassette rather than from the Word of God. That type of laziness produces spiritual blindness. No wonder they can't see it. It's so much easier to slap in a tape than spend time studying the scriptures. It may be easier, but that sure doesn't make it right.

SKILLFUL?

Played skillfully? Wrong again! There is not much skill involved in playing rock music. Any twelve-year-old can learn the eight basic chords of rock and soon be playing songs from records and radio. Oh, but what about those fantastic solos! You'd be amazed what $10,000 worth of electronic effects will do for the most mediocre guitarist and keyboard player. There are a few rock musicians who know more than eight basic chords, but they are in the minority. Hordes of imitators quickly crop up to copy their style note-for-note until the next "guitar hero" hits the scene. Like hairy apes, they simply imitate what has already been done again and again and again. If you dig in and find out who the C-Rock stars' early musical influences were, you'll see that the "Christian" Rockers learned their licks from the same stable of guitar gonzos that inspired their worldly cousins.

Loud, new and skillful. C-Rock fails on all three counts.

3.) I have to be like the world to save the world.

232

Can this be true? A favorable verse quoted to "prove" this point is:

> ". . . I am made all things to all men, that
> I might by all means save some."
> I Corinthians 9:22

When the Apostle Paul wrote those words, how far do you think he went in his pursuit of lost souls? Did he become an alcoholic to win the drunkards at the pagan feasts? Did he wallow in sexual sin so he could better present the gospel to the temple harlots? Did he swear and curse like the foul-mouthed sailors at the docks so he could become "one of the boys?" Obviously this was not what Paul was talking about by becoming all things to all men. We cannot ignore verses like:

> "Because it is written, Be ye holy; for I am
> holy." I Peter 1:16

Let's make something clear. Sin is sin. Nowhere in the Bible does God ever condone sinning to win others to Christ. If a Christian wishes to preach the gospel to drunks in a bar, that is his privilege. But drink that first beer and he's blown it! We are to reach out and draw lost sinners up from their mudholes, not jump in and wallow with them while we preach (Jude 23). Few things today are more vile than Rock & Roll and all the trappings that surround it. Participating in the world's sin in Christ's name is not holiness by any stretch of the imagination. Jesus never stooped that low. Neither should you!

4.) Rock music is a neutral force. It can be either good or bad, depending on how you use it.

This is an occult concept, not a Christian one. The

witchcraft doctrine of "The Force" says that there is a neutral power within all of nature which can be directed by the person controlling it. For example, witchcraft can be either good or evil, depending on whether it's white or black. Actually, both powers come from the same source – Satan. What does the Bible say? In Genesis 1:31, when God looked on all of His creation, He said, "Behold, it was very GOOD." No neutral ground with God! According to "The Force" theory, good or evil is in the eye of the beholder. Thus, the concept of Christian Rock cannot be scripturally sound. C-Rockers are so desperate to defend their music, they have even resorted to the use of occultic principles in their vain attempts to do so.

5.) We must use rock music to reach lost kids because that's the language they understand best.

> "Christian music is becoming more accepted by the general audience more than ever before, primarily because our artists are using a language most people understand and want to listen to. It's a lot easier to get a rock-loving non-believing friend to listen to Christian rock than to some hymns or heavily-orchestrated praise music. And if that friend is used to the top-of-the-line sound on the general Top 40 charts or front-line video, then you'd better have something technically as good, or you'll find yourself defending low production values rather than sharing the gospel. Besides – doesn't God deserve the best!" Commentary from a Word Records publication.[2]

> "The exciting thing now about where we're

at with contemporary Christian music is
that we don't have to apologize anymore.
We Christian artists can get up and do our
music and sing our tunes that communicate something in a language that people
are going to understand . . . "

C-Rocker Kenny Marks[3]

Baloney! I don't know about Kenny or the people at
Word Records, but I'll never apologize for my Lord
Jesus Christ, nor the ministry He has called me to.

"Whosoever therefore shall be ashamed of
me and of my words in this adulterous and
sinful generation; of him also shall the Son
of man be ashamed, when he cometh in the
glory of his Father with the holy angels."

Mark 8:38

There are no C-Rockers who will admit it, but there are
scriptural limits to our evangelism. Jesus told his
disciples in Matthew 10:14, Mark 6:11 and Luke 9:5
and 10:10-11, to "shake the dust off their feet" and
move on when their preaching was falling on deaf ears,
NOT to keep watering down the gospel, making it
easier and easier to accept! The Apostles put this into
practice in Acts 13:51. C-Rock's "Gospel" is just the
opposite – win a convert at any price and use the beat
as bait to reel 'em in! What a sad state of affairs that
this is what passes for modern evangelism.

I have a question: If "Christian" Rock is such a great
conversion tool, why is there no mention of musical
evangelism in the Bible? How did young people get
saved in the centuries before rock music came on the
scene? Almost 2,000 years of successful soul winning
have gone by without the help of beat-baiters. Music

has always been a mighty medium of expression for mankind. Music moved people just as powerfully in the days of the Apostles as it does now. If putting the Gospel to music to win souls is such a great idea, why didn't Paul, one of the greatest soul winners of all time, do so? Why didn't he, Timothy and Silas get down on the drums and tambourine and rustle up some converts in Ephesus and Philippi? Why? Because music has never been nor will it ever be an evangelistic tool.

6.) "Christian" Rock makes me feel so good. How could it be wrong?

This perverted philosophy infests not only C-Rock today, but the rest of the church as well. Christians are so concerned with feeling good, they have forgotten all about the importance of a holy fear of God. The fear of God is a subject that Christians avoid like the plague. When was the last time you heard a sermon on the fear of God? The emphasis today is not on obedience to the Lord, but on feelings.

Our contemporary Christian mind-set focuses almost entirely on what has become known as "The Love Gospel," whose philosophy is, "Jesus LOVES you; God LOVES you and we LOVE you too. If you accept Christ, you will feel peace and love beyond your wildest dreams. Accept Jesus and feel His loving presence come into your life." "Christian" Rock is the natural result of this.

The "Love Gospel" preaches the exact opposite of the old fire-and-brimstone "Fear Gospel," which has been used so extensively in past generations. We now want no part of it. NEITHER of these gospels is complete without the other. Like a lopsided scale, the love, love, love philosophy is meaningless unless it is balanced by obedience, holiness and righteousness.

236

Why should we fear God? BECAUSE HE HAS THE POWER TO UTTERLY DESTROY US, AND THAT IS ALL WE DESERVE! (See Genesis 6:11-17 and Romans 3:10-18.) C-Rockers wouldn't be caught dead preaching this part of the Word. That would be too offensive, too depressing and too "judgmental." Thus, there is no real fear of God in their message or in their music. The Bible says in Psalm 111:10:

> "The fear of the Lord is the beginning of wisdom: a good understanding have all they that do his commandments: his praise endureth for ever."

This is why the "Love Gospel" of "Christian" Rock is neither wise nor fair to the lost kids they are trying to reach. The reverent, face-in-the-dust fear of the Lord is missing, and without it, wisdom perishes. Please consider the following scriptures:

> "Specially the day that thou stoodest before the Lord thy God in Horeb, when the Lord said unto me, Gather me the people together, and I will make them hear my words, that they may learn to fear me all the days that they shall live upon the earth, and that they may teach their children."   Deuteronomy 4:10

> "O that there were such an heart in them, that they would fear me, and keep all my commandments always, that it might be well with them, and with their children for ever!"   Deuteronomy 5:29

> "Wherefore, my beloved, as ye have always obeyed, not as in my presence only, but

now much more in my absence, work out
your own salvation with fear and trembling."   Philippians 2:12

Sinners need to hear both the "Love" and the "Fear of
God" messages. (The redeemed could use a good dose
of this once in a while too.) No one in the Bible preached
about Hell more than Jesus Christ. Study His par-
ables, like the wheat and the tares (Matthew 13:24-
43), the rich man and Lazarus (Luke 16:19-31) and the
sheep and the goats (Matthew 25:31-46). They mince
no words about the destiny of the lost. Like dead wood,
they shall be burned (Revelation 20:11-15).

Occasionally, some Heavy Metal C-Rock groups throw
out a lyric or two about Armageddon or facing a
Christless eternity alone. The words sound valid until
you match them with the music. At that point, visions
of headbanging saints wildly boogeying before the
judgment throne take over. These kinds of songs
project images of recycled *Black Sabbath* clones "praising" the Lamb while kids raise their clenched fists in a
holy salute to the Lord. What blasphemy!

7.) But kids are getting saved through C-Rock. How can you condemn it?

How crass it is to fire up gullible kids with a high
powered rock show and then hit them with an "altar
call" as their peaking emotions push them over the
edge. Christ wants us to come to Him under the right
conditions. He wants humbled and broken spirits,
hearts heavy with a hateful knowledge of our sins. He
doesn't want half-deafened star-struck kids throwing
in their lot with the "Jesus" their idols have just
manufactured. No holiness. No conviction of sin. No
repentance. No nothing.

All C-Rock groups echo the same claim about saving thousands of souls though their music. If so many multitudes are coming to Christ through "Christian" rock, are you seeing the results in your church? Do your youth show the spiritual depth and growth that comes from true conversion? Or are they the same old kids? (Except for their C-Rock T-shirts, worldly attitudes, and C-Rocking cassette tapes, that is.) To hear the "Christian" rockers tell it, so many thousands have been saved at their concerts, churches all over the country should be constructing new youth buildings by now just to handle the crush. How about it? Has C-Rock changed YOUR church for the better?

Another point to consider. Jesus said,

> "And I, if I be lifted up from the earth, will draw all men unto me."   John 12:32

How can these kids be getting saved when Jesus is barely even mentioned, let alone "lifted up?" The ones who are being lifted up and worshiped during these concerts are the rock gods. Who are C-Rock fans coming to worship when they attend a concert? Jesus Christ, or the hard-rocking headliners? The Bible says that you can't have it both ways (Matthew 6:24).

If these groups and singers are really serious about giving Jesus Christ the glory for everything they do, why do they seem ashamed to even mention His name? Why do they pattern their concerts after their pagan counterparts? Simple. It wouldn't make much of a "show" if they didn't. Too many ticket buying fans have come to see the circus and give THEM the glory, not the Lord Jesus. They've come to worship their visible rock stars, not Jesus Christ.

239

Also, if the performers who have dedicated themselves to C-Rock evangelism are really interested in lifting up Christ only, why do they have fan clubs that promote themselves, advertise themselves and increase their own following? (All done in the name of Jesus, of course.) The answer is obvious. Their only interest lies in promoting themselves. Some fan is sure to fire back, "Well, it takes a lot of money to produce those tours, albums and concerts. They have to raise the bucks somehow." Sorry. These people are using Jesus Christ as a money-making gimmick, plain and simple.

Men can't save you, only Christ can. Since Christ is not being lifted up, true conversion isn't taking place. The "altar calls" are just one more side show in the religious carnival called "Christian" Rock.

8.) Even the Apostle Paul said that nothing was unclean of itself. Rock's just a different style. There's nothing wrong with it. What about Romans 14:14, which says:

> "I know, and am persuaded by the Lord Jesus, that there is nothing unclean of itself: but to him that esteemeth any thing to be unclean, to him it is unclean."

According to the misuse of this scripture, "Christian" Rock cannot be unclean and unacceptable to God because "nothing is unclean of itself." Before we can make that assumption, we must do two things: (1) Put Romans 14:14 into the context of the entire chapter and, (2) Name some things that the Bible says are unclean by their very nature and existence. If nothing is unclean of itself, then our list should be empty. Obviously it isn't. Here are just a few examples:

240

1.) Sex with animals is unclean.
2.) So is sin.
3.) So is witchcraft and devil worship.
4.) So is enchantment with drugs (sorcery).

In fact, a long list of unclean things is found in Galatians 5:19-21. These are the works of the flesh, and "uncleanness" is one of the seventeen sins mentioned! If we take Romans 14:14 as the C-Rockers say we should, those fleshly works from Galatians 5 are only filthy if our conscience tells us so. What a perversion of scripture! According to the WHOLE Word of God, there are indeed some things which are by their very nature unclean.

Paul's message in Romans was directed toward some specific items, namely meats and vegetables (herbs), and special days of worship to the Lord. Those in the faith were not to judge their brothers on such disputable matters as eats, drinks and holy days. Quarreling over such things wasn't worth the time it took. That's the gist of Romans 14. Check me on it. Research it.

Rock music is vastly different than questions about foods and ceremonial worship. We know from scripture that what goes into the body through the mouth cannot make anyone clean or unclean (Matthew 15:10-11). But what goes into the mind (heart) through the eyes and senses is a different matter entirely.

Rock music has proven itself to be evil over and over again. It has broken down the barriers of decency and smeared smut all over radio, television and movie screens. Rock music is almost always used as the sound track for pornographic movies. Rock & Roll has splintered families and fired up teenage rage since its beginning. It has preached rebellion, hatred, drug abuse, suicide, fornication and the dark things of Satan for too many years.

Hear this warning from scripture about those who hold positions of spiritual responsibility and fail to teach the difference between the unclean and the clean. "Christian" Rockers, this is what the Word says:

> "Her priests have violated my law, and have profaned mine holy things: they have put no difference between the holy and profane, neither have they shewed difference between the unclean and the clean, and have hid their eyes from my sabbaths and I am profaned among them . . . Therefore have I poured out mine indignation upon them; I have consumed them with the fire of my wrath: their own way have I recompensed upon their heads, saith the Lord God." Ezekiel 22:26 & 31

Rock music is unclean.

9.) God can use anything to reach souls, so why can't He use rock music?

God can do anything He pleases with whomever He wants. He is God. To claim anything less is to show irreverence toward our Lord. The question that should be asked, though, is not CAN God use Rock music, but rather, WILL He use it? The Bible says:

> "Abstain from all appearance of evil." I Thessalonians 5:22

The Lord calls us to maintain holiness (separation) from the world. When C-Rock groups have the same

242

hairstyles, outfits, jewelry, concerts, light shows, fog machines and musical noise as their secular doubles, they are presenting an APPEARANCE of evil. God will NOT bless that. That's a long way from holiness; it's outright deception.

> "Ye adulterers and adulteresses, know ye not that the friendship of the world is enmity with God? whosoever therefore will be a friend of the world is the enemy of God." James 4:4

Rock music is of the world. If you love rock music, you love the world. If you love the world, you are the enemy of God, says James 4:4. "Now hold on," the C-Rock fans shout, "I love 'Christian' Rock and I love Jesus too!" What they're really saying is, "I love Jesus but I love the devil's music too." You can't have it both ways.

> "Love not the world, neither the things that are in the world. If any man love the world, the love of the Father is not in him. For all that is in the world, the lust of the flesh, and the lust of the eyes, and the pride of life, is not of the Father, but is of the world." I John 2:15-16

If this produces a spirit of argument in your heart, please argue with God. He wrote these scriptures.

10.) If Jesus is preached, nothing else matters.

> "What then? notwithstanding, every way, whether in pretence, or in truth, Christ is preached; and I therein do rejoice, yea, and will rejoice." Philippians 1:18

C-Rock fans use this verse to argue that as long as Jesus Christ is preached, nothing else matters. Is such a stand correct? Let's see.

If someone takes off their clothes to draw a crowd and begins preaching the gospel of Christ, is that permissible since the gospel is being preached? Obviously not. If a woman works as a topless dancer so she can preach Christ to the men she meets, would God be happy with her? No way. Paul never meant that ANYTHING goes. Sin is still sin. And God will never resort to using sin to proclaim the wonderful message of salvation.

Paul was in a Roman prison when he wrote his letter to the church at Philippi. His confinement caused many to preach the gospel for a variety of different motives. As far as Paul was concerned, the reasons didn't matter, because the bottom line made it all worthwhile. Christ was being preached. But he sure didn't condone sinning to get the job done.

11.) Why should the devil have all the good music? Doesn't God deserve the best?

This very popular view is so absurd it's hard to even take seriously. Who can name ten good things about rock music? How about five? One? For every "good" thing mentioned, (makes me feel good, blows off steam, helps me cope, etc, etc.) there are three bad: (devils, drugs, death, smut, noise, violence, callousness, vulgarity, disrespect, etc. etc.) Anyone with an ounce of sense and two brain cells knocking together can clearly see there's nothing "good" about Rock & Roll.

To suggest giving such filth to God as the best is nothing short of absurd, whether you're talking about the music, the message or both. Even without words, rock is a loud, grating, obnoxious blast of confusion and dissonance. It instantly projects an ungodly message, no matter what words may be included. There's no way a Christian can indulge in C-Rock and still enjoy the "peace of God which passeth all understanding" (Philippians 4:7).

There is no doubt that rock is the devil's music. Let him keep it. Why would any true disciple of Jesus Christ want it in the first place? Isaiah 5:20 slams the door on this whole issue:

> "Woe unto them that call evil good, and good evil; that put darkness for light, and light for darkness; that put bitter for sweet, and sweet for bitter!"

10

CHRIST OR CONFUSION

"Not everyone that saith unto me, Lord, Lord, shall enter into the kingdom of heaven; but he that doeth the will of my Father which is in heaven. Many will say to me in that day, Lord, Lord, have we not prophesied in thy name? and in thy name have cast out devils? and in thy name done many wonderful works? And then will I profess unto them, I never knew you: depart from me, ye that work iniquity."

Matthew 7:21-23

"Any band who says they are in a ministry and they don't want to be popular are talking through their mouth. If I can't feed my family then I'm in the wrong business. The

bible teaches us that ministry comes second."   Richard Lynch, of *Saint[1]*

It may shock you to learn that the Jesus we Christians
serve is not the only "Christ" loose in the world. There
are even demons who go by the name and appearance
of Jesus Christ![2] Our Lord warned us that in the last
days many would come in His name, claiming to be
Christ, and deceiving many (Matthew 24:5, Mark 13:5-
6). This will increase as world conditions worsen
(Matthew 24:24). We have ample evidence of this
sweeping deception today through dozens of false cults
that are attracting millions of deceived followers
world-wide.

These days, the name of Christ is being thrown around
like an irreverent lucky charm. Whenever discerning
Christians question the motives, goals and results of
C-Rock's style of "evangelism," fans and performers
fire back with: "We're preaching Jesus!" (Philippians
1:18). But my question is, "Which Jesus are you
preaching?" There are many Christs in the world, but
just one is the only begotten Son of God (John 3:16).

The true Jesus was born of a virgin, and was tempted
in all ways as we are, yet without sin (Luke 1:34-35 and
Hebrews 4:15). He was handed over to sinners, beaten,
scourged, mocked, tortured and killed for the sins of
lost mankind (Matthew 27:1-54). He was laid in a tomb
but was resurrected three days later by the power of
the Holy Spirit. He now sits at the right hand of God
the Father in heaven (John 19:40-42, 20:1-17).

Is this the Christ of "Christian" Rock? To get the
answer, let's take a look at some albums by two of the
biggest names in the C-Rock business:

STRYPER

"To Hell With The Devil" (1986) (See Figure 21.)

Songs:

"To Hell With The Devil" – Jesus is not mentioned once.

"Calling On You" – Christ not mentioned. The lyrics are so ambiguous, they could be written to the Lord, someone's girl friend or the family dog.

"Free" – Jesus is not discussed. The song is about believing in true-blue friendship.

"Honestly" – Christ is called by name in this one. How does *Stryper* say we should receive Him?

> "Change all my ways, Give up my life . . .
> Reading his word helps me to see . . .
> Rockin' for the one who is the Rock . . ."

I have a couple of questions: Where's the fear of God which prompts conversion? And if changing all your ways and giving up your life is necessary to be saved, then why didn't *Stryper* give up playing Rock & Roll?

"Sing Along Song" – A patriotic ditty where the only use of Christ's title is in the line, "Let's lift our voices to the King of Kings." Absolutely no gospel message.

"Holding On" – We should believe in a vague "one from above" if we want to feel good.

"All Of Me" – A love song. Jesus is not even named, much less discussed.

248

Figure 21

"More Than A Man" – Jesus is described as a man who died for us. God created us, and if we ask, we can receive Jesus into our heart. They're getting close. Too bad it took seven songs to reach that point.

"Rockin' The World" – They're Rockin' the world for the Holy One, but they don't say who "He" is!

MICHAEL W. SMITH

Figure 22. "The Big Picture" (1986)

Songs:

"Lamu" – There is nothing in this song that even remotely resembles the gospel of Jesus Christ. The theme here is about heading to an island off the coast of Africa for a vacation.

"Wired For Sound" – No Jesus here, either. This

tune points out that Bible reading has been discarded, as electronic head knowledge takes over. Smith fails to mention that "Christian" Rock is the reason why!

"Old Enough To Know" – Holding on to virginity is the message. It's a noble attempt to keep youth pure, but what's that got to do with being saved?

"Pursuit Of The Dream" – Is full of vague lyrics about staying true to your goals as long as you let "him" guide you. Too bad we never find out who "him" is.

"Rocketown" – A change in the heart will relieve your inner emptiness. A non-violent stranger walks silently away, praying for Rocketown. Is this supposed to be Jesus Christ? Maybe it's about the Lone Ranger.

"Voices" – The idea here is to make your own choice. About what is anybody's guess.

"The Last Letter" – The name Jesus is used one time in the next-to-the-last line. Pray to him and you won't have to commit suicide.

"Goin' Through The Motions" – Double standards and compromise in the game of life. A really neat theme. If you're looking for the gospel, though, don't look here.

"You're Alright" – Full of generic jargon about God the Father and a price He's paid. It doesn't even come close to the cross of Calvary as the ransom for sin.

In this entire album, the name of Jesus is used just ONCE in nine songs. There is not one clear call to accept Jesus Christ as Lord, Master and Savior. Nothing is said about Christ's sinless life, why He died, our need for repentance, or why we should even care about any of it.

C-Rock's goal is to present its "gospel" in such a way that no one gets offended. However, the first word Jesus spoke as He began His earthly ministry was, "Repent" (Matthew 4:17 and Mark 1:15). The very idea of having your rock cake and eating it too, just because the icing is "Christian," flies right in the face of true biblical repentance.

The two records we have examined are just the tiniest tip of the C-Rock iceberg. Dozens of similar groups and singers are out there peddling the same brand of worldly junk – a "Christian" gospel with the name of Jesus barely mentioned. Spurred on by the success of newly crowned C-Rock superstars, the entire Contemporary Christian Music industry has jumped on the bandwagon, pumping out records by the thousands that usually "preach:"

   1) No Jesus at all.
   2) A cardboard cutout of Christ.
   3) An inoffensive love gospel designed to
      make you feel good.

Here's how the "Christian" Rock stars feel about what they're doing:

> "I'm not connected to Christian music at all. I can't stand Christian radio stations, and Christian tv makes me barf. Our music is a vehicle for our Christianity, but I'm not so quick to prostitute that as a lot of bands."   Joey Taylor, of *Undercover*[3]

> "We're not religious fanatics who are

252

trying to convert everybody we meet. We're not trying to shut down rock radio stations or make magazines go out of business. We honestly believe that Jesus Christ is the Savior, but we're about the most unreligious Christian band you could imagine. Religion is real for us, but so is rock and roll . . . "

Robert Sweet, of *Stryper*[4]

" . . . The key is to entertain and not to limit myself. Music has to fit the scene, just like movie music does. I have hard-driving words to fit hard-driving music, so that it ministers and people get the point."

Carman[5]

" . . . I'm really sick of all this heavy-handed Christianity. Musicians take themselves too seriously. They should have more fun, and they should stop preaching unless that's what God has called them to. If I want to hear a sermon, I'll go to my church, thank you."

Rich Mullins[6]

"I'll have a *Foreigner* 4 album going in my car and then the next minute I'm on my knees talking to the Lord about something that is very personal in my life . . . And I don't feel that my life style with my friends should be the type of life style that I'm demonstrating on stage . . . Some guy will just say, 'I'm only a Christian entertainer.' Bull@#%! These guys have a responsibility to talk to these kids as if they were speaking the very words of God themselves in their theology . . . " Steve Camp[7]

" . . . So I've made a definite decision now that I'm no longer in the Sandi Patti kind of groove. I love Sandi. I think her music is great, and she needs to do her thing. But my goal is not to speak to the church. I want to talk to the kids and address the whole peer pressure thing."

Michael W. Smith[8]

" . . . Everybody pushes a point of view. Is Madonna's music just for whores? Is Prince's music just for sexual deviates? . . . Don't worry about what people think about you. And work on saying something different. I've got to say that when my songs started drawing fire, and they were too controversial, I knew that I was on the right track . . . " Steve Taylor[9]

"I want them (the fans) to know that being a Christian doesn't mean that you have to stop enjoying life or become a nerd and wear unstylish clothes." Amy Grant[10]

"Our first priority is getting out there into an opening slot with *Iron Maiden*. Our direction is to the world. Christians are going to find it wherever it is. That is a problem for a lot of Christian bands. They get categorized and they go straight into the gospel sections."

Steve Whitaker, of *Barren Cross*[11]

Is THIS what the Apostle Paul gave his life to preserve? He who was beaten, stoned, whipped, attacked and executed for the cause of Christ would surely weep over the shameful musical muck being produced today in the name of Jesus. Let's not forget that the same man who wrote Philippians 1:18 also said:

> "Brethren, be followers together of me, and mark them which walk so as ye have us for an ensample. (For many walk, of whom I have told you often, and now tell you even weeping, that they are the enemies of the cross of Christ: Whose end is destruction, whose God is their belly, and whose glory is in their shame, who mind earthly things.) For our conversation is in heaven; from whence also we look for the Saviour, the Lord Jesus Christ:"
>
> Philippians 3:17-20

> "Now I beseech you, brethren, mark them which cause divisions and offences contrary to the doctrine which ye have learned; and avoid them. For they that are such serve not our Lord Jesus Christ, but their own belly; and by good words and fair speeches deceive the hearts of the simple."
>
> Romans 16:17-18

One thing we can be very sure of. The C-Rockers quoted above are not preaching the same Jesus Christ the Apostle Paul preached. Their "Jesus" is a counterfeit Christ of confusion sent straight from the devil. Though the icing tastes good, C-Rock's musical cake was baked in hell, and is full of hidden poison. Let the C-Rockers eat their fill if they want to, but the fans deserve to be told the truth. What is that truth? There is nothing Christian about "Christian" Rock.

11

PRAISING GOD

"Praise ye the Lord. Praise God in his sanctuary: praise him in the firmament of his power. Praise him for his mighty acts: praise him according to his excellent greatness. Praise him with the sound of the trumpet: praise him with the psaltery and harp. Praise him with the timbrel and dance: praise him with stringed instruments and organs. Praise him upon the loud cymbals: praise him upon the high sounding cymbals. Let every thing that hath breath praise the Lord. Praise ye the Lord."   Psalm 150

"People are tired of Christian songs that are only praise and worship. The church forced the 'old' taste in music on kids. We're breaking the stereotype."

Leslie Phillips[1]

The issue of praising the Almighty is central to exposing the doctrine of devils called C-Rock. All Christians want to praise their Lord. This is a natural longing every brother and sister in Christ shares. Our God is good. He gives us much more than we deserve. He is worthy of our praise. But there are more important things to God than just praising His name. Obeying the Bible is one of them (Psalm 138:2). According to God's Word, obedience is better than sacrifice:

> "And Samuel said, Hath the Lord as great delight in burnt offerings and sacrifices, as in obeying the voice of the Lord? Behold, to obey is better than sacrifice, and to hearken than the fat of rams."   I Samuel 15:22

This point was hammered home in the life of King David, a man famous for his godly praise. I Chronicles 13:1-14 and II Samuel 6:1-9 tell the story. Though David and the others were praising God with all their might, someone died because of their disobedience to God. God did not honor the praise because of the disobedience. I have a feeling the praising came to an abrupt stop when God's judgment fell, and David's friend Uzzah was struck dead.

Such harsh treatment seems unfair until we realize that God's Word was available to David and all Israel, just as it is to us today. They knew that obedience was better in God's sight than the sacrifices of men. Yet they thought God wouldn't mind since they were putting out such a praise-worthy effort on His behalf. It took someone's death to wake them up to the truth.

257

The modern application between I Chronicles 13 and "Christian" Rock is this: Obedience to God's Word is more important than all the praise put forward at all the unholy C-Rock concerts ever held. Dozens of scriptures command God's people to separate themselves from the profane. Rock music is an abomination to God, and Christians are supposed to maintain holiness from the world's filth. The C-Rock concept erases that line.

Will God have to deal with you like He did with David to teach you that valuable lesson? Is this view too legalistic? The man God struck dead probably would have thought so, had he been given the chance.

Habakkuk 2:20 is worth reading here:

> "But the Lord is in his holy temple: let all the earth keep silence before him."

Other scriptures have the same sobering message:

> "Be still, and know that I am God: I will be exalted among the heathen, I will be exalted in the earth."   Psalm 46:10

> "Be silent, O all flesh, before the Lord: for he is raised up out of his holy habitation."
>   Zechariah 2:13

"Christian" Rockers and their fans are so hung up on this idea of praising the Lord, they overlook verses like these. Praise has its place, but there is also a time to shut up and keep silent before the Lord. C-Rock concerts would certainly sound different if these commands were put into practice!

Holiness Is The Answer

Praise that is pleasing to God can only come from a holy heart and life. The Bible tells us how to obtain both:

> "Having therefore these promises, dearly beloved, let us cleanse ourselves from all filthiness of the flesh and spirit, perfecting holiness in the fear of God."
>
> II Corinthians 7:1

> "But now, after that ye have known God, or rather are known of God, how turn ye again to the weak and beggarly elements, whereunto ye desire again to be in bondage?" Galatians 4:9

> "For God hath not called us to uncleanness, but unto holiness."
>
> I Thessalonians 4:7

> "Follow peace with all men, and holiness, without which no man shall see the Lord:"
>
> Hebrews 12:14

Without holiness, praise is meaningless. The Lord has already shown from His Word that He will not honor sacrifice without obedience, no matter how loud the hosannas may ring. Until "Christian" Rockers and their fans understand this simple truth, all their "praises" will continue to blow away with the wind. Why? Because God's not listening.

12

TELLING THE DIFFERENCE

> "For God is not the author of confusion, but of peace, as in all the churches of the saints."   I Corinthians 14:33

> "(Our music) it's well-directed violence."
> Stephen Streiker, of Stryken[1]

Godly parents today are asking difficult questions like: "If C-Rock is not of God, then what IS Christian music? How do we define and test it? Where do we draw the line?"

Though it may seem confusing, a careful study of God's Word will clear up the matter.

PEACE

There are several basic requirements before music can truthfully be considered godly.

The first is a quality of PEACEFULNESS. There is nothing peaceful about rock music. Rather, it is by nature a crashing, bashing, screaming bomb blast of utter confusion. Genuine peace is an important key to godliness of music. If music is not peaceful, but confusing, God is not the author of it, according to I Corinthians 14:33. Apply that verse to all "Christian" Rock and you will find groups and singers dropping like flies by the dozens.

Some C-Rocking fans will say, "What about the milder ballads on my favorite group's album? Doesn't that prove they're peaceful and of God?" NO. The Lord doesn't want just two songs out of every ten to be godly. Christ doesn't want a mere twenty percent of our devotion. He wants everything we've got. To say, "I only serve Satan eighty percent of the time and the rest of the time I serve God," is hardly acceptable.

JOY

Another attribute that must be addressed is JOY. This much misunderstood concept is one of the nine fruits of the Spirit found in Galatians 5:22-23. Joy is often confused with happiness, but they are not the same thing. Happiness charges us up and pleases our flesh. It uplifts us for awhile but circumstances determine whether we will stay happy or not. When a C-Rock fan finally sees his favorite group in concert after a month-long wait, he is happy. When he has to go back to school the next morning, the happiness vanishes.

Joy is quite different. We experience joy from the inside-out. It is a blessed and blissful assurance that no matter what storms swirl around us, we remain calm and confident because the Holy Spirit inside us will be our faithful guide. A key element to obtaining true joy is found in I Corinthians 14:40:

> "Let all things be done decently and
> in order."

That verse doesn't describe a typical C-Rock concert. The ones I have attended were barely controlled chaos. Rock music is confusion. Just because the fans and performers act deliriously happy, that doesn't mean true joy resides in their hearts.

Apply both biblical peace and joy to your favorite music, song by song, group by group, album by album. As a matter of fact, you can use all nine of the fruits of the Spirit in your testing. With the Lord's help, you will be able to objectively determine their anointing or lack of it. The hardest part comes when the music is found lacking and you must cut it out of your life to obey scripture and pursue holiness.

What IS Christian music?

The Bible tells us plainly. All we need to do is be willing to believe and accept it. I have heard many ways to judge religious music. Some say look at the lifestyles. Measure the message and the anointing is another suggestion. What church does the group go to? How long have they known the Lord? What does their pastor think? It seems like we're told to do everything except match them up against the Word of God.

Above ANYTHING else, we must know what the Bible

says about godly music. If you objectively study the Word, you will find that true Christian music is very narrow in focus, but never ending in scope:

> "Let the word of Christ dwell in you richly in all wisdom; teaching and admonishing one another in psalms and hymns and spiritual songs, singing with grace in your hearts to the Lord."   Colossians 3:16

> "Speaking to yourselves in psalms and hymns and spiritual songs, singing and making melody in your heart to the Lord; Giving thanks always for all things unto God and the Father in the Name of our Lord Jesus Christ;"   Ephesians 5:19, 20

First and foremost, Christian music is for Christians, not for the lost. According to the scriptures just mentioned, we are to sing those psalms, hymns and spiritual songs in our heart "to the Lord." Remember, Paul was speaking to Christian churches here. He never told us to sing to the lost. When the choir sings during Sunday morning worship, the soloist should not be singing to the congregation, seeking their praise. He or she should be singing to the Lord God Himself. Anything less is mere men-pleasing eye service.

This fact, when combined with the glaring absence of musical evangelism in the Bible, pretty much pulls the plug on C-Rock's greatest "strength" – outreach to the lost. Let's think about this for a minute. How can those who don't know Christ appreciate "Christian" music in the first place? All the things true Christians express in song – salvation, devotion, comfort, thankfulness – are utter foolishness to the unsaved:

"But the natural man receiveth not the things of the Spirit of God: for they are foolishness unto him: neither can he know them, because they are spiritually discerned."   I Corinthians 2:14

THANKFULNESS

An expression of thankfulness is another basic requirement of Christian music, says Colossians 3:15,16 and Ephesians 5:19,20. If C-Rock's purpose is evangelism, how can the lost be thankful when they don't even know Christ? Only a Christian can appreciate the miracle of salvation and enjoy real thankfulness for it.

The world always despised Christian music, that is until it became worldly enough to attract them. This is why C-Rock artists and their managements are crowing about finally producing a style of music they don't have to "apologize" for. It appears that they are embarrassed and ashamed of being Christians, instead of being thankful. Are they?

GRACE

Grace is another facet of Christian music that should not be overlooked. The fact that everything God has given us is unearned and undeserved is GRACE. This fact should ring out loud and clear in the music we listen to and sing. It should come straight from our heart and fill every inch of our being. If grace isn't there, pride will take its place. And one thing no one can deny, pride is splattered all over everything C-Rock produces. Where does "Christian" Rock fit into this attitude of grace? The answer to that question is very simple. It doesn't!

264

TEACH AND ADMONISH

Music worthy of Christian acceptance must be rooted in the Word of God as we use it to TEACH and ADMONISH one another. "Admonish" means to warn, reprove, (express disapproval of) or exhort. Our Christian music, then, should also be a tool to keep us on the straight and narrow path. Rather than teaching and admonishing Christians according to the Word, C-Rockers are more concerned with the crass worries associated with fees, production costs, light and stage set-ups and tour expenses. They are consumed with printing and advertising outlays, management percentages, demographic printouts and gospel chart popularity polls. Such worldly junk has nothing to do with teaching and admonishing from God's Word.

Believe it or not, there IS genuine Christ-centered music, but it is a small percentage of everything produced. It would be easy to give you a list of groups and singers with my stamp of approval. But YOU must take your music and match it against the scriptures. YOU must talk to God and continually seek His will about each record, tape, group, singer and song.

It is up to you to dig into the mass of music called "Christian" and separate the holy from the profane. Most will not measure up to the Word and should be dumped into the trash. But that small, sparkling segment of beautiful, pure, praiseworthy music will make it all worthwhile.

Young people, I have a message particularly for you. "Christian" Rock has grown to its present state of popularity because you have abused your freedom in Christ. Perhaps you think church music is stupid and boring. Maybe you'd rather have some good old crash-bang Rock & Roll to liven up your day. If it's called "Christian," so much the better. If that's the case, then Satan has you right where he wants you. Your devotion to Christ is just so much lip service. You cannot serve two masters. It's either 100% Jesus Christ, or it's Satan's worldly music.

Make your choice.

Parents, this one's for you. As Christians, if you have enslaved yourselves to the music of the world (that includes country and pop), don't expect your kids to meet your double standard. The old "do as I say, not as I do" philosophy will never cut the mustard. Before your kids will ever learn to enjoy genuine godly Christian music, you will have to set the example.

Perhaps you're ready to pull your hair out as you sincerely try to provide godly music for your family. Maybe secular rock offended you and "Christian" Rock seemed like a good bridge to fill the gap. That's nothing but compromise, and God is never for that.

But don't despair. Keep in mind one very important truth. There is hope. Good Christian music is available. And the rewards for searching it out make it all worthwhile.

13

DRINKING THE CUP OF DEVILS

"Ye cannot drink the cup of the Lord, and
the cup of devils: Ye cannot be partakers of
the Lord's table, and of the table of devils.
Do we provoke the Lord to jealousy? are
we stronger than he?"

I Corinthians 10:21,22

"Our metal tells God's side of the story.
Our goal is to show that you can rock and
roll and serve God at the same time. We
don't compromise Jesus, but we don't
compromise being heavy metal either."

Robert Sweet, of *Stryper*[1]

Since 1984, *Stryper*, a California Heavy Metal quartet,
has utterly smashed down every barrier that previ-

267

ously existed in Christian music. Since dozens of C-Rock groups now imitate them, *Stryper* holds an incredibly powerful position and snowballing influence over hundreds of thousands of young believers. Because of this awesome responsibility, *Stryper* deserves a special in-depth examination.

They claim the Lord called them to perform Heavy Metal music for the glory of God and to spread the gospel of Christ. If that's true, everything they say and do will be in accordance with the Bible, since the Lord will never lead anyone to act contrary to His Word. Are they really serving God, or causing confusion? Let's examine the facts to find to the answer.

Stryper consists of four young men in their mid-twenties . . . lead singer Michael Sweet, his older brother Robert (drums), bassist Tim Gaines and guitarist Oz Fox (real name Richard Martinez). The Sweets form the backbone of the band, having performed together in secular rock groups since their high school days in the Los Angeles suburb of Whittier, California. Their parents were part-time performers of gospel and country music. Though the Sweets claimed to be Christians, Robert remembers things this way:

> "You know, it was like the (Sunday School) bus pulls up, and mom and dad put the kids on to get a break from them for a couple of hours."[2]

At age eight, he received his first drum set – a present from his grandparents. Like countless young people everywhere, Robert began worshiping Rock & Roll:

> "My influences were the same as most everybody else's. I didn't listen to religious

268

music. I was into *Zeppelin* and *KISS*. All
the hard rock bands were playing the music
I loved. Religious music always disappointed me . . ."[3]

In an Associated Press article by writer Richard De
Atley, Robert expanded on those comments:

"I was not interested in any Christian
music I heard. I could not buy one Christian record, put it on the turntable and say,
'That is awesome. I gotta hear that again!'"[4]

By the time he was 17, Bobby Sweet was playing
regularly with his own rock band. His group had one
small problem – no lead singer. Finally giving in to
pressure, he allowed his kid brother Michael a shot at
the microphone and the Sweet musical partnership
began. They honed their musical skills while attending Whittier's Pioneer High School. The Sweet boys
spent much of their time trying to recruit fellow student Richard Martinez into their group. *Stryper* fans
today know Richard by another name – Oz Fox. How
did Dick become Oz?

"In high school I had long hair, to my
shoulders. I used to wear torn jeans and
shirts and walk down the halls singing all
the time. I'd get crazy at lunchtime and do
my Ozzy Osbourne imitations."   Oz Fox[5]

Robert Sweet had this to say about his good buddy, Oz:

"In high school (Oz) was very much into
Black Sabbath and a band called *Rest In
Peace*. His thing was to wear black clothes
and come out of a coffin."[6]

On their 1984 "Reason For The Season" record, *Stryper's* lead guitarist is listed as "OZZIE Fox." These quotes show that Richard Martinez was so infatuated with Ozzy Osbourne that he took the demented singer's name for his own. It's also plain to see that *Stryper* cut their musical teeth on three of the most satanic bands ever – *Black Sabbath, Led Zeppelin* and *KISS*.

By 1982 the Sweet brothers plus Oz Fox were fronting their own Heavy Metal group, a secular outfit called *Roxx Regime*. For almost three years they opened concerts for worldly brain bashers like *Ratt* and *Quiet Riot*. At this point their much publicized religious conversion occurred, thanks to their friend Kenny Metcalf. At his urging, the boys started rocking for God. The band was quickly reorganized to make room for incoming bassist Tim Gaines. The son of a Christian minister, Tim had his fill of religion as a youth and sought rebellious refuge in booze and dope instead:

> "I got into drugs and alcohol so heavily, I'd wake up in the morning and grab a beer, and then I'd do a few lines or some speed . . . The lifestyle almost killed me. I had to get out of it . . ."[7]

Recent photos of Tim Gaines show just how true that statement is. With his hollowed out eyes, skeletal face and emaciated, whippet-thin frame, years of drug abuse have indeed left their ugly mark.

> "My dad is a Presbyterian minister, and that kind of turned me against the whole Christianity thing. I was pretty bad off – ruining my nose with cocaine, and I was an alcoholic . . ." Tim Gaines[8]

> "Back when I used to party, I got really
> smashed one night and I passed out in this
> guy's bass cabinet. I thought that was cool
> so I decided to play bass. I really got into
> it. It was my whole life. I quit school and
> played eight hours a day."   Tim Gaines[9]

United by their desire to "Rock for the Rock," this new
group needed a fresh name to match their enthusiasm.
"*Stryper*" was chosen. Why? Because it rhymed with
"hyper." It wasn't until later that the boys discovered
Isaiah 53:5, "And with his stripes we are healed,"
making it their foundation verse. Robert Sweet has
declared that "*Stryper*" is an acronym meaning
"Salvation Through Redemption Yielding Peace, En-
couragement, and Righteousness." Sure sounds good,
but the hype came first.[10]

Oz Fox admitted:

> "Enigma wanted us to come up with a new
> name because the old name didn't have
> what it needed. One day Robert came up
> with '*Stryper*' because it rhymed with
> 'hyper' and because we were already using
> stripes in our outfits and on the equip-
> ment. So we spelled it with a 'Y.' "[11]

In 1984, *Stryper* hit the concert trail with their new
image and a six song record, "The Yellow And Black
Attack." They dressed in wild, two-toned spandex
outfits, teased their hair to the moon and applied
foundation, blush, eyeliner and lip gloss to their faces.
The sight of four prancing, dancing, striped peacocks
mixed with the volcanic roar of their mountain moving
music made *Stryper* look like pretty bumblebees on a
military search and destroy mission.

271

Christian kids had never seen anything like it. (Christian parents still wish they hadn't.) Their debut record sold 150,000 copies and cracked Billboard Magazine's Top 20 Inspirational chart – a minor miracle for such a conservative music market. The limited edition "Yellow And Black Attack" album became a collector's item and was re-released in 1987 to meet heavy demand.

Riding high on the crest of their new-found success, *Stryper* followed up with 1985's "Soldiers Under Command." The cover of this record featured Bob, Mike, Dick and Tim brandishing pistols, machine guns and automatic weapons in front of a yellow and black armored personnel carrier. Bob is clutching a Bible, but it's tough to spot amidst all the other hardware. When asked about endorsing violence under the guise of Christianity, Michael Sweet replied:

> "We're not blind to the evils of the world; we were just showing we're ready to go to any lengths to make sure that our message is heard. We are soldiers under God's command, at war with Satan. And soldiers use whatever means necessary to win their war."[12]

Sweet's answer stands in direct opposition to the Word of God. II Corinthians 10:3,4 says:

> "For though we walk in the flesh, we do not war after the flesh: (For the weapons of our warfare are not carnal, but mighty through God to the pulling down of strong holds;")

> "But I say unto you, Love your enemies, bless them that curse you, do good to them that hate you, and pray for them which

despitefully use you, and persecute you;"
Matthew 5:44

"Soldiers Under Command" proved that lightning can indeed strike twice, selling more than 280,000 copies as it climbed into Billboard's Top 5. Numbers like these were unheard of in the "Inspirational" marketplace. (Billboard magazine doesn't like to use the word "Christian" for some reason. Must be too offensive.) Suddenly, record industry bigwigs, retailers and chart watchers everywhere fixed their eyes on *Stryper* to see what would happen next.

Though fans of the "God Squad" doubled and tripled, Christian parents and leaders knew this wasn't what the Bible meant by "making a joyful noise unto the Lord" (Psalm 98:4). Dozens of fundamentalist ministers joined the outcry over *Stryper's* "prancing and display of the flesh." The fans dug in and hurled back their own loud and angry defenses of those "Righteous Rockers," the boys from *Stryper*.

As a result of the controversy, a wedge has been driven into Christian families and churches that is growing wider every year. Cracks in the generation gap have become chasms, with Satan smashing his sledgehammer of division deeper and deeper, creating utter chaos. But God is not the author of confusion. (See I Corinthians 14:33.) This kind of uproar comes from only one source – Satan (I Peter 5:8). He is the only one who gets anything out of this entire C-Rocking mess. The best way to expose the devil's dirty work is to rip away his "Christian" mask and hit him with the pure, intense Light of God's Word. Let's start with *Stryper's* 1986 blockbuster album, "To Hell With The Devil."

With the release of this record, *Stryper* shot straight

into the major leagues of Rock & Roll superstardom. The album hit Billboard's Top 40 two weeks after its debut. Two new *Stryper* videos became MTV's most requested minifilms – "Calling On You" and "Free." ("Free" was the number one most requested video on MTV in May, 1987.) Thus a brand new doorway opened wide for these misfit makers of "Heavenly Metal." They walked right through it into a wonderland of fame and frenzy that made their previous efforts look like a good garage sale. All this on the strength of one album. Why?

Let's zero in on some things that really stand out about this record. First, there's the title. Satan is a master at turning phrases to cause confusion. Almost everyone assumes that "To Hell With The Devil" means that Satan can go back where he came from. The meaning changes drastically, though, when read with the emphasis on a different word: "To Hell WITH The Devil." Used this way, the phrase shows that fans are being dragged to Hell along with the devil because of their *Stryper* idolatry.

Stryper has created a very dangerous situation by portraying Satan as some kind of harmless dodo who can be sent back to Hell by merely singing a Rock & Roll song. Satan loves the fact that hundreds of thousands of young fans think he's weak, powerless and puny. The Bible teaches that we are to RESPECT our enemy, even as we wage war against him. Anything less would be stupidity. When Jesus was tempted by the devil in the wilderness, He didn't tell Satan to go to hell. He simply said:

> "Get thee behind me, Satan: for it is written, Thou shalt worship the Lord thy God, and him only shalt thou serve." Luke 4:8

Even the archangel Michael, when disputing with the devil over the body of Moses, dared not bring a railing accusation against him but said, "the Lord rebuke thee" (Jude 1:9). For *Stryper* fans to think they can use the strength of their flesh plus Rock & Roll to blow Satan out of the water and tell him where to go is nothing short of ridiculous.

Another deceitful part of this album cover has to do with the four angels surrounding Satan as he falls into the pit. The one on the upper right is wearing blue eye shadow and has on a 777 necklace, a symbol *Stryper* claims is godly. Do angels really wear mascara and jewelry? Both this winged messenger and his long-haired partner have earrings dangling from their holy lobes. Do angels really have pierced ears? What about all that hair? One word describes this picture perfectly: Blasphemy.

In I Corinthians 11:14, we read that long hair on a man is shameful. We're talking New Testament here, not Old Testament "legalism." What is "long?" The members of *Stryper* wear their hair long and woman-ish by anyone's definition, and so do the angels on their album cover. This is a perversion of nature, according to the Bible.

What about earrings on angels (or men)? Few people remember the biblical significance of pierced ears on a man (voluntary slavery). But in today's society, it means only two things: Homosexuality or loyalty to Rock & Roll.[13] One of the unwritten laws of our culture is that gay men pierce their ears in only one lobe as a silent signal to attract new partners. This is usually done in the right side. The only other reason men wear earrings today is to imitate their rock gods. Keith

Richards of the *Rolling Stones* started the trend fifteen years ago. So with *Stryper's* angels, which is it? Are two of them gay, or just fans of the band?

What about the 777 necklace? Is it really a sign of godliness as *Stryper* claims? The number 7 has always been associated with the Lord throughout the Bible, from Genesis to Revelation. It represents God's perfection. The number 7 is indeed a godly sign. But it is also a powerful number in the occult, ESPECIALLY when combined in threes, as used exclusively by *Stryper*.

Need proof? The following quote comes from a book called "Treasury of Witchcraft:"

> "SEVEN: this number, in occult rites, possessed mystic implications . . . The number 7 has special significance in magic ritual; while repetition is the essence of conjuration . . . POWERFUL: triple repetition is characteristic of magic ritual."[14]

The ancient Egyptians and Assyrians both worshiped astrology and revered 7 as being religiously significant. They knew that there were 7 chief luminaries in the sky, and bowed down to them (sun, moon and five planets). They also realized that the moon changes its phase every seven days. The heathen worshiped 7, and when any number is tripled in witchcraft, it signifies deity, or godhood. This is obviously NOT the godhood of Father, Son and Holy Spirit!

Things get even more sinister. One of the most evil and influential satanists of the last century was an Englishman named Aleister Crowley. Before his death in 1947, he had gained a world-wide reputation as a Black Magician, demonologist, bisexual, drug addict, devil worshiper and murderer. He has many devoted followers of his teachings in the realm of modern Rock & Roll, including *Led Zeppelin's* Jimmy Page, the demented Ozzy Osbourne and Daryl Hall of *Hall & Oates.* Members of the *Beatles*, the *Doors* and the *Rolling Stones* have also been on the fringes of Crowley's power and influence.

During his wretched life, the "Great Beast 666" as he liked to be called, wrote many books about ritual magic, the Tarot and the occult in general. One of these was titled, "Liber 777!"[15] One day, I was stopped dead in my tracks at a local bookstore by a thick white paperback that caught my eye in the "Parapsychology" section. The title? "777 And Other Qabalistic Writings of Aleister Crowley," published by Samuel Weiser, Inc., 1973, York Beach, Maine.

Both *Stryper* and their fans have adorned themselves with the 777 by sewing it on their clothing. It's also on the cover of both "The Yellow And Black Attack" and "Soldiers Under Command." Inside the "To Hell With The Devil" album, Michael Sweet's triangular belt buckle has a 7 etched at each of the three corners. Flip the record cover over and guitarist Oz Fox is wearing a pyramid patch on his chest with the same numbers set in the same places. So is Tim Gaines. I'd like to know how wearing a satanist's sacred number gives glory to the Lord Jesus Christ.

What about other occult emblems on this album sleeve? Inside, Oz Fox has a machine attached to his outfit that is flashing a digital message in the viewing screen: "Dimension 4," an occult term for the spirit world.[16]

While browsing through a shopping mall, I stumbled upon an album by *David Lee Roth Band* guitarist Steve

Vai. Titled, "Flexable," the back featured a huge, intricately drawn symbol that also incorporated a pyramid with three sevens, one at each corner. Steve has never claimed to be Rocking for Jesus, so why does he have a sign of "godliness" on his record?

Vai settles any doubt about which god he serves in the May, 1988 issue of "Guitar World." On the front cover he wears a pyramid necklace with a 7 in each corner. On page 51 he's shown making a sign of satanic allegiance!

I wrote to David J. Meyer, a brother in Christ whose specialty was witchcraft/astrology before being saved. I asked him about the similarity between *Stryper's* triple 7 pyramid and Steve Vai's logo. Here is part of his reply to my letter:

> "The triangle is a favorable sign or aspect in astrology. . . The trine aspect in the drawing would indicate, in my opinion, the Age of Aquarius. The "7" refers to the 7th solar house of the heavens. Remember the song "Age of Aquarius," and the words; 'When the moon is in the seventh house and Jupiter aligns with Mars.' . . . I see definite druid witchcraft involvement here. The druids referred to themselves as the Holy priesthood of the "Septenary" or Seven. The equilateral triangle with one point up represents the male or good side of the force (principle of the Tao, yin and yang). The downward pointing triangle (not shown here) represents the female or dark side of the force. When the male triangle penetrates the female triangle it produces the six pointed crest of Solomon

or hexagram, the most wicked symbol in witchcraft. The sevens then disappear and we end up with the geometric mark of the beast. All lines that angle right are 6, all that angle left are 6 and the core is a hexagon with six lines. Thus we have a geometric 666 instead of a triangular 777. In short, the symbol that you sent is one of the most powerful of all satanic symbols and is pointing to the New Age of Antichrist . . ."

When I questioned Brother Meyer more closely over the telephone, he told me that the triangle/pyramid containing three sevens as used by *Stryper* and Steve Vai showed a "spirit of blasphemy," man reaching upward to become God. This inner "god-self" is the basis of New Age Movement teaching. Look at the thousands of fans who have been duped into thinking that they can come to God through *Stryper*, instead of going directly to the Lord Jesus (John 14:6). The bottom line here is: *Stryper* is using a bona fide witchcraft sign to identify themselves to their fans. And those symbols didn't appear on that record by accident.

One last thing about *Stryper's* "To Hell" cover. The electric guitar is being torn from Satan's grasp, which would indicate that rock music belongs to the devil. Does *Stryper* really think they can take this demon-drenched evil medium and claim it for the Lord? Michael Sweet says:

"I don't think a lot of those secular bands really understand what they're singing about. They're going for shock value – and they're succeeding. If they do know what they're doing, I fear for them. They're

279

dealing with very powerful forces."[17]

I believe *Stryper* knows exactly what kind of forces they're dealing with.

Oz Fox adds:

> "We listen to just about everybody. From Whitney Houston to *Judas Priest*. We like music in general. If we closed our minds to one particular way or one particular thing in music we wouldn't be artists. We wouldn't be able to write the kind of music we write. Of course, we're rooted and grounded so it doesn't hurt us. Somebody who can't handle themselves, listening to that kind of music might make them want to go out and booze and party and whatever."[18]

The Bible has a stern warning for people who believe such foolishness. I Corinthians 10:12 says:

> "Wherefore let him that thinketh he standeth take heed lest he fall."

In conclusion: "To Hell With The Devil" twists the Word of God to fit the band's image. Angels do NOT have long hair, make-up or earrings. Satan is NOT some harmless pussycat we can sing back into the pit; the *Stryper* pyramid logo is NOT a godly symbol and the triple 7 number is outright witchcraft blasphemy. Though *Stryper* slapped a disclaimer sticker on the album, no matter how it's explained away, deception and confusion is being fostered here . . . and they know it! That's exactly how Satan works.

We must look at still another disturbing aspect of *Stryper's* career – their record company. Enigma Records is a California conglomerate that helped give secular rock monsters *Ratt* and *Motley Crue* their start.[19] They produce some of the most disgusting and obviously satanic rock filth in the marketplace. They handle groups with names like *Obsession*, *Sodom* and *Poison*. How can a "Christian" band be part of a Satan-spewing machine like Enigma records? Obviously, *Stryper* has no problem with it. Michael Sweet proves his loyalty with these comments about the "To Hell" album:

> " . . . Now with good label distribution on this record, we feel we've stayed loyal to our principles. So if we make a lot of money for the label this time, that's okay."[20]

The waters get deeper. A special logo appears on every product Enigma puts out, including all *Stryper* records and tapes. In fact, on the original "Yellow And Black Attack" album, this trademark filled the entire circular center of one side of the disc. No song titles, no credits, just the puzzling Enigma picture. What is an enigma, anyway? Webster's New World Dictionary calls it "a riddle, a perplexing or baffling matter." At first glance, this symbol looks like a meaningless blob. Shortly after I wrote **"The Devil's Disciples - The Truth About Rock,"** a brother from Iowa sent me his finding on the matter. Based on his research, the Enigma trademark represented a crude triangle combined with the occult/demonic name for God – "The Yod." Depending on which direction the pyramid pointed, one could call on the god of "good" or "evil."

The Lord told me to get it straight from the horse's mouth – write Enigma Records and ask them about their mysterious little logo. I did so. I take the Lord's commandment in Matthew 10:16 very seriously, so I used my wife's name as the return address. Two weeks later I received a reply enclosed in an Enigma envelope. Here is what it said:

> "Oh Paula – it's an ENIGMA. I can't tell you, but if you turn it upside-down and use your imagination you might be able to figure out that it's one of the greatest, most beautiful, most amazing things on earth – maybe in all the universe! And YOU and I use it everyday, see it all around us, and we take it for granted. It's really beautiful when you figure it out! (Oh – all right! It's two parts of the female anatomy.)"

Please read that again. Do you fully understand what this means, young person? Anyone who owns *Stryper* records or tapes also has crude pornographic drawings as well! This should disgust you!

There is much more going on with *Stryper's* career than their fans realize. Evil is not a game Christians should play, seeing how close they can come to the flames without getting burnt. *Stryper's* deception is leading countless multitudes of "God Squad" fans astray. The facts show that Robert and the boys have never repented of their original carnality. Bob even admits his sin in this quote:

> "As a matter of fact, the band was one thing that was making us turn and walk the opposite direction from Christianity, because, let's face it, when you're out there playing rock 'n' roll, and you're having a real good time doing your own thing – it's

not that you hate God or anything – you just don't want to think about Christ, because what he does is he exposes a lifestyle. If you're doing something you like doing, and God says not to do it, then you're not going to pay attention."

Robert Sweet[21]

Truer words were never spoken. Like stiffnecked hardheads, Bob and the band continue to perform and promote rock music, even though God condemns it.

Stryper has talked about appearing with a major secular act for some time. Robert Sweet even wanted to tour with devil-rocking *Motley Crue*:

"Well there's been a lot of talk about it. Maybe someday. A heaven vs. hell tour. I think it might be kind of neat. We both are bands that really want to get up and entertain, we both stress trying to look as good as we can and put on a good show."[22]

Motley Crue sing about Satanism, sexual perversion and violent killing. Lead singer Vince Neil caused a person's death through drunken driving. Pentagrams, fornication and Jack Daniels whiskey are well-known symbols of the band.

What are *Motley Crue* concert tours like? This excerpt from a 1987 Tacoma, Washington newspaper story titled "It's Too Heavy For Their Mettle" explains:

"About 150 police officers signed a petition telling superiors they no longer will work at heavy metal concerts in the Tacoma Dome following an incident in which a fan

283

licked blood off the floor. The petition started out as a letter from Det. Bill Belante, who said the *Motley Crue* concert three weeks earlier was the last straw. Belante said he saw drug use, assault, open sex and half naked girls. Then, after the victim of a vicious beating was taken away, a young man crouched over the spilled blood and licked it . . . His protest letter described the concerts as 'sanctioned war zones . . . ' "

Sweet must have been disappointed but *Motley* didn't make it onto *Stryper's* 1987 tour. Instead, a new group from the Enigma stable called *Hurricane* opened their show. On March 26, 1987, I attended a *Stryper / Hurricane* concert at Clowes Hall in Indianapolis, Indiana. I can honestly say it was an utter reproach to the name of Christ. *Hurricane* didn't even pretend to be a Christian band. (For a look at their debut album, see Figure 23.) During the concert, Michael Sweet declared that the members of *Hurricane* were his "**brothers**." (To Christians, this means united in spirit and purpose, joint-heirs of eternal life.) Does *Hurricane* fit that description? Judge for yourself from the songs they performed that night:

"Hot And Heavy"

"Party's just started and we're all on fire
And your temperature's risin' till it can't
   get higher
Hey now don't you worry if she will or she
   won't, no
Cause you'll never know the answer till
   you ask her what she wants
She'll say she wants it hot and strong

She wants it all night long
Let's get hot and heavy . . ."

"Take What You Want"

"Thrill me and do it like you mean it
And tell me that it feels so good
Show me that you know how to do it . . ."

Figure 23

**Michael Sweet called _Hurricane_ his "brothers."
You judge whose family they're both in.**

"Girls Are Out Tonight"

"Struttin' down the sidewalk
Causin' heartache wherever she goes
Zippers and lips and high cost sins
You know I don't want to know
My eyes are burning bright
Wanna go round, round, round to her house
   tonight . . ."

What was the crowd's reaction to such smut? They loved it! Wild screams, fists in the air and Il Cornuto devil-signs were all over the hall. It was hard to remember this was supposed to be for the glory of God.

In fact, for a "Christian" concert, there was precious little Jesus to be seen, onstage or off. Before the show, I passed one of the band's buses in the parking lot. A yellow and black sign hung in the driver's window: "INSURED BY SMITH & WESSON." Great witness.

As I waited in line, ticket in hand, hundreds of excited young people milled about the entrance. Some were dressed *Stryper*-style, wearing sparkly yellow and black parachute pants, jackets, scarves and bandanas. Many others advertised their favorite rock gods on their T-shirts – a degenerate list including *KISS, AC-DC, Bon Jovi, Cinderella, Ratt* and *Iron Maiden*.

Crosses dangled from the ears of some young men and one ten year old boy's shirt had this blasphemous message on the back: "JESUS CHRIST ROCKS." Why is this blasphemy? A rock can be a solid foundation, braced and immoveable. Or "rock" can mean to move back and forth, to sway from side to side. When used as a verb, as in "JESUS CHRIST ROCKS," this indicates that Christ is not the dependable and unchang-

286

ing cornerstone all true disciples depend on. Rather, He is a moving, swaying branch blown back and forth by the wind. Maybe these C-Rock fans think our Lord tunes in to the Top 40 on His Heavenly transistor radio and boogies on over to the four and twenty elders for a jam session. Jesus on drums?

Blasphemy! I wonder where this ten year old picked up such a blasphemous idea. I wonder if he saw the article in People magazine titled, "Holy Rock & Rollers!" that shows Robert Sweet seated before his massive drum kit. The words on the back of his chair read, "JESUS CHRIST ROCKS."

Inside the auditorium, the usual pre-concert chaos reigned. A booth of over-priced *Stryper* stuff was doing a land office business, with fans crowded around four deep on all sides. You could get a T-shirt for $20.00 or a button for a buck. Bumper stickers were $2.00.

Secular Heavy Metal rock noise was blasting from the onstage P.A. system as hundreds of kids slowly took their seats, waiting for the "show" to begin. They knew every hard rocking song by heart and screamed with wild caveman yells when the latest David Lee Roth, Bon Jovi and *Van Halen* hits were played.

The lights went out, the fists went up, and *Hurricane* hit the stage to the sound of monstrous, over-amplified, booming thunderclaps. The crashing chords of their first song felt like a knife in the brain. Having attended a *Petra* concert some months earlier, my wife and I knew what to expect this time around, so we reached for the brand new earplugs we had brought with us. As I opened the package, these words caught my eye: "Sonic II hearing protectors are also ideal protection from high impulsive noise associated with rock music, aircraft, chain saws, snowmobiles, lawn mowers, race cars and tractors." Rock music had beaten everything, including airplanes. We got a big laugh out of that.

By the time *Hurricane* finished, I felt like a Florida homeowner who had forgotten to buy flood insurance. But the concert crowd loved every blistering, ear peeling minute. Christian? Non-Christian? Nobody cared. It was Rock & Roll! And that was all that mattered.

During the intermission, a teenage girl in the balcony to my right took off her shirt while boys crowded around her. A young man stood and screamed into the air, dancing and jumping to music only he could hear. The road crews swarmed over the stage like busy ants, removing the leftovers of *Hurricane's* attack and setting up *Stryper's* equipment, including Robert Sweet's multi-drum extravaganza. Unlike other rock drummers, Bob turns his set sideways so his fans can get a good look at him. Most rock percussionists are so buried in tom-toms and cymbals, the crowd is lucky to see the top of their Heavy Metal head. But Robert's sweethearts are treated to a nice profile of their favorite rock god. Hey, wait a minute. I thought Jesus was supposed to get the glory here, not Bobby Sweet.

By the time the crowd heard the first eerie chords of "Abyss" (the instrumental lead-in of "To Hell With The Devil") they were primed to the bursting point. A hundred hands openly flashed the devil-sign of satanic allegiance. Screams and howls filled the air. One young man right in front of me formed the Il Cornuto with both hands, then brought them together, using his fingers to produce a pyramid in the middle. (This sign is used by singer Sammy Hagar in the *Van Halen* video, "Best Of Both Worlds.")

When *Stryper* hit the stage, the multitude went nuts. They knew every word of "To Hell With The Devil" and sang the chorus till the walls rocked. Oz Fox's curly perm stuck out an astounding three feet. Robert and Tim's lank locks hung well past their shoulders. Michael was wearing a pretty blush on his mascaraed face, which was beautifully framed by a cascading waterfall of curls. If *Stryper* doesn't get signed up to do shampoo commercials, someone at Enigma is missing a real opportunity.

They boogied, they leaped and they danced until the roar from the audience even drowned out their music (not an easy thing to do). Oz spun in circles like a hairy zebra-striped top as he played. After a couple of songs, the band stopped to catch their breath. That's when Michael Sweet said, "Let's hear it for *Hurricane*! We're brothers and we love these guys a lot, and we love you. You'll be seein' more bands Rockin' for the man upstairs, I'm sure. You sure are a Rockin' crowd! How many Rock & Rollers have we got out there? Come on! LOUDER!"

(Who's the "man upstairs," their landlord?)

The deafening screams of *Stryper's* congregation, the blinding banks of strobing floodlights and the stomach -flapping volume created a scene of complete chaos. Michael looked up at his drum-pounding brother and yelled, "Robert! Robert! Come on down!" Bob descended from his platform and stood on the lip of the stage. As Mike handed him an armful of books, he shouted, "Here's something we always throw out to the crowd." Bob pitched Bibles like baseballs, but no one bothered to mention it was the holy Word of God or that it had the power to change lives forever. I knew that throwing out Bibles like red-hot concert souvenirs was their idea of "evangelism" because of the many rock magazine articles I've read. They even slap their own customized yellow and black logo on the cover, giving it that "personal" touch.

After Robert returned to his drummer's perch, Michael screamed into the microphone, "YEAH! He's the one and only way!" Then the band launched into "The Way" and "Calling On You." Long, drawn out bass, drum and guitar solos followed, just like at any other rock concert. Oz Fox fell to his knees, mouth open, head bobbing and hair flying as he cranked out a sizzling and scorching mega-decibel lead that quickly degenerated into white noise. It sounded like a saw-mill that had just been hit by a Cruise missile. All this was your basic brand of rock star ego-tripping. I asked myself; "How does this junk glorify Jesus Christ?

When the band lit into "You Won't Be Lonely," girls screamed until their voices gave out, spurred on by Michael's hip bouncing wiggle. "Battle Hymn Of The Republic" finally closed the concert. As the boys from *Stryper* walked into the wings, Clowes Hall erupted into a deafening bellow – "STRY-PER! STRY-PER! STRY-PER! STRY-PER!" The Lord Jesus was the last thing on anyone's mind.

> "We don't like to tell people we're a Chris-
> tian band, because the metalheads would
> be turned off. I'm not saying Christian
> bands are bad, but a lot of times it's not
> what the kids want to hear. The kids'll
> say, 'I don't want to go see THAT, I don't
> want to have somebody preaching at me .
> . .' So we tell people we are 'God rock.' "
>
> Oz Fox[23]

After five minutes of roaring pandemonium, *Stryper* returned. A thunderous ovation shook the roof. A sweat-soaked Michael Sweet declared, "We don't sing about sex and booze, and we don't sing about drugs." *Stryper* may not sing about sex, booze or drugs, but they sure didn't say much about Jesus Christ, either! It seems impossible, but the volume of their final encore increased to the point that the inside of my ears began to hum.

Finally, after the last atom bomb crash of head-ripping, lightning blast of thunder, Michael Sweet, his back to the crowd, lifted his guitar high above his head in the classic pose of Rock & Roll defiance. Grabbing the microphone, he shouted, "Anyone who's not a Christian, try our God, Jesus Christ!"

And then they were gone.

There was no altar call and no plea to accept Jesus Christ as Lord, Master and Savior. All *Stryper* could manage was a half-hearted yodel to "try Christ" like some kind of new improved anti-perspirant. And no wonder, they didn't want to share their glory with anyone. The guitar gods were the only ones worshiped at this concert. There was no room left for the true King of Kings.

As the theme from the old Perry Mason TV show played over the PA, the tired and happy crowd filed out of the auditorium. Two young boys passed me, trying to talk to each other. With one finger wiggling in his ear, the first boy shouted, "Huh? I can't hear you." They had both been thoroughly deafened. Even with plugs in place the entire night, my ears rang for the next twelve hours.

The final comment I heard as I walked out said it all: "Yeah, I think they're PROBABLY Christians."

That is exactly what happened at Clowes Hall on March 26, 1987. No Christian witnessing was done. No instruction was given about the importance of the Bible, repentance, salvation, forgiveness or holiness. Many say, "It's all in the music, man." No, it's not. I know it's not because I was there and I heard it with my own two ears. Robert Sweet puts it this way:

> "You can say 'I believe in God' but if you don't do what He asks you to do, big deal. So we made the decision to go all the way – not to turn anybody off, not to force anybody, but to make sure we never backed down."[24]

Bob Sweet's contempt for the church is evident from the following quote:

> "We always had this attitude that we didn't want to be characterized as this little religious band sold in religious bookstores and happy and content to play in a church for love offerings. I mean, all that's wonderful, but our whole goal and vision was to be a real rock 'n' roll band to reach a real world . . ."[25]

But the Bible says:

> "For do I now persuade men, or God? or do I seek to please men? for if I yet pleased men, I should not be the servant of Christ."
> Galatians 1:10

292

Before you tell me not to judge *Stryper*, read Leviticus 19:15. Match *Stryper's* philosophy, actions and comments with the Bible, then you decide who's right:

> "And have no fellowship with the unfruitful works of darkness, but rather reprove them." Ephesians 5:11

The wild, cram-packed concert crowd that thronged the front of the stage waved the Il Cornuto devil-salute left and right. Why didn't any of the band members stop them? I realize the stage lights were blinding, but *Stryper* could still see the first few rows as they performed. Were they afraid of "turning someone off" and losing a record-buying fan?

How does a *Stryper* concert match up against these verses?

> "What? know ye not that your body is the temple of the Holy Ghost which is in you, which ye have of God, and ye are not your own? For ye are bought with a price: therefore glorify God in your body, and in your spirit, which are God's." I Corinthians 6: 19,20

If *Stryper* truly love their fans, why do they play megadecibel, dive-bombing music that destroys temples of the Holy Spirit – the bodies, minds and ears of their fans? Because that's just the way Rock & Roll is? What a strange way of showing love. No one should have to lose their hearing to accept Christ.

Stryper is often quoted as saying that Heavy Metal is "the best" and "the greatest:"

"We know that a lot of the people who come to our shows are there because we play good, loud rock and roll. But hopefully some of our message is rubbing off on them as well. We all owe so much to the power of God, and we see no reason that His virtues shouldn't be extolled through the greatest music there is, heavy metal . . . We don't consider ourselves to be overly religious when we say that. In fact, religion has nothing to do with what *Stryper's* all about. We're just trying to communicate the word of Jesus Christ."

Michael Sweet[26]

By repeatedly making these ridiculous claims, they are proving that they have been brought under metal's power. They have become slaves to the music, which is wrong (II Peter 2:19).

Let's have a pity party for poor Robert Sweet as he tries to justify the abominable music he makes:

"And I feel that in today's Christian realm of music - I'm not knockin' anybody now – but I feel so much of the music production, the show, everything to do with it is inferior. The production's lousy. Why does Michael Jackson sell 50 million "Thriller" records? Why does Prince sell 17 million "Purple Rain" records, and Christian artists are doing good to go gold? It's not because of what they're saying, it's because of how they're saying it. And why should the world want to hear about God through music when it's inferior music?" [27]

But I thought it was the MESSAGE that mattered, Robert, not the music. Mr. Sweet has just contradicted one of C-Rock's main "defenses," that the message is all that matters. I wish he would decide what he believes. Is the music important or isn't it? You can't have it both ways, Bob.

> "And another thing, most Christian music today draws primarily Christians. That's like teaching Spanish in Mexico to me. We're supposed to win the Lost. We're supposed to go after the sick that need the doctor, not the well. And this is another reason why we look the way we do. Because people out there who don't have Jesus can relate to this, and when you have relatability, they'll listen to you because they respect you ..." Robert Sweet[28]

If Robert ever glanced at Ephesians 5:18-20 or Colossians 3:15-16, he would see that Christian music is SUPPOSED to draw Christians! "Relatability" to win respect can be summed up in one word – "compromise." You don't win people to Christ by sinning against God. Fans may love *Stryper*, but God's Word condemns them (Romans 12:2). Is a rock star's logic more important than the Lord's command to be holy?

The Bible also condemns *Stryper* because of their appearance. *Stryper* says, "appearances don't matter; it's what's in the heart that counts. Don't judge me by the way I look; it's unscriptural." I don't have to, God already did. I Corinthians 6:9-10 says those who are "effeminate" (a man who makes himself look like a woman) will NOT inherit the Kingdom of God. The members of *Stryper* have long, womanish hair, wear foundation, eyeliner, lip gloss and blush. New fans have often mistaken them for girls at first glance. Thus, *Stryper* stands condemned by the Word of God.

Here is a quote from *Stryper* keyboardist Kenny Metcalf that was taken word-for-word from a taped interview. Can you honestly look to a man like this to gain your spiritual insight?

> "So I encourage people to listen to stuff that's got a positive message, a good message. It doesn't even have to sing and say Jesus in it. Y'know, if it's got a good message behind it . . . if it's just a positive song. I've met so many Christians that, since they came to the Lord, they didn't have any music to listen to. And they don't, y'know, they listen to the church stuff, but I mean it's not what they really like to listen to, and like they've found, y'know, like y'know, it's not an alternative. But y'know, even we need to give the kids out in the world an alternative, y'know, to music. Because they're gonna listen to the kind of music that they like. And if it's got evil influence, if it's just got negative stuff, then that's what they're gonna listen to because they like that style of music. So we might as well give them something that's gonna encourage them to do something with their life instead of tear their life down . . . "[29]

Sorry Kenny, your boat doesn't hold water, y'know.

Christ didn't come to do a nonstop song and dance for poor little Christians longing for their favorite Rock &

Roll fix. Saints across the world are losing their freedom and even their lives for the cause of Christ, and *Stryper* is worried that some of the "King's Kids" might have a boring day? How selfish. How absurd! You'll NEVER find the "give 'em what they like" philosophy in the Bible!

Let's follow this teaching to its logical conclusion. How about "Christian" porno? It'll help us reach those enslaved to the secular stuff by giving them an alternative. Let's start making "Holy Ghost" whiskey. It's sure to save millions who otherwise wouldn't set foot in a church. (Make lots of money, too!) Then there's "Christian" cigarettes, with a scripture verse on every pack. It would be a great way to witness and besides, doesn't God deserve the best? They're just gonna do it anyway, so why not give them the most positive alternative possible? Right?

This is no more absurd than trying to use something as filthy, stinking and evil as rock music for God's glory. He doesn't need Satan's junk to assert His majesty. And we don't NEED it either. We just WANT it because it feeds our ungodly flesh. Sticking the "safe" tag "Christian" on it doesn't make it any more holy than a piece of pornography.

How does the unsaved world look at these Metal "missionaries?" Here are two letters printed in a secular Heavy Metal magazine. One is about *Stryper's* famous yellow and black uniforms, colors they claim represent caution. Draw your own conclusion:

> "Methinks someone should tell all you God-loving, Christian-loving metalheads: the livery of the Devil is black and yellow, black indicating death, yellow implying

quarantine (Treasury of Witchcraft, Harry E. Wedeck, 1961, Citadel Press, pg. III and other sources) So if they know what livery means or if they can read, they may really have a black and yellow or yellow and black attack. In any case, maybe *Stryper* is the most satanic band ever – fooling all the fools. But only a fool would call such limpy lame soggy bull#@%! metal anyway! So #@%! off. Thank you Bye."

Little Ted, Oakton, VA [30]

" . . . I'd like to say to *Stryper* that they @#%! so bad that they make grown men weep. When I played their new album, my dog ran whimpering into the street. Where do these self-proclaimed evangelists get off throwing Bibles into the audience at their concerts? If I was a 'gung-ho' Christian – which I am not! – I would feel sick to my stomach watching *Stryper* make a mockery of my religion. They are a total and absolute joke! To hell with *Stryper* – and soon!!!   A. Moya, Simi Valley, CA."[31]

Stryper's "relating" philosophy just doesn't work because everything *Stryper* stands for is against what the Bible teaches. And no matter how slick the package, true converts to Christ aren't made through the devil's music. The ONLY thing it produces is more slaves for Satan. Where does this leave *Stryper*? Unless they repent, they will continue to be servants of antichrist . . . and the enemies of God.

14

WHO GAVE ROCK & ROLL TO YOU?

"Beloved, believe not every spirit, but try
the spirits whether they are of God: because many false prophets are gone out
into the world."   I John 4:1

"Music was part of warfare in the Old Testament, as the singers went to set the tone
for the battle. We relate that, of course, to
our warfare now. More directly to how
Petra is involved in warfare against Satan
through our ministry of music."
                    Bob Hartman, of *Petra*[1]

Though worshiped as C-Rock saints, much needs to be
said about *Petra*, a group that flashed the internation-
ally known Il Cornuto devil-worship sign during one of
their 1986 concerts. Believe it or not, that's exactly

what my wife and I saw with our own eyes. But first, a little background.

Petra is one of the oldest C-Rock bands around. They began in 1972 as a four-man, electrified Jesus-Rock outfit from Ft. Wayne, Indiana. The folky Jesus music of the sixties was getting out-dated when *Petra* started playing their own brand of "Christian" Rock. Though despised by most believers, *Petra* hung on for nearly a decade and eventually hit the big time.

Figure 24

"More Power To Ya" Back Cover

Their 1974 self-titled debut album on Myrrh Records died a quick death on the Christian bookstore racks. Only a few hard core fans were willing to accept such a loud bombastic blast of "Christ-Rock." The next album (Come And Join Us) fared no better and Myrrh dumped *Petra*. The band eventually hooked up with a Texas based record company called "Star Song." Thanks to the production of studio whiz Jonathan David Brown and the massive nationwide distribution of A & M/ Word Inc., *Petra* finally began getting radio play.

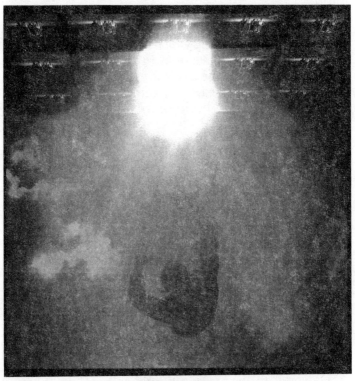

Figure 25

"Beat The System" Album Cover

The "Never Say Die" album, released in 1980, was their turning point. Touring extensively throughout the early eighties, *Petra* found a whole new generation of Christians who had been raised on rock. These kids had no trouble accepting the devil's music, though it now wore a Christian mask.

More records followed, including 1982's "More Power To Ya." (See Figures 24.) This album contains an intentional backmasked message at the beginning of the song, "Judas' Kiss," that says, "WHAT ARE YOU LOOKIN' FOR THE DEVIL FOR, WHEN YOU OUGHTTA BE LOOKIN' FOR THE LORD?" Fans were delighted. Smiling youth leaders laughed at such cleverness. No one seemed to care that *Petra* was slavishly imitating the secular groups who intentionally backmasked praises to Satan on their own devilish records. "Christian" backmasking. How cute!

> "Cursed be he that doeth the work of the Lord deceitfully, and cursed be he that keepeth back his sword from blood."
> Jeremiah 48:10

According to a note at the bottom of "More Power To Ya," the cover illustration was done by "Petragram." What is a "Petragram," anyway? I have no idea, but change one letter and the word becomes "Pentagram," one of the most evil symbols in satanism/witchcraft.

Though six albums and twelve years of touring helped, 1984's "Beat The System" record and video pushed *Petra* over the top. It was the biggest breakthrough of their career. (See Figure 25.) They had already sold well over a million records, and more than 900,000 after 1981. Two of the most popular tunes from "The System" raise serious questions about *Petra*:

"Witch Hunt"

"Another witch hunt looking for evil wher-
    ever we can find it
Off on a tangent, Hope the Lord won't
    mind it
Another witch hunt, Takin' a break from
    all our gospel labor
On a crusade but we forgot our saber . . .
So send out the dogs and tally ho . . .
No one is safe, No stone is left unturned
And we won't stop until somebody
gets burned . . . "

Is the message of "Witch Hunt" a stinging and sarcas-
tic rebuke aimed at anyone who doesn't like "Christian" Rock, or *Petra* in particular? Are they afraid
someone might investigate the facts and find out who
they are really serving? Song writer Bob Hartman's
lyrics suggest that Christians should blind their eyes
to evil all around them and overlook it. This is the very
method satanists use to keep their own evil deeds
concealed. For a group that starts every song with a
verse of scripture, this is a very strange attitude.

Another song from "Beat The System" is even more
deceptive to undiscerning C-Rock fans:

"God Gave Rock And Roll To You"

"You can learn to sing
You can play guitar
You can learn to rock
You can be a star
But where will you be when the music's
    gone
God gave Rock and Roll to you

303

Gave Rock and Roll to you
Put it in the soul of everyone . . . "

There are several dangerous and deceptive lies here.
First, the song was not even written by *Petra*. It was
recorded in 1973 by a secular group of re-fried rockers
called *Argent*. *Petra* is using a heathen song to push a
supposedly "godly" point of view – that the Lord has
put Rock & Roll in all our souls. Which do you want in
YOUR soul? The Lord Jesus Christ or the devil's
wicked rock? (See II Corinthians 4:14-17.) Secondly,
Petra changed the words to make the song say what
they believe to be true, that God has put Satan's vile
sludge into our souls. Can you think of a more vicious
and ridiculous lie?

Unlike every other song on "Beat The System," "God
Gave Rock And Roll To You" has no scripture verse
above the lyrics on the inner sleeve. Why not? Can't
a theme this important be backed up by the Bible? Of
course it can't, because Rock & Roll is Satan's perversion of God's music. The GOD OF THIS WORLD made
Rock & Roll! HE puts it in the soul of everyone he can,
where it burns like a malignant, flaming cancer.

Here's a trivia question for *Petra* fans: What does the
name "Petra" mean? "Oh, that's easy" you say. "Petra
means 'Rock' in Greek. It's based on Simon Peter's
Good Confession found in Matthew 16:15-18." True.
But the word Petra also stands for something much
more evil. Petra was the capital of Edom, a land full of
pagan people whom the Lord detested (Malachi 1:3,4).
Petra was one of the highest of the "high places," where
human sacrifices were performed:

> "Several High Places have been discov-
> ered by those interested in Biblical archae-

304

ology . . . The first to have been found is the so-called "Great High Place at Petra." It is situated on the top of one of the highest hilltops which surround Petra, the capital of ancient Edom. It is cut out of the solid sandstone rock. . . Near the center of this court there is a raised but undetached platform of rock. On this slab victims for sacrifice were probably slain . . ."[2]

In short, the name Petra is synonymous with ungodly paganism and human sacrifice.

Petra singer Greg Volz quit to go solo around 1985 and was replaced by a man named John Schlitt, who got his start in a secular band called *Head East*. (One of their early albums featured a huge blow-up of a Marijuana bud on its cover.) John and *Petra* produced a new album in 1986 called, "Back To The Street," and together they hit the concert trail.

I saw them perform live at Hulman Center in Terre Haute, Indiana, on October 9th, 1986. What I saw and heard there was not what I expected. It was one of the loudest concerts I've ever attended. Since being saved two years earlier and having repented of all involvement in Rock & Roll, I had almost forgotten what 110 decibels of live rock did to the ears, mind and body. Both *Petra* and their opening act, *DeGarmo & Key*, were so incredibly loud that I found it amazing to see mothers, fathers and even little children soaking up wave after wave of crunching, eardrum-busting C-Rock without complaint.

C-Rock idolatry was everywhere, as evidenced by dozens of fans wearing T-shirts and other trappings supporting their favorite "Heavenly Metal" stars. One young man even sported studded *Motley Crue* armbands draped with dangling chains. With his pierced ears and biker boots, he was one very strange character indeed. A hand painted, glowing cross covered the back of his jacket. With his clenched fists held high in the air, he hung on the railing above the stage all night, a real "headbanger for Jesus."

The Bible tells us that we will know false prophets by their fruits (Matthew 7:15-20). Most people point to the lifestyles of the C-Rockers as their "fruits," but there's more to it than that. The real fruit of groups like *Petra* are found in those who turn out for the concerts. THERE is the real fruit. Before the night was over I saw first hand the effect *Petra's* brand of Christianity was having on their congregation.

For example, keyboardist John Lawry programmed his synthesizer to "speak" the name "Jesus" in a rapid-fire, machine gun stutter, rising from a foggy hollow bass to a screaming, Alvin & the Chipmunks falsetto. The crowd cheered, laughed and screamed until the walls shook. I couldn't help wondering how making a joke of the name of our Lord could possibly give Him Glory. What a blasphemy of that powerful scripture, Philippians 2:9-11:

> "Wherefore God also hath highly exalted him, and given him a name which is above every name: That at the name of Jesus every knee should bow, of things in heaven, and things in earth, and things under the earth; And that every tongue should confess that Jesus Christ is Lord, to the glory of God the Father."

The stage set-up, synthesizer solo, band outfits, fog-banks, and thundering bomb-rock brought back very bad memories for me. The verses that immediately flashed into my mind were II Peter 2:20-22:

> "For if after they have escaped the pollutions of the world through the knowledge of the Lord and Saviour Jesus Christ, they are again entangled therein, and overcome, the latter end is worse with them than the beginning. For it had been better for them not to have known the way of righteousness, than, after they have known it, to turn from the holy commandment delivered unto them. But it is happened unto them according to the true proverb, The dog is turned to his own vomit again; and the sow that was washed to her wallowing in the mire."

Amid the chaos, *Petra* singer John Schlitt stepped forward and declared that Jesus Christ was his one and only Lord. How impressive that must have been to the star-struck kids who hooted and howled. But midway through their set, Schlitt and guitarist Bob Hartman both did something that floored me. First John lifted his hand straight up and made the Il Cornuto sign of allegiance to Satan! (See Figure 26.) This is a bona fide symbol of satanism and is on the back of Anton LaVey's "Satanic Bible." (LaVey founded San Francisco's First Church of Satan in 1966.)

Schlitt's open use of the Il Cornuto sign shocked me so much that I kept my eyes glued on his hand for the next half hour. I thought, "Maybe it was an accident." But John settled the question beyond any doubt by making the sign again and again and again. At one point, he held his arm straight out, still forming "the Horn," and

307

pointed at Bob Hartman, who stepped forward and began a guitar solo. Hartman then lifted his hand high, making the devil's salute.

RONNIE JAMES DIO

Figure 26   "Metal Edge," Dec. 1986, p.64

Satan Rocker Dio, making Il Cornuto, the same sign Petra flashed over and over.

This was NOT the sign language for "I love you," where the thumb is also openly extended. I had excellent seats and there was no problem with obstructed vision. My wife was beside me and she also saw both Hartman and Schlitt make those hand motions of allegiance to Satan. The Lord Jesus Christ is my witness. I know what I saw and never in a million years did I expect to see such a thing at a "Christian" concert.

I sought out Schlitt and Hartman's testimony on the matter. I wrote their office in Tennessee and asked them about it. I received a letter of reply in which Hartman denied doing such a thing. Schlitt said that he may have used the "love" symbol but could not remember specifically. My question is, why would they use a deaf language symbol at a concert? The kids could hear fine when they went in. They weren't deaf until they came out. Both men said they would never do anything like that again to avoid confusion. To promise never to do something again is an admission that they did indeed do SOMETHING.

Three seats to my right sat a young man about 17, obviously a strong *Petra* fan. The band was playing one of their songs from "Beat The System" called, "It Is Finished," about the crucifixion of Christ. As they sang about the thudding nails being hammered home, the gambling soldiers, and blackening skies, I watched the teenager on my right closely. No love or compassion showed on his face – only a pop-eyed rage. His concentration was fixed firmly on the band. Every time that thundering chorus "IT IS FINISHED!" came, he screamed out the words at the top of his lungs, his clenched fist punching the air. He had lots of company. This was going on all over the arena. He was not worshiping Jesus Christ or contemplating the Master's sacrifice, he was worshiping Rock & Roll, man! And the people who make it – in this case, *Petra*.

That teenager is typical of the many tens of thousands who are bowing to the idols of C-Rock. They think they can come to Jesus through the stars of popular music, but that's a lie (Matthew 7:13, 14, John 10:1-9).

There was an "altar call" at the end of *Petra's* concert, if that's what you want to call it. Those who went forward followed arena staff who had passed out *Petra* mailing forms earlier. The staff people headed down the aisle first, pretending to be responding to the invitation. If the lost see others leading the way, then perhaps they won't be too "embarrassed" to go. Lovely thought, isn't it? "AH HA! We've got you now. Tricked into the Kingdom, but at least you're saved!" But were those kids who responded led into the kindgom of Jesus Christ, or the cult of "Christian" Rock? The answer is obvious.

In the fall of 1987, *Petra* released their tenth album, entitled "This Means War." It zoomed up the Christian charts like greased lightning. The album also provided *Petra* with a mass market goldmine. LTM Marketing in Knoxville, Tennessee produced a special newsletter with all the details called "Battle Plan." Disguised as a " . . . learning experience in the area of spiritual warfare," *Petra* offered THIS MEANS WAR balloons, THIS MEANS WAR stickers, THIS MEANS WAR buttons, THIS MEANS WAR bookcovers, THIS MEANS WAR posters, a THIS MEANS WAR cassette, promotional flyers, a leaders' guide, a P.O.W. rescue plan, and oh yes, Bible studies. Can't forget those. Costs for these marvelous "spiritual warfare" materials was steep. One of every item on the order blank ran over $200.[3] God pity the poor kids who think they will learn spiritual warfare against Satan by flying *Petra* balloons and wearing a *Petra* T-shirt.

Using the promo packs *Petra* sells, THIS MEANS WAR youth events were held, supposedly to teach kids spiritual warfare. Let's look at what went on. Youth groups were "inducted," and given "draft cards, wristbands, and other military goods." They were assigned to "battalions," where they played games and went through "life simulations." They entered contests pretending to play the guitar and sing (visualization) as one of *Petra's* new songs blasted away. Finally, there was a Bible study/challenge, followed by prayer. Then the kids "turned in their draft cards."

This stuff teaches spiritual warfare all right. But it teaches it from the other side. They are using purely occultic principles just as satanic fantasy games like Dungeons & Dragons do. Visualization, role playing, life simulations ... these are all thinly disguised spiritual exercises designed to make contact with the spirit world. These things come straight from the devil.

Is *Petra* really serious? Battle Satan with balloons, buttons and stickers?

Another disturbing issue that must be addressed concerns two envelopes I received from *Petra* during my correspondence with them. Both envelopes were stamped "Firstborne Productions Incorporated" as a return address. This is the name of the management agency that handles *Petra's* business. Directly beneath these words is a very strange little picture, consisting of an inverted triangle with a circle in the center. A solid rectangular bar pierces both the triangle and the circle.

311

I sent a copy of this logo to a Christian brother who practiced witchcraft many years before being saved. Without knowing anything about *Petra* or Firstborne Productions, here are his findings:

> "Now in regard to the downward equalateral triangle with a circle in the middle and a diagonal line, the meaning is very clear to me. This has been used and is being used by witches continually. The triangle with one point down is the female reproductive area. The circle inside represents the son of the sun god (Baal) and the bar entering the female triangle is the phallus of Baal impregnating the female to bring forth Tammuz. This has the same meaning as the heart with the arrow through it except for the circle inside which indicates that the conception of the "firstborn" of Baal has taken place . . ."

When I confronted *Petra* by mail with this, Bob Hartman swore that no occultism was involved with the making of that logo. He insisted that no one connected with *Petra* had anything to do with the occult. There's just one thing Bob didn't say. He never told me what the logo does mean. Isn't that strange? If there is a perfectly good explanation, why not say so? Why beat around the bush unless it's really true?

From start to finish, bloodstains of the occult are sprinkled all over *Petra's* "ministry." Despite their clean-cut image, their actions speak much louder than their words. While they talk about serving God Almighty, their actions reveal that Satan is the true master behind their music.

15

THE CULT OF 666

"Little children, it is the last time: and as
ye have heard that antichrist shall come,
even now are there many antichrists;
whereby we know that it is the last time."

I John 2:18

" . . . and if I rearrange it
It remains the same
I'll change the way I say it
But never what I say
The message must remain the same
Don't stop, don't stop the music
You've got to let it play . . . "

DeGarmo & Key[1]

DeGarmo & Key was considered at one time to be a very bad joke by most of the gospel music industry. Their brand of high octane Rock & Roll noise masquerading as Christian music was just too absurd to take seriously. But publicity generated from their work on the 1981 Amy Grant tour changed things drastically. *D & K* went on to become the first C-Rock band to receive a Grammy nomination.

They also produced the first "Christian" video ever shown on MTV. Entitled, "Six, Six, Six," it was all about the antichrist. Scenes of sizzling human beings being burnt to skeleton crisps were so bizarre, the bigwigs at "anything goes" MTV refused to play it until the grisliest parts were cut out.

Today, Ed DeGarmo and Dana Key are seen by thousands of fans as devout musical ministers for the Lord Jesus Christ. But who's side are they really on? Read the following lyrics from the song and video that made them famous and decide for yourself:

"Six, Six, Six"

" . . . I said Jesus won't you save me
From this evil man of sin
I have read about his future
I don't want to go with him
And when I looked up he had gone
But he had left a note that said
'My number is, my number is . . .
Six, Six, Six . . . '
Flight 666 . . . departing – WELCOME"

The message in this song is amazing to me. A "Christian" band is suggesting that even Jesus can't rescue people from the antichrist. This poor man begged

314

Jesus to save him but ended up aboard Flight 666, headed straight for hell. What a gruesome final line for a supposed Christian song – WELCOME TO HELL! And these words come from a group whose mission is to win people to the Lord? Ed DeGarmo said:

> "It's all a matter of what you're called to do. We've always felt we were called to win kids to Jesus Christ. That's our mission. That's our goal. There are a lot of people out there who are called to make great music and entertain people, and I'm not arguing that. Please don't misunderstand me. But evangelism is our original mission. And as long as we keep winning kids to Christ I know we're in the Lord's Will."[2]

Before *D & K* say, "Hey! That's just one song," let's look at an entire *DeGarmo & Key* album and see what kind of job they do at winning kids to Jesus Christ:

"Street Light" (1986) (See Figure 27)

Songs:

"Every Moment" – A nostalgic look backward into the memories of childhood. God gets thanked for the good times, but His Son and the sacrifice He made for lost mankind doesn't even rate a nod.

"War Zone" – The message here focuses on the problems of two desperate people in a big city ghetto – "Dancing Jimmy" and a red-dressed transvestite. The solution to their confusion? "Somebody just like Jesus." Not the only begotten Son of God, you understand, but somebody just like Him. All this would probably make a good plot for a "Miami Vice" episode.

315

"Addey" – Addicted to drugs? The song says to just "trust in God," and He won't lead you astray. Now if only the junkies listening to this tune knew how to put that into practice. *DeGarmo & Key* don't bother to tell them that Jesus has the power to change lives, or how to receive that power.

Figure 27

"Soldier Of Fortune" – Drug pushers are heartless and cruel people. What's this got to do with Christ? We never find out, since Jesus isn't mentioned even once.

"Don't Stop The Music" – This song is a snotty reply

to *DeGarmo & Key's* critics. They're going to keep on C-Rockin' no matter who doesn't like it, while they sing "the songs that set men free." It's hard to imagine how that's going to be accomplished, though, as the cross of Calvary is not mentioned, discussed, described or even hinted at in 10 of the 11 tunes on this album.

"Don't Throw Your Love Away" – Please stay a virgin, little Janie; but if you don't, I'll love you anyway. What a great uncompromising attitude! No Jesus here, either.

"Video Action" – The heavy spiritual message of this tune consists entirely of deciding which video cassette to rent - James Bond, Sherlock Holmes, or Jane Fonda.

"She Believes" – Inner strength comes through belief. Belief in what?

"Holy Hustle" – Good works will make people happy; they'll see the Savior in you. Wonderful. Now how do those same people GET that Savior? Who knows?

"Up On A Cross" – This is *DeGarmo & Key's* token stab at evangelism. The crucifixion is described, as well as the fact that Christ died for all. But the final line of the tune leaves you wondering who they're communicating with when they say, "I heard the devil's voice today."

"Inside Out" – The nameless force described here searches through our inner selves and knows everything about us. Great! What does that have to do with the plan of salvation? They don't bother to say.

Dana Key offers this lame excuse for their watered down whitewash that they call "Christian:"

> "On 'Street Light' we were trying to stick to
> the street theme and deal with problems
> people were dealing with. They weren't
> biblical themes, and they didn't talk about
> God a lot . . . "[3]

The "Street Light" album is a perfect example of the
pasteurized pap masquerading as Christian soul winning. No one could get saved through this slop. Jesus
is a mystery man, a kind of galactic Santa Claus. He's
never presented as the personal Lord, Master and
Savior all true disciples know. Compromising "Christian" Rock like the "Street Light" LP has turned true
Christianity into a fairyland of mass market religion.
Blinded by the bright lights and deafened by the roar,
the fans never know the difference.

In the face of a 20% drop in nationwide C-Rock music
sales, *DeGarmo & Key* hit upon a sure-fire gimmick to
launch their tenth LP, 1987's "D & K." The first
100,000 copies contained a free "evangelism cassette."
They also gave 1,000 church youth groups a free
promotional *DeGarmo & Key* video.

The albums release date was October 31, 1987, a day
hundreds of churches hold youth lock-ins as an alternative to traditional Halloween celebrations. How sad
that multitudes of kids protesting the devil's holiday
were still bopping to his music through the brand new
D & K album. "Debut parties" like these are just one
more coin in the C-Rock money machine.

Where did the idea for the "evangelism" tape come
from? Was it out of a deep concern for lost souls on their
way to hell? Dana Key answers the question for us:

> "The people who work in the marketing

318

department with Vince Wilcox suggested the evangelism cassette. When he came up with the idea we said, 'Sure. We'd love to do that. But it's kind of insane, isn't it?' "[4]

What a vivid picture of *D & K's* spiritual condition! Their money-making people come up with an idea to scrape in a few extra bucks, but *DeGarmo & Key* think the idea of an evangelism tape is "insane."

The lyric sheet of their 1984 "Communication" album tells the true story:

"Communication"

"There came a technological lion
With a deafening roar
I heard a king & kingdom
Knocking at my door

I saw a selfish spirit
Turn wise men into fools
I found a timeless message
And joined it with a tool."

These lyrics clearly show the sly vagueness found in all C-Rock music. What is really being said here? I'm sure Dana Key would say he's using the technological roar of rock music to preach the timeless message of the gospel. But this poem can be taken quite another way:

I Peter 5:8 describes our adversary, the devil as a roaring lion, seeking whom he may devour. We also know that Satan is a king and has a kingdom. He is the god of this world. Selfish spirits come straight from the devil and his timeless message has always been "WORSHIP ME!"

319

My question is, what exactly did *D & K* join? Every single line of that song can refer directly to Satan and his demons. An album supposedly designed to bring kids to Christ should never have this kind of problem. At best, *DeGarmo & Key* are creating confusion. Since God is not the author of confusion, there can be only one other mastermind behind their music. Without question, *DeGarmo & Key* are giving glory to Satan.

16

AMY SELLS OUT

> "I will therefore that the younger women marry, bear children, guide the house, give none occasion to the adversary to speak reproachfully. For some are already turned aside after Satan."   I Timothy 5:14-15

> "My hormones are just as on key as any other twenty-four-year-old's. I know the deep need in a marriage for sex. But I see sex not just as a way to get your nuts off but to say, this is an integral part of our working relationship."   Amy Grant[1]

Despite comments like this, there are few stars in the C-Rocking heavens bigger or brighter than Amy Grant. The shy southern teenager who started her career a dozen years ago singing sweet, simple songs about the Lord has become the reigning Princess of pop/rock. She was one of the first "gospel" artists to successfully move into the secular music realm, keeping her original popular base, while doubling her overall audience. This is called "crossover," a phenomenon most performers dream about, but few ever achieve.

Since signing her first recording contract at age 15, Amy has appeared on every major talk show in the nation, aired her own T.V. special and set a Grammy Awards first by being named Top Female Gospel Vocalist three years in a row. She is also the leader in C-Rock platinum album sales (one million copies). Both "Age To Age" and "Unguarded" went platinum. "Age To Age" stuck like glue to Billboard's Inspirational chart for nearly three years!

Another Grant album, 1984's "Straight Ahead" ruled the gospel roost at number one for 53 consecutive weeks. In that year alone, her tours reached 500,000 fans and grossed almost $1.5 million. She was even more successful in 1985, adding another million bucks from live concerts. This shocked everyone in the industry because Christian artists aren't supposed to BE that popular. Why Amy?

As she blasted into the realms of C-Rock superstardom, conservative Christian leaders and fans raised bitter, disappointed cries of anger over her "sellout." Did Amy dump biblical holiness for a mountain of fashionable dollars served up on the world's silver platter? Let's dig into Amy's past and present to get the answer.

Compared to most secular rock stars, Grant had it good from the start. She was born November 25, 1960, the fourth daughter of a well-bred family that could trace its rich Tennessee roots back three generations. Her father was a radiologist specializing in cancer treatment, and her great-grandfather founded the multimillion dollar Life & Casualty Insurance conglomerate. Amy spent her childhood and adolescence in the best private schools Nashville had to offer. Spiritual instruction came from the non-instrumental Church of Christ, whose Sunday singing services were a far cry from her favorite folk and pop artists – Elton John, James Taylor and John Denver.

Though baptized in her teens, Amy began rebelling against the strict discipline of her family's church:

> "I was pretty much a good kid. But when I left my parents' church and went searching on my own I thought I was rebelling in the biggest way. It felt good. When you're young and discover any sort of truth, it suddenly makes you want to tell your parents how to live . . ."[2]

She ended up joining a charismatic group called the Belmont Assembly, one of the most liberal Christian organizations in Nashville. She found her spiritual niche just when her musical talent began blooming. Turned off by the boring routine of daily morning devotionals at her posh all-girl high school, Amy wanted to sing instead. She gave her first public performance one morning before a group of students. For 30 minutes, she sang folk songs and original tunes she had composed on her acoustic guitar.

Through her Belmont Assembly Bible study group, Amy met a man named Brown Bannister, who worked in a local recording studio. It wasn't long before the two began putting her tunes on tape. Under Bannister's watchful gaze and professional coaching, Grant soon had a rough demo, a special present for her parents.

Brown Bannister's boss was an up-and-coming force in the budding pop/gospel music business named Lon Christian Smith. Such diverse artists as Elvis Presley, B.J. Thomas, Olivia Newton-John and Sheena Easton have recorded Smith's tunes, making him one of the most successful songwriters in Nashville. Somewhere along the line, Lon changed his name to "Chris Christian," a move he swears was purely coincidental.

Part of Smith's job was to spot and develop new talent for the Texas-based gospel music giant, Word Records. As he met with Brown Bannister one day at the Nashville recording studio, Amy Grant's demo tape was playing. Smith flipped his wig over it and immediately burned up the phone lines to Texas. The executives at Word Inc. were also impressed, and at age 15 Amy signed her first recording contract.

Lon Smith went on to become a huge maker and shaker in the C-Rock industry. As head of the LCS Music Group, he later produced and promoted twenty gold and platinum albums by a variety of artists. In a 1986 Associated Press article, the man who discovered Amy Grant defined the phenomenon he had helped create:

> "There's no such thing as Christian music. Music is generic. People get caught up on whether Christian music can be rock. We're just a bunch of normal people that happen to have a message . . . worth hearing. We as companies and artists, we want to give as quality a musical package as pop can give. We don't want it to be corny."
> Lon Smith[3]

Amy's self-titled debut record sold over 50,000 copies, an unheard-of success in the gospel music world of 1977. Though superstardom was still years away, the door for the shrewd management and media hype to come was now open. As green as grass at age 17, Grant trusted both Bannister and Smith with every aspect of her career. They updated her laid-back, soft-rock style with the electrified crunch of Top 40 pop.

Her brother-in-law, Tennessee banker Dan Harrell, took an active interest in the performing aspect of Amy's career. All eyes were firmly fastened on the gaudy goal of making it big in the Gospel/Rock business like no one had ever done before. They had a talented, hot property on their hands who just might crack that market wide open. Naive and idealistic, Amy went along for the ride.

Harrell puts it this way:

> "We never played many churches with Amy. That was the way everyone else had done it, and nobody had ever made it."[4]

"Making It" involved continuing changes in Grant's image. She was encouraged to dance and prance around the stage during performances, rather than stand nailed to one spot. By the time her second album, "My Father's Eyes," was released in 1979, her sound had become slick and glossy. The man who wrote the title song was Gary Chapman, Amy's future husband.

Chapman was a guitar picking whiz kid from Oklahoma who journeyed to Nashville to make his mark in music. Barely into his 20's, he had already toured with gospel greats *The Rambos*, and written a number one hit for country star T.G. Sheppard called, "Finally." In

1981, Chapman was named Songwriter of the Year by the prestigious Gospel Music Association. The lyrics of his tunes were so ambiguous they could mean anything. All C-Rock has since imitated the watered-down style he pioneered. "My Father's Eyes" pushed Amy up another notch on her way to the big time.

A solo performer in his own right, Chapman toured with the Grant road show in 1980 as a warm-up act. When the two young stars became romantically attracted, Dan Harrell had him fired. Smitten by love at first sight, Gary chased Amy across the country for the better part of two years. She finally said yes to his proposal and they were married on June 19, 1982.

Even without Chapman, more Amy Grant records were made, including a double album set of live 1981 concert appearances. Her backup band were the incredibly loud, ear-piercing rock music "ministers" *DeGarmo & Key*. Amy's show (and the audience's ears) were never the same.

More barriers came crashing down with the release of "Age To Age" in 1982. It quickly became the biggest record of Amy's career, at one point selling 6,000 copies a week. Word Inc. named it their fastest moving album of all time. Finally, "Christian" Rock had matched secular pop in sales figures. The C-Rock industry cheered loud and long as they bowed before their new queen – Amy Grant.

Another record, another tour. But this time things were different. Established secular rock concert promoters were used instead of the smaller organizations that had given Grant her start years before. They dumped $20,000 into the light and sound production, making the "Age To Age" concerts major undertakings.

Gary Chapman and keyboardist Michael W. Smith joined the show. More staff and personnel were hired, and a video was made.

Their eyes popping, the Nashville hype machine geared up in earnest. Because of money-hungry madness for more of that dollar-doubling "C-Rock," secular recording giants CBS and MCA jumped on the bandwagon in a big way. They signed new gospel artists by the dozens, enviously imitating the management and marketing strategies that had boosted Amy to the top.

But Grant's own management team still had more headline-raising, money-making tricks up their sleeve. Though Amy denies it, her career was carefully designed from the beginning to make her a secular pop star, free from the confining limits of "stuffy old gospel cornpone." Her 1984 album, "Straight Ahead," was one of the final steps toward that goal.

The likes of the "Straight Ahead" tour had never been seen before in gospel music. Amy's stock with secular rock promoters rose considerably as she sold out some of the biggest concert halls in the nation and opened dates with country music god Kenny Rogers. The crowds that turned out in record-breaking droves to see her eye-dazzling, ear-splitting production were not disappointed. Her sound system was one of the loudest in the business. An expensive, sophisticated series of mechanical graphics featuring a giant stoplight and a looming golden cross was the show's highlight.

With the "Straight Ahead" tour, the Grant management team beat the secular music world at its own game. Gospel Music Association executive director Don Butler put it this way:

"(Amy) doesn't want the conservative
fundamentalists coming to the concerts.
She wants young people who will get up
and move to the beat, people who want to
be pinned against the back wall by the volume for two hours. That's what she gives
them. Besides, Amy never had the traditional Gospel music fans, so how could she
turn them off? She has never been the
darling of the fundamentalists."[5]

The Grant media blitz took off with a vengeance. A
historic distribution deal between secular giant A & M
Records, Word Inc. and Grant's management helped
whip up dollars by the millions. The non-Christian
market had been cracked, smashed, and utterly broken through. A & M received exclusive rights to stock
Amy's records in secular retail outlets nationwide. No
longer would her product be limited to tiny Christian
bookstores in the middle of nowhere. Amy could now
be found in every record shop in the country.

Appearances on T.V. talk shows and prime-time T.V.
programs, combined with newspaper and magazine
articles by the score threw Grant feet first into the
world's spotlight. All this carefully cultivated hoopla
was the final countdown to the biggest blastoff of her
career – the "Unguarded" album. (See Figure 28.)

Over $200,000 was spent making this record. "Age To
Age" was a breakthrough, but "Unguarded" became a
landmark. Her sound had never been slicker or more
polished. Full of layered keyboards, keening guitars
and thumping bass beats, Christian youth finally had
something both hip and popular to listen to. Who cared
if it didn't really dig in to Jesus Christ? At least you
could dance to it. Amy admitted:

"I wanted to make a record that musically would fit right between Madonna and Huey Lewis."[6]

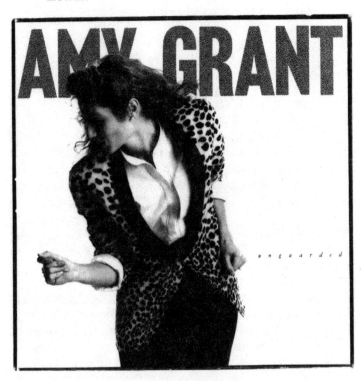

Figure 28

Wiping out almost all mention of the name of Jesus, "Unguarded's" lyrics became the new standard for "Christian" Rock. For "gospel" music, there sure wasn't much gospel in it: Take "I Love You," for example:

> "You were pretty crazy
> Back when we fell in love
> Wanting to be everything

That I would be proud of
Hours we spent dreaming
How we'd beat the odds
Now the truth has hit us
Life is very hard . . ."

"The Prodigal"

" . . .But still the days drag on
Why did you decide to go
Did you only need to see
What only time can show . . .
And even if
You never do return
Still I will have learned
How to love you better . . ."

I sure hope she's not talking about the Lord Jesus Christ. If not, then who IS she talking about and what's it doing on a "gospel" album?

This shiny, sugary-sweet, pop package was eagerly devoured by millions as the guiding lights behind Amy put together a ferocious media campaign. The songs were so shallow no one could possibly be offended – no one except narrow minded "Bible thumpers," that is.

"Unguarded" videos, buttons, posters and ad promotions flooded the market. Four different covers of the album were made, increasing its value to collectors. The usual follow-up tour was an extraordinary event with fog machines, smoke bombs and a computerized light show that launched C-Rock into the musical space age.

"Unguarded" rocketed into Billboard's Top 40, and stayed on the Hot 100 chart for the better part of a year with every radio format possible playing her songs. Musically speaking, 1985 belonged to Amy Grant. With the success of "Unguarded," the ten year plan to make Amy a worldly pop star was fulfilled. There was no turning back now. She could never again be the sweet little guitar-strumming Christian, singing love songs to the Lord. Her recording and video work with secular artist Peter Cetera of the rock group *Chicago* cemented her fresh position as a super pop performer. The song they recorded together, "The Next Time I Fall," became a number one hit.

One horrendous example of the "new Amy" is found on Grant's "Stay For Awhile" video. As the eerie, synthesized background music swells like winter wind whistling through bare-boned trees, Amy's bleached-out ghostly face floats through a leafless forest. Her unblinking eyes burn holes right through you as a voice whispers, "Please stay." The last thing we see is her pale and dead face. She looks like some kind of vampire, glaring straight into the camera with a mesmerizing stare of icy evil. A wailing scream fills the soundtrack and just before the screen goes black, the insistent whisper returns. "Please stay." That's it, folks. Many words could be used to describe this video, but "Christian" certainly is not one of them.

Husband and co-producer Gary Chapman sums up Amy's intentions this way:

> "I think she wants to say that it's O.K. to be a Christian and have fun. Not completely separate yourself from humanity just because you don't believe exactly like everyone else."[7]

Her manager Dan Harrell said of Amy:

"She doesn't wear chiffon dresses and have a beehive hairdo and that breaks down the gospel music stereotype. She can't be churchy. The records in the past were made for people who had a Christian experience and were very involved in the Church. Now we're assuming we're going to communicate with people who may not have had that experience or even been exposed to it."[8]

Secular writer Cliff Jahr notes the difference between Amy and her worldly counterparts:

"With her successful blend of gospel and rock, Amy's Christian music could easily pass for secular. Its hard driving arrangements, featuring guitar riffs, and her impassioned delivery sound exactly like today's mainstream pop . . . She has attracted hundreds of thousands of well-scrubbed young fans . . . who know every lyric by heart. Like rock fans everywhere, they clap, cheer, join hands, sway in their seats and boogie in the aisles."[9]

These are all quotes from people who have observed and worked with Amy Grant. Let's look at some statements from Amy herself. If she is truly a positive role model for Christian youth, then everything she says and does should uplift and give glory to God:

"I remember years ago – it sounds so mundane now – the first time I smelled anybody smoking a joint at a concert, I was thrilled. I thought, this is incredible. Not that there aren't some Christians that smoke pot– yes, it does exist – but it meant to me that obviously this person is not affected by the church peer pressure. A lot of people smoke like haystacks, but if they're in a gathering that they know is all Christians, they will not totally be themselves."[10]

"Why isolate yourself? Your life isolates you enough. I'm isolated when I walk into a room and somebody says, 'She's a Christian' and nobody offers me a joint and all the coke (cocaine) disappears. I don't want it anyway, but it doesn't mean that we can't be friends."[11]

"Petting happens. It's part of growing up, finding out who you are, how men and women work. As a teenager, when I gave part of me to someone, I knew I was just going to flirt, have a little fun, and do whatever I could rationalize, but go no further, because there is only one first time."[12]

"People say, 'Prude, prude, prude,' but I'm glad I didn't cross certain barriers, because I wouldn't want to compare Gary's moans with some other guy's . . . I have friends who did cross those barriers and don't seem to be the worse for wear. They continue to love and honor each other."[13]

"I have a healthy sense of right and wrong, but sometimes, for example, using foul, exclamation-point words among friends can be good for a laugh."[14]

"It seems to me that people who are most adamantly against premarital sex have experienced some kind of pain in their own lives. Like the people who say absolutely NO to rock 'n' roll. Chances are it has something to do with a past sadness . . ."[15]

"I'm trying to look sexy to sell a record. But what is sexy? To me it's never been taking my shirt off or having my tongue sticking out. I feel that a Christian young woman in the eighties is VERY sexual."[16]

"For maybe five or ten minutes (during concerts) I'll say who I am and what Jesus means in my life. I don't want to browbeat a crowd for two hours."[17]

Another shocking revelation about Amy's personal life came in a 1985 Rolling Stone magazine article. While talking about her African vacation, she mentioned being surprised by some men as she and a girlfriend sunbathed naked on the beach.[18]

From rich, pampered preppie to pop/rock superstar, Amy Grant has become the adored idol of millions. Without her proven example of the dollars to be made, the big secular record companies would never have pumped oceans of bucks into their own gospel divisions. Old-fashioned praise music would still be the order of the day. Though it wouldn't be as popular as the worldly stuff Amy so shamelessly grinds out, popularity and making big bucks has never been the yardstick for measuring biblical holiness.

Did Amy Grant sell out? I think we all know the answer to that one.

BUILDING FROM SCRATCH

"And a man's foes shall be they of his own
household."   Matthew 10:36

"Your Pop's caught you smokin'
And he says, 'No way!'
That hypocrite smokes 2 packs a day
Man, livin' at home is such a drag
Now your Mom threw away your best
    porno mag
You gotta fight for your right
To party . . . "   *The Beastie Boys*[1]

The purpose of rock music is to split, splinter and
destroy your home. While you are working to mend
broken bridges between you and your children, the
sleazy rock monsters are doing everything they can to

tear those bridges to shreds and widen the gap. This comment from Gene Simmons of *KISS* is typical:

> " . . . you don't need those people around, and that includes your parents. If people aren't supporting you, they are your enemies . . . "[2]

A February, 1988 newspaper article in the L.A. Press-Telegram tells about a Minnesota boy whose dad wouldn't let him listen to a particular tape. The teen's response? He took an ax and chopped his entire family to pieces with it. The very next day, he shaved his head into a punk rock style.

If you don't believe rock music breeds rebellion, just try to take rock away from a youngster who is enslaved by it. You'll find yourself in the middle of World War III. Rock music has always fueled rebellion, and wherever you see rebellion, you can be sure Satan is successfully at work. Rebellion is the devil's trademark. It is always found in people under his control. When destroying a family, Satan and his demons continually throw more rebellion, rebellion, rebellion onto the raging family fires. And rock music is the gasoline they use to feed the flames.

Occultist *Sting* and *The Police* sing a song called "Murder By Numbers:"

> "Because murder is like anything you take
>   to
> It's a habit-forming need for more and
>   more
> You can bump off every member of your
>   family
> And anybody else you find a bore"

Mom and Dad, if your child happens to feel you are bugging him, these rockers suggest your kids get a .44 and blow your brains out! As if that wasn't bad enough, this song goes on to suggest that once you've killed one person, you "must try a twosome or a threesome."

Rock music is Satan's greatest crowbar to pry children away from their parents and more importantly, away from God. Ultimately, all rebellion is disobedience toward God. If the devil can breed enough rebellion into a teenager, he can destroy not only a family, but he can also damn that young person's soul, leaving them to burn forever in the lake of fire. That's what Satan is really after, and rock music is his best tool to accomplish that goal.

Why does rock bring such rebellion with it? Because when you as a parent allow rock music into your house, you are allowing Satan and his demons to come in too. Former satanists have testified that witchcraft rituals are held in recording studios to place demons on the master tapes of new records for one purpose . . . to get demons into homes and people.

The following lyrics by rockers *Mercyful Fate* are the actual oath people recite when they enter satanism. Every time a young person sings this song, they renew their allegiance to the devil, whether they realize it or not:

"The Oath"

"By the Symbol of the Creator, I swear
    henceforth to be
A faithful Servant of his most puissant
Arch-Angel The Prince Lucifer . . .
I deny Jesus Christ, the Deceiver

And I abjure the Christian faith
Holding in contempt all of it's Works
As a Being now possessed of a human Body
In this World I swear to give my full
   Allegiance
To it's lawful Master, to worship Him
Our Lord Satan, and no other . . .
I swear to give my Mind, my Body and
   Soul unreservedly
To the Furtherance of our Lord Satan's
   Designs . . ."

Before peace can ever come to your family, you must get Satan and his demons out of your kids, and out of your house. As far as removing demons from your children, to detail all aspects of deliverance would take an entire book in itself. To help you in that area, I highly recommend: "Pigs In The Parlor" by Frank and Ida Mae Hammond (Impact Books) as well as "He Came To Set The Captives Free" and "Prepare For War" by Rebecca Brown, MD (Chick Publications).

Once your child has been set free, great care must be taken to make sure the demons do not return. The Bible says they will try. (See Luke 11:24-26.) To keep your child spiritually clean, you must do everything you can to get your house in order and keep it that way. Here are ten steps toward that goal:

1.) **Trust Jesus Christ As Your Savior.** Step one is the most important of all. Both Dad and Mom must trust Jesus Christ as their personal Savior. Without Christ, your home and your children have no chance. Admit you're a sinner (Romans 3:23). Believe with all your heart that Jesus Christ is God's only begotten Son, that He was born of a virgin, was crucified for your sins, and rose again from the dead. Ask Jesus to come into your heart and save you (Romans 10:9-10). Accept Him as your Savior and Master. Ask Him to cleanse and forgive your sins (Romans 10:13). Repent (turn away) from the lifestyle that now enslaves you (Luke 13:5). Obey Christ's command and be baptized (Mattthew 28:19).

2.) **Burn All "Familiar" Objects In Your House.** A familiar object is anything which is made by, used for, or dedicated to Satan and his demons. This includes rock records, tapes, CD's, posters, books, magazines, jewelry, clothing and videos. Anything dedicated to rock music is dedicated to the devil. As a result, it should be burned because Satan and his demons exercise control over humans through these "familiars." (See Acts 19:19.) Here are two bedrock principles to keep in mind:

> 1. The Bible says you can be cursed through possessing unclean and accursed things (Deuteronomy 7:25, 26 & Joshua 6:18).
>
> 2. Removing those things brings spiritual freedom and cleansing.

3.) **Put On The Whole Armour Of God.** This literal spiritual covering is available to all Christians, and can stop demonic attack dead in its tracks (Ephesians 6:13-18). Ask the Lord for this armour every morning, and for the protection of mighty angels around your home day and night (Psalm 34:7; 91:10,11).

4.) **Increase Your Daily Prayer Time.** You should at least double the time you spend in prayer. (See I Thessalonians 5:17.) Don't have time? Turn off the television and you'll have more time than you know what to do with (II Chronicles 7:14).

5.) Rebuke Satan Whenever He Attacks. Deliverance doesn't end the battle; you must keep fighting. Jealousy, fear, lust and depression are just some of the signs that demons are striking you. When this happens, rebuke Satan and his demons out loud and tell them you stand in the power of the Lord (Ephesians 1:19-23; 2:6). Command those foul spirits to leave immediately in the name of Jesus Christ (Philippians 2:9-11).

6.) Have A Consistent "Family Altar." This is simply daily Bible reading, study and prayer as a family. You are to teach your children the Word of God and write it on their hearts and minds. In most families, this job has been shamefully neglected (Joshua 1:8 and Deuteronomy 6:6,7). Correct this situation and you'll see some real, positive changes start to happen.

7.) Don't Neglect Worship. Sunday morning is a time for **everyone** to be together in the Lord's house, whether in a church building or private home. Parents should NOT drop the kids off, then go back home to read the paper or take a nap! (See Hebrews 10:25.)

8.) Study Your Bible Individually. In addition to holding family altar, the father is to STUDY the Bible on his own and encourage the rest of the family to do the same. (See II Timothy 2:15.) Too busy? You'll wish you had made time when your child passes out from bad drugs at the next rock concert.

9.) Don't Compromise With The World. Jesus didn't compromise. Neither should you. God honors an unflinching stand, especially in the midst of persecution. Stay holy (II Timothy 3:12).

10.) Quit Being Passive. The biggest problem with

most Christians can be summed up in one word . . . passivity. A passive Christian is no threat to Satan and is cursed by God. (See Jeremiah 48:10.) The message here is simple, Christians. Fight! Rock music is one of Satan's primary weapons in this warfare. To win, you must be willing to fight it forever.

Conclusion

Jesus Christ has the power to heal your broken and battered family. He will bring you complete victory over the evil one if you cling to Him and obey His commands. You must be willing to stand up for God against Satan, as a firm and faithful servant to the end. Though the price is high, seeing your children rescued from the ravages of the devil's destruction will make it all worthwhile. Take a stand against rock, and refuse to budge an inch.

Will you do it, Dad? Mom? How about you, young person? Start down the right path today by dumping all the devil's pollution back where it belongs . . . into the raging flames. If this filth bears the label, "Christian," then dump it all the faster. Don't be deceived. There is nothing "Christian" about rock music.

Rock & Roll is a **deadly** poison.

Jesus Christ is the one and only cure.

The choice is yours.

POSTSCRIPT

After reading this book, you may be wondering, "Just who is Jeff Godwin, and what gives him the right to put down "my" music? Hopefully, my testimony will answer that question:

For thirteen years I was a slave to Rock & Roll music. All through my teens and early twenties, it was my god. I spent almost half my life worshiping before the altar of rock. I played in Heavy Metal bands on a local level for seven years, and spent thousands of dollars on everything connected with the rock lifestyle.

The music and the demons behind it cast such chains of darkness over my mind that I became a reprobate and degenerate abuser of drugs, alcohol and women. I threw violent rages against anyone who opposed me, was engaged in much sin, and was often in trouble with the law. Every thought of my heart was only evil continually. The music fed this perverse attitude until I was stuffed to the gills with wickedness.

Such was my life until I repented of my sins and made Jesus Christ my Lord, Master and Savior. Thank God, He set me free! Once saved, I dumped everything associated with rock music. The more I got rid of, the less hold Satan and his demons had on me, and for the first time in my life, I clearly saw the true wickedness of rock music.

The Lord is now using the knowledge I gained while still in rock's bondage to wage war against Satan and those who serve him by exposing their dirty work in popular music.

If you think that my case is an extreme, one-in-a-million rarity, I've got news for you. There are thousands upon thousands of young people who are caught in the same deadly trap – pawns of the devil taken captive to do his evil will (II Timothy 2:24-26).

I was raised in a Christian family and taught right from wrong at an early age, but nothing mattered when the music and the devil took over. Once Satan had his clutching claws into me, he wouldn't let go. If you will take a look, you'll see that the same thing is happening all around you.

Rock music is of the devil – don't let anyone tell you it isn't. It's a spiritual battle and Jesus is the ONLY one who can break those chains which Satan has wrapped around you. I'm living proof of that. You can't say, "he doesn't know what he's talking about," because I do. I've been on both sides of the fence. I've lived it.

I urge you right now to sever all your connections with rock music – "Christian" or otherwise. There is nothing Christ-like about Rock & Roll, and it should have no place in your life. Please follow the straight and narrow path of holiness the Lord has marked out for all who trust and obey Him.

The Rock Ministries
P.O. Box 2181
Bloomington, Indiana 47401

FOOTNOTES

About The Cover
1. Encyclopedia Britannica, Inc., 1968, Vol. 17, p. 199
2. Ibid.
3. Ibid.
4. Last Trumpet Newsletter, January, 1988, p. 2
5. Encyclopedia Britannica, op. cit., p. 199
6. Ibid.

Chapter 1
1. *Blue Oyster Cult*, Lyrics to the song, "Burnin' For You"
2. Denver Post, June 21, 1970, and The Independent Baptist Voice, August 13, 1987, p. 2
3. HIMknowledgy Ministries Report, Independent Baptist Voice, August 13, 1987, p. 2
4. Mark Grant, *Can Rock & Roll Lead To Rack & Ruin?* Los Angeles Times, Feb. 5, 1978
5. James Strong, Abingdon's Strong's Exhaustive Concordance of the Bible, (Nashville, 1986) pp. 59, 142
6. John H. Steele, *World Of The Unexplained*, (Ripley Museum Inc., 1977) pp. 9, 10
7. David Henderson, *Scuse Me While I Kiss The Sky*, (Bantam Books, 1978) pp. 60-61
8. Ibid., pp. 214-215
9. Ibid. pp. 250-251
10. Last Trumpet Newsletter, Vol. IV, Issue XIII, August, 1985, pp. 3-4

Chapter 2
1. *KISS*, Lyrics from the song, Tomorrow And Tonight
2. Toby Goldstein, *Twisted Sister*, (New York, 1986), p. 13
3. Ibid., pp. 12-13
4. Ibid., p. 13
5. Faces Rocks, December, 1986, p. 24
6. Record, December, 1984, p. 38
7. Circus, March 31, 1985, p. 86
8. Concert Shots, November, 1987, p. 10
9. Toby Goldstein, op. cit., p. 68
10. Circus, April 30, 1985, p. 76
11. Record, December, 1984, p. 37
12. Hit Parader, April, 1985, p. 68
13. Circus, March 31, 1985, p .86
14. Musician, September, 1984, p. 42
15. Toby Goldstein, op. cit., p. 122
16. Musician, September, 1984, pp. 42-43
17. Dee Snider and Philip Bashe, *Dee Snider's Teenage Survival Guide*, (New York, 1987), pp. 34-35
18. Ibid., p. 40

19. Rip, February, 1988, p. 44
20. Charles White, *The Life And Times Of Little Richard*, (New York, 1984), pp. 8-9
21. Spin, October, 1986, p. 63
22. Charles White, op. cit., p. 71
23. Victoria Balfour, *Rock Wives*, (New York, 1986), p. 50
24. Charles White, op. cit., p. 189
25. Ibid., p. 197
26. Hit Parader, August, 1983, p. 17
27. Best Of Rock, December, 1984, p. 66
28. Faces Rocks, June, 1984, p. 14
29. Musician, June, 1984, p. 50
30. Hit Parader, April, 1985, p. 37
31. Musician, June, 1984, pp 51-52
32. Hit Parader, April, 1985, pp. 37-38
33. Ibid., March, 1987, p. 6
34. Ibid., August, 1984, p. 16
35. Circus, March 31, 1984, p. 64
36. Rolling Stone, No. 445, April 11, 1985, pp. 26, 61
37. Ibid., p. 24
38. Hit Parader, August, 1983, p. 17
39. Best Of Rock, December, 1984, p. 67
40. Circus, October 10, 1978, p. 26
41. Hit Parader, January, 1985, p. 6
42. Faces Rocks, June, 1984, p. 19
43. Creem, October, 1981, p. 35
44. Spin, April, 1986, p. 66
45. Rolling Stone, No. 445, April 11, 1985, p. 24
46. Faces Rocks, June, 1984, p. 16
47. Best Of Rock, December, 1984, p. 67
48. Creem, July, 1980, p. 45
49. Musician, June, 1984, p. 54
50. Hit Parader, November, 1985, p. 43
51. John Phillips with Jim Jerome,*Papa John - An Autobiography*, (New York, 1986), p. 54
52. Ibid., p. 127
53. Ibid., p. 338
54. Ibid., p. 411
55. Faces Rocks, May, 1987, p. 27
56. Spin, May, 1987, p. 46
57. Martin Torgoff, *American Fool - The Roots And Improbable Rise Of John Cougar Mellencamp*, (New York, 1986), p. 31
58. Hit Parader, August, 1984, p. 22
59. Barbara Charone, *Keith Richards - Life As A Rolling Stone*, (New York, 1982), p. 32
60. Faces Rocks, December, 1984, p. 25

Chapter 3
1. Bob Dylan, Lyrics from the song, "Gotta Serve Somebody"
2. Musician, August, 1980, p. 98

345

3. Ray Coleman, *Lennon*, (McGraw-Hill, 1984) p. 256
4. Peter Brown & Steven Gaines, *The Love You Make - An Insider's story Of The Beatles*, (McGraw-Hill, 1983), pp. 249-250
5. Ibid., p. 250
6. Rolling Stone, No. 482, September 11 1986, pp. 101- 102
7. Ibid., p. 101
8. Rolling Stone, No. 320, June 26, 1980, p. 11
9. Wilson Bryan Key, *Media Sexploitation*, (Prentice-Hall, New Jersey, 1976), p. 137
10. Ibid., pp. 134-135
11. The Rolling Stone Interviews - 1967-1980, (New York, 1981), p. 305
12. Rolling Stone, No. 482, September 11, 1986, p. 48
13. Peter McCabe & Robert D. Schonfeld, *John Lennon: For The Record,* (Bantam, 1984), pp. 78-79
14. Tina Turner with Kurt Loder, *I, Tina,* (New York, 1986), p. 25
15. Ibid., p. 42
16. Rolling Stone, No. 485 October 23, 1986, p. 52
17. Tina Turner with Kurt Loder, op. cit., pp. 140-141
18. Ibid., pp. 154-155
19. Ibid., p. 156
20. Ibid., p. 172
21. Rolling Stone, No. 485, October 23, 1986, p. 106
22. Ibid., p. 106
23. Record, No. 2, Vol. 4, December, 1984, p. 21
24. Penthouse, March, 1987, p. 66
25. Ibid., p. 66
26. Ibid., p. 74
27. Ibid., pp. 60, 62
28. Rolling Stone, No. 439, January 17, 1985, p. 20
29. Ibid., p. 22
30. Ibid., p. 22
31. Faces Rocks, May, 1985, p. 48
32. Ibid., p. 50
33. Rolling Stone, No.435, November 22, 1984, p. 16
34. Ibid., p. 20
35. Spin, April, 1987, p. 57
36. Faces Rocks, May, 1985, p. 50
37. Faces Rocks, July, 1984, p. 49
38. Rolling Stone, September 17, 1981, p .57
39. Timothy White, *Rock Stars,* (New York, 1984), p. 250
40. Ibid., p. 257
41. Faces Rocks, July, 1984, p. 48
42. Rolling Stone, September 3, 1981, p. 18
43. Bam, September 11, 1981, p. 4
44. Mike Warnke, with Dave Balsiger & Les Jones, *The Satan-Seller* (Plainfield, New Jersey, 1972), pp. 33-34

Chapter 4
1. LL Cool J, Lyrics from the song, "Dangerous"

2. Rolling Stone, No. 488, Dec. 4, 1986, p. 62
3. B. Adler, *Tougher Than Leather*, (New York, 1987), p. 11
4. Ibid.
5. Time, Sept. 1, 1986, p. 20
6. Rolling Stone, No. 488, Dec. 4, 1986, p. 62
7. Spin, August, 1986, p. 56
8. Rolling Stone, No. 488, Dec. 4, 1986, p. 102
9. Ibid.
10. Creem, December, 1986, p. 31
11. Spin, April, 1986, p. 12
12. Rock Scene, August, 1987, p. 4
13. Rolling Stone, No. 435, Nov. 22, 1984, p. 86
14. People, March 9, 1987, p. 31
15. Rock Scene, August, 1987, p. 10

Chapter 5
1. Lines from the movie, "Trick Or Treat."

Chapter 6
1. *Whitesnake*, Lyrics to the song, "Children of the Night"
2. Bob Larson, *Rock*, (Wheaton, Illinois, 1984), p. 41
3. Ibid., p 41
4. Circus Rock Immortals #1, 1980, p. 23
5. Circus, April 30, 1981, p. 46
6. Rip, February, 1988, p. 50
7. Hit Parader, July, 1986, p. 61
8. Ibid., p. 61
9. Circus, January 31, 1988, p. 37
10. Ibid., p. 37
11. USA Today, December 1, 1987, p. 4D
12. Hit Parader, November, 1979, pp. 35, 60
13. Hit Parader, August, 1982, pp. 6, 7
14. Circus, August 24, 1976, p. 18
15. Hit Parader, November, 1979, p. 35
16. Creem, September, 1987, p. 38
17. Ibid., p. 38

Chapter 7
1. Metal-Creem Close-Up, March, 1987, p. 57

Chapter 8
1. *The 5th Dimension*, Lyrics from the song, "Aquarius," from the Broadway musical "Hair."
2. Constance Cumbey, *The Hidden Dangers Of The Rainbow,* (Shreveport, Louisiana, 1983), p. 143
3. Ibid, p. 58
4. Chris Salewicz, *McCartney*, (New York, 1986), p. 191
5. Joseph J. Carr, *The Twisted Cross*, (Shreveport, Louisiana, 1985), p. 281

6. Constance Cumbey, op. cit., p. 179
7. Ibid., p. 49
8. Ibid., p. 50
9. John Lennon & Paul McCartney, Lyrics from the song, "The Ballad Of John & Yoko"
10. Jann Wenner, *Lennon Remembers*, (San Francisco, 1971), p. 11
11. Peter McCabe & Robert D. Schonfeld, op. cit., p. 30
12. Ibid., p. 94
13. The Playboy Interviews, p. 95
14. Ibid., p. 99
15. Hunter Davies, The Beatles, Second Revised Edition, (McGraw-Hill, 1985) p. 103
16. HIMknowledgy Ministries Report, The Independent Baptist Voice, July 30, 1987, p. 2
17. The Playboy Interviews, p. 133
18. Ibid., p. 169
19. Vincent Bugliosi & Curt Gentry, *Helter Skelter,* (New York, 1974), pp. 195-196
20. Ibid., p. 196
21. The Playboy Interviews, p. 106
22. John Lennon, Yoko Ono, & Andy Peebles, *The Last Lennon Tapes,* (New York, 1981), p. 113
23. Last Trumpet Newsletter, Vol. VII, Issue I, January, 1988, p. 2, & SPELLBOUND, (Chick Publications, Chino, California, 1978), p. 24
24. Ibid., Vol. IV, Issue VII, July, 1985, p. 4
25. Rolling Stone, No. 454, August 15, 1985, p. 31
26. Ibid., p. 32
27. Spin, July, 1986, p. 75
28. Ibid., p. 80
29. Faces Rocks, October, 1985, p. 37
30. Ibid., p. 39
31. Circus, December 31, 1985, p. 86
32. Constance Cumbey, op. cit., p. 24
33. Creem, August, 1984, p. 15
34. D. Scott Rogo, *UFO Abductions - True Cases of Alien Kidnappings,* (New York, 1980), pp. 93, 94, 118, 119, 162, 163, 170, 171
35. Constance Cumbey, op. cit., p. 176
36. Creem, August, 1984, p. 15

Chapter 9
1. Lyrics from the song "Believe" by *Barren Cross*
2. Echoes, Vol. 2, 1986, p. 14
3. Ibid., p. 16

Chapter 10
1. Faces Rocks, May, 1987, p. 23
2. Johanna Michaelsen, *The Beautiful Side Of Evil*, (Eugene, Oregon, 1982), p. 77
3. Contemporary Christian, June, 1986, p. 15
4. Hit Parader, November, 1986, p. 21

5. Echoes, Vol. 2, (1986), p. 7
6. Contemporary Christian Music, April, 1987, p. 12
7. Ibid., November, 1986, pp. 20-21
8. Contemporary Christian, June, 1986, p. 18
9. Glen Berteau, *Christian Or Religious Rock-The Controversy Confronted*, July, 1986, Tape # 2
10. Bob Millard, *Amy Grant,* (New York, 1986), p. 179
11. Faces Rocks, May, 1987, p. 23

Chapter 11
1. Carol Leggett, *Amy Grant*, (New York, 1987), p. 112

Chapter 12
1. Contemporary Christian Music, March, 1987, p. 12

Chapter 13
1. Hit Parader, February, 1985, p. 31
2. Rip, April, 1987, p. 49
3. Hit Parader, November, 1986, p. 21
4. Richard De Atley, *Stryper plays heavy metal with a halo,* (Associated Press, 1986)
5. Gerri Miller, *Quotable Revelations From Metal's Righteous Rockers,* p.47
6. Rip, April, 1987, p. 49
7. Gerri Miller, op. cit., p. 47
8. Rip, April, 1987, p. 49
9. Gerri Miller, op cit, p.49
10. Richard De Atley, op. cit.
11. Youth!, January, 1987, p.10
12. Hit Parader, April, 1987, p. 51
13. Albert Svenddal, *What Does God Say About Christian Rock? Lyrics, Lifestyles & Appearance,* (Minnesota, 1986), p. 6 (unpublished)
14. Harry E. Wedeck, *Treasury Of Witchcraft,* (Citadel Press, 1961), p.23
15. Marty Tingelhoff, *Expose' On Rock, Soul and Country Music,* (cassette tape #4,) Living Word Ministries, Kingsport, Tennessee
16. Rebecca Brown, M.D., *Prepare For War*, (Chino, Calif., 1987), p.136
17. Hit Parader, April, 1987, p. 51
18. Youth!, January, 1987, p. 11
19. Richard De Atley, op. cit.
20. Hit Parader, April, 1987, p. 51
21. Rip, April, 1987, p. 49
22. Hard Rock's Metal Studs, February, 1987, p. 30
23. Youth!, January, 1987, p. 8
24. Hit Parader, March, 1987, p. 60
25. Milwaukee Journal, August 25, 1987, p. 11
26. Hit Parader, February, 1987, p. 41
27. The Peters Brothers Interview Stryper - Whose Side Are They On?, (St. Paul, Minnesota, 1987)
28. Ibid.

29. Ibid.
30. Creem Metal, June, 1987, p. 61
31. Ibid.

Chapter 14
1. Media Update, Vol. 6, Issue 5, Sept.-Oct., 1987, p. 4
2. Holman Master Study Bible - Authorized King James Version, (Nashville, Tennessee, 1983), p.1524
3. "Battle Plan," LTM Marketing, (Nashville, Tennessee, November 1, 1987), p. 1

Chapter 15
1. *DeGarmo & Key*, Lyrics to the song, "Don't Stop The Music"
2. Contemporary Christian Music, November, 1987, p. 20
3. Ibid., p.20
4. Ibid., p.20

Chapter 16
1. Rolling Stone, June 6, 1985, p. 9
2. Bob Millard, *Amy Grant*, (New York, 1986), p. 31
3. Houston Chronicle, December 27, 1986
4. Rolling Stone, June 6, 1985, p. 10
5. Bob Millard, op. cit., p. 154
6. Rolling Stone, June 6, 1985, p. 10
7. Ibid., p. 10
8. Bob Millard, op. cit., p. 169
9. Ladies Home Journal, December, 1985, p. 98
10. Bob Millard, op. cit., p. 30
11. Ibid., p.169
12. Ibid., p.30
13. Ibid., pp. 128-129
14. Ladies Home Journal, December, 1985, p. 100
15. Ibid., p. 210
16. Rolling Stone, June 6, 1985, p. 10
17. Bob Millard, op. cit., p. 168
18. Rolling Stone, June 6, 1985, p. 10

Chapter 17
1. *The Beastie Boys*, Lyrics to the song, "Fight For Your Right (To Party)"
2. Faces Rocks, December, 1984, p. 25

BIBLIOGRAPHY

1. Michelle Phillips. *California Dreamin*. New York: Warner Books, 1986
2. John Phillips with Jim Jerome. *Papa John*. New York: Dolphin Books, 1986
3. Tina Turner with Kurt Loder. *I, Tina*. New York: William Morrow & Co., 1986
4. Toby Goldstein. *Twisted Sister*. New York: Ballantine Books, 1986
5. Ethlie Ann Vare. *Ozzy Osbourne*. New York: Ballantine Books, 1986
6. Charles White. *The Life And Times Of Little Richard*. New York: Pocket Books, 1984
7. Susan Dworkin. *Desperately Seeking Susan*. New York: Harmony Books, 1985
8. Christ Salewicz. *McCartney*. New York: St. Martin's Press, 1986
9. John Lennon, Yoko Ono, & Andy Peebles. *The Last Lennon Tapes*. New York: Dell Publishing Co. 1981
10. Peter McCabe & Robert D. Schonfeld. *John Lennon: For The Record*. Bantam Books, 1984
11. David Sheff & G. Barry Golson. *The Playboy Interviews With John Lennon & Yoko Ono – The Final Testament*. New York: Berkley Books, 1981
12. John Green. *Dakota Days*. New York: St. Martin's Press, 1983
13. May Pang & Henry Edwards. *Loving John*. New York: Warner Books, 1983
14. Ray Coleman. *Lennon*. McGraw-Hill, 1984
15. Peter Brown & Steven Gaines. *The Love You Make – An Insider's Story Of The Beatles*. McGraw-Hill, 1983
16. Victoria Balfour. *Rock Wives*. New York: Beech Tree Books, 1986
17. Curtis Knight. *Jimi*. New York, Washington: Praeger Publishers, 1974
18. David Henderson. *Scuse Me While I Kiss The Sky*. Bantam Books, 1978
19. Henry Edwards & Tony Zanetta. *Stardust – The David Bowie Story*. McGraw-Hill, 1986
20. Robert Feiden. *Light Of Day*. New York: Signet Books, 1987
21. Bob Millard. *Amy Grant*. New York: Dolphin Books, 1986
22. Bob Larson. *Rock*. Wheaton Illinois: Living Books, 1984
23. The Peters Brothers with Cher Merrill. *Why Knock Rock*.

Minneapolis, Minnesota: Bethany House Publishers, 1984

24. Lowell Hart. *Satan's Music Exposed*. Salem Kirban, 1981

25. Winkie Pratney. *Devil Take The Youngest*. Shreveport, Lafayette, Louisiana: Huntington House Inc., 1985

26. Mike Warnke with Dave Balsiger & Les Jones. *The Satan-Seller*. Plainfield, New Jersey: Logos International, 1972

27. Johanna Michaelsen. *The Beautiful Side Of Evil*. Eugene, Oregon: Harvest House Inc. 1982

28. Joseph J. Carr. *The Twisted Cross*. Shreveport, Lafayette, Louisiana: Huntington House Inc., 1985

29. Constance Cumbey. *The Hidden Dangers Of The Rainbow*. Shreveport, Lafayette, Louisiana: Huntington House Inc., 1983

30. D. Scott Rogo. *UFO Abductions – True Cases Of Alien Kidnappings*. New York: Signet, 1980

31. Wilson Bryan Key. *Media Sexploitation*. New York: Signet, 1976

32. Albert Svenddal. *What Does God's Word Say About 'Christian Rock' Music*??? Cloquet, Minnesota: 1986 (unpublished)

33. Albert Svenddal. *The #1 Christian Heavy Metal Rock Group Exposed by God's Word*. Cloquet, Minnesota: 1986 (unpublished)

34. Gene & Earline Moody. *Basic Deliverance Manual*. Baton Rouge, Louisiana: (unpublished) 1986

35. "The Independent Baptist Voice" newspaper, (January 22, 1987 through June 25, 1987)

36. David J. Meyer. Last Trumpet Newsletter. Beaver Dam, Wisconsin: September, 1984 - July, 1987

37. Steve Bell. *Passivity*. Hot Springs, Arkansas: December, 1986 (cassette tape recorded at Lake Hamilton Bible Camp.)

38. Michael K. Relfe. *Rock Music – The Five Level Attack*. New Jersey: 1986 (unpublished)

39. B. Adler. *Tougher Than Leather*. New York: Signet Books, 1987